SELFISH
GIFTS

SELFISH GIFTS

Senegalese Women's Autobiographical Discourses

LISA McNEE

State University
of New York
Press

Published by
State University of New York Press, Albany

© 2000 State University of New York

Production by Susan Geraghty
Marketing by Fran Keneston

Printed in the United States of America

For information, address State University of New York
Press, State University Plaza, Albany, N.Y., 12246

Library of Congress Cataloging-in-Publication Data

McNee, Lisa.
    Selfish gifts : Senegalese women's autobiographical discourses /
Lisa McNee.
        p.   cm.
    Includes bibliographical references and index.
    ISBN 0-7914-4587-9 (hc. : alk. paper). — ISBN 0-7914-4588-7 (pbk.
: alk. paper)
        1. Wolof literature—Women authors—History and criticism.
    2. Wolof literature—Senegal—History and criticism.
    3. Autobiography in literature. I. Title.
PL8785.5.M35 2000
896'.3214—dc21   99-39903
                                                                              CIP

10 9 8 7 6 5 4 3 2 1

To my mother,
who taught me
that all things are possible
with love

CONTENTS

ACKNOWLEDGMENTS

First, I wish to give thanks to all of the many women who shared their knowledge and their artistry with me. I owe special thanks to Anta Bouna Dieng, Besse Dieng, Ami Guèye, Arame Caane Seck, and Kenn Sène. I also wish to express my great gratitude to those who helped me very actively in gathering data, transcribing, and annotating it in Senegal. My thanks to Cheikh Hamallah Traoré, Abdoulaziz Diaw, Rokhaya Diouf, Fatou Samba Diouf, Oumar Guèye, and Ami Diène for their help in these activities. The personnel at Radio-Télévision Sénégal, the Archives Nationales du Sénégal, and the Archives Culturelles du Sénégal also deserve my thanks for their kind assistance. Chérif Thiam, Saxiir Caam, and Papa Samba Diop also offered their assistance and discussed my interpretations of the poems with me at length.

My fieldwork in the Republic of Senegal (November 1992 to December 1993) was made possible by a generous Fulbright-Hays Doctoral Dissertation grant from the Department of Education. The German Academic Exchange Service offered me a fellowship that allowed me to analyze my data and write part of the thesis that was the basis for this book during the 1994/1995 academic year at the African Studies Center of the University of Bayreuth. Prior to my fieldwork, further funding from FLAS and FLEP allowed me to study Wolof, the language of my research, at the University of Illinois at Champaign-Urbana. After my fieldwork, the University of Illinois awarded me a Regional Africanist grant that made further library research possible.

From the moment I seriously considered undertaking this project, Albert Wertheim and Nancy Schmidt offered their support and advice. In addition, Eileen Julien, Matei Calinescu, John Eakin, János Riesz, Ruth Stone, and Patrick O'Meara offered their advice as I was writing the thesis that was the basis for this study. My thanks to all of them for making this work possible.

I also wish to express my heartfelt thanks to the editing and production team. Indeed, Zina Lawrence's encouragement and faith in this book project made a mere possibility into a reality. She and the other members of this team—Susan Geraghty, Fran Keneston, and others—have made it possible through this book to widen the circles of cultural exchange that began in Senegal.

A NOTE ON TRANSCRIPTION AND TRANSLATION

I am grateful to Abdoulaziz Diaw and to Cheikh Hammallah Traoré for the transcriptions of all Wolof texts (with the exception of those quoted from studies of Wolof oral literature) that appear in this dissertation. Mr. Diaw has long been employed by the Centre de Linguistique Appliquée (C.L.A.D.) at the University of Dakar-Cheikh Anta Diop as a researcher. He has published two lexicons of Wolof vocabulary,[1] and is now working on a lexicon of maritime vocabulary. Mr. Traoré is currently completing a doctorate in African linguistics at the University of Dakar.

Their transcriptions follow the official Senegalese guidelines, set in 1972. The official alphabet conforms very closely to the International Phonetic Alphabet (IPA). Typographic problems have forced me to use "ng," rather than the IPA sign for this sound. The following table attempts to compare IPA representations to American English equivalents as closely as possible.

Vowels

i	ee
e	open e (pair)
é	closed e ("sir")
ã	nasalized a
a	open a
à	closed a
ó	open o (o)
o	closed o
ë	euh (*kër*, pronounced like **cur**)
u	ou, as in "you"

Consonants

c	**ch**, as in chair
j	as in jump
x	"**ch**," as in German, or Spanish "jota"
ñ	ny

Linguists have yet to agree upon the factors that distinguish open from closed vowels in Wolof; some argue that it would be more appropriate to speak of long or doubled vowels in contrast to short vowels. For further information on transcription, I recommend the introduction to the *Dictionnaire wolof-français* by Arame Fal, Rosine Santos, and Jean Léonce Doneux (Paris: Karthala, 1990).

I myself translated the corpus of texts into English. My translations rely in part on performers' and audience members' interpretations, and

---

1. *Un Vocabulaire wolof de la faune au Sénégal. Les Langues nationales au Sénégal* 67 (Dakar: Centre de Linguistique Appliquée de Dakar, 1976), and *Un Vocabulaire wolof de la flore au Sénégal. Les Langues nationales au Sénégal* W16 (Dakar: Centre de Linguistique Appliquée de Dakar, 1981).

in part on annotations provided by Abdoulaziz Diaw, Rokhaya Diouf, and Mohamadou Guèye. Given that performers compress a great deal of information into dense, complex texts, I have found it necessary to translate somewhat freely. Although I have attempted to stay as close to the original texts as possible, I have sometimes added a word in brackets to make the text easier to understand, or added an American image or proverb that expresses a similar idea. All additions have been carefully noted for the readers' sake.

The Other's Face
Might Be Your Own

The voices of Senegalese women, lifted to share their lives in various autobiographical discourses, provide the basis for this study of the relevance of lived experience to literature. In order to translate these voices into print, I have found that I must first retrace my experiences during my fieldwork in Senegal. This is so because we can only know an Other through the often blurry lens of our own subjectivity, as the history of anthropology and of travel writing teaches us. Indeed, the anthropologist Michael Jackson's theories on fieldwork and radical empiricism suggest[1] that individual experience has a great deal to do with the empirical project of ethnographic fieldwork. No pure empiricism can exist in a world subject to contingency, for researchers must interact with the object of inquiry, just as researchers in the natural sciences have already concluded. This suggests that conventional western notions of subject and object in research rarely apply[2] in the field. The paradoxical relationship between the voices of Senegalese women and my own thus foregrounds problems of subjectivity and identity for this reason. This preface, then, presents the shifts in my understanding of subjectivity and the autobiographical representation of the self that came about because of my research in Senegal.

My subject has led me to view fieldwork, as well as identity, as a process predicated on collaboration and interaction. Other researchers' experiences confirm this view. When Sylvia Ardyn Boone conducted her research on the Sòwò mask in a Mende community in Sierra Leone, for example, she found that it was impossible to penetrate the secrecy surrounding the Sandè society that organizes the masquerade. As a result, she adopted an indirect method of inquiry that not only resolved her immediate, practical problem, but also led her to modify her research project. This decision resulted in her perceptive study on Mende esthetics.[3] As I understand her explanation of this fieldwork experience, her interactions with informants led her to reshape her project. As a result, an individual's project became a collective work, then returned to the individual as a book project that again became a collaborative effort

1

linking reader(s) and author. This process of exchange linking the individual agent and a community makes knowledge of others possible, releasing the researcher from a certain ethnocentric narcissism, if only for a moment in time.

Such exchanges demand much of participants in research, for they must choose a mutually acceptable framework for interaction. Within a culture, groups may rely on shared cultural models that ease interactions, but cross-cultural groups must create new models or adapt to one particular culture's framework. During my fieldwork, I attempted to do both. I soon discovered that it would be necessary to adapt to another spatial framework, for instance, as performers often travel. I adapted by commuting between Senegal's current capital, Dakar, and Louga, a regional capital on the highway between Dakar and Saint Louis, the colonial capital, since many performers follow this route. On occasion, I accompanied performers to Saint Louis, but most of my research took place in Dakar and Louga and its surrounding villages. This adaptation was relatively easy, as I basically controlled the framework.

Adapting to my collaborators' cultural models was far more difficult, as my western attitudes were an obstacle to my research on praise poetry. Research on panegyric, particularly in West Africa, demonstrates that attempts to impose a western, mercantile framework, or a bourgeois conception of art that considers art invaluable,[4] not only bypass the functioning of this poetry, but also make its performance impossible. Gift-giving is an integral part of the performance itself. Rather than compromising research, then, recompense makes performance and research on the performance of praise poetry possible.[5] From a western perspective, however, it is all too easy to misunderstand the relationship between gift-giving and performance by interpreting gift-giving as a form of commerce. My own mistranslations of cultural terms thus affected the first stage of my fieldwork in Senegal. As a result, when women told me that I should give gifts, I did not truly hear or understand their words. My own understanding of my role as a researcher diverged too sharply from theirs for me to grasp the importance of gifts. Gift exchanges were also related in ways that I did not then understand to the cultural exchanges that made collaboration with informants and research assistants possible.

The problem of exchange thus became the touchstone of my attempts to understand my fieldwork in Senegal. If secrecy was Boone's obstacle, my initial blindness to the patterns of exchange in Wolof communities and to my own place in global exchanges as a *white* American[6] were the principal barriers to my research. However, problems sometimes offer their own solutions. In an indictment of the American ideology of individual self-sufficiency and the colonialist myth of white status,[7] Maivân Lâm suggests that gift exchanges undermine both. It follows that an understanding and an acceptance of gift exchange could make true collaboration possible.

SUBJECTIVE FIELDWORK

As I have already noted, my own lack of understanding regarding my role in global patterns of exchange was an important obstacle to my research. This was so because of my personal history. Class issues, above all others, have influenced my perceptions of my own academic training and of the fieldwork that I conducted in Senegal. I grew up in a small industrial town in the Midwest, where working-class children were not expected to pursue a higher education. My certitude that I would go to college, as my older siblings had, marked me as different. All the same, many of the children growing up in my town faced the same dilemma of class identity: improving one's standard of living via education also involves leaving familiar moorings of identity and finding new ones as part of the process of constructing a new social identity.

These issues impinged upon my fieldwork more strongly than might otherwise have been the case, because I was unexpectedly obliged to spend three months in my hometown before untying the final bureaucratic red tape and leaving for Senegal. In many ways, then, the trip to Senegal echoed earlier departures, for it also affected my social identity. In fact, fieldwork involved constructing several new social personae—those of the professional researcher, the student abroad, the boarder, the newly adopted "sister," and the fledgling *taasukat*, or poet, among others. All of these personae were just as real as those that I incorporate in more familiar social situations; however, they also represented something quite different simply because adults seldom face the need to construct several new and often foreign "selves" on short notice.

Of course, this type of identity crisis is well known as "culture shock," the stress involved in adapting to another culture. My need to create a social persona or social personae that would make communication possible with the people around me was intense, as I had almost no contact with other westerners in the field until the last few months of my stay in Senegal. Communication, of course, cannot be limited to language. Although I had studied Wolof intensively before leaving the United States, I still communicated from my own fields of reference. I was only able to start communicating from another field of reference after gaining further knowledge of the community that I inhabited for a year.

As a foreign researcher adrift, I was supremely lucky to meet a few people who invited me to join their community for a time and who taught me much about their social codes. In the process, they helped me to translate my self into Wolof. This included more than just working intensively on language skills. The family that "adopted" me also expected me to behave as a member of that family. This meant that I, too, was expected to visit relatives and follow Wolof social norms. Since I inevitably failed to do so many times, they corrected me as they would one of their own (with the understanding that a foreigner probably would always make mistakes). These informal classes in etiquette and social obligations were all the more important because my behavior had an effect on the status of the family in question, just as the behavior of any of its members would. Their acceptance was thus a precious honor.

Since this framework sometimes clashed with my goals as a researcher, increased understanding did not always make research easier. This seems to have been a consequence of the friction between the self I construct *for myself*, and the selves I must construct in order to relate to others. In spite of frequent misunderstandings—or because of them, as Johannes Fabian might argue[8]—my Senegalese friends led me to an understanding of the complex codes that regulate gift-giving as well as interpersonal communication in their community.

As a result of the contradictory demands of my social context and my research goals, I floated between different identity positions. My image as a Caucasian westerner sometimes wavered, because I usually wore Senegalese clothing, spoke Wolof at least as often as French, and associated with ordinary people faced with the grinding economic difficulties of life in Senegal. I rented a room for 3,000F CFA (at the time, about US$10) a month in an ordinary neighborhood, and lived frugally. People in the area are very familiar with the Peace Corps program; however, only in Dakar (where I usually wore western clothing) did people ask if I was a member of the Peace Corps. At one wedding, a griot who believed I was a Moor began singing the praises of the Haïdara family (which claims descent from the Prophet Muhammed) to me.

I cannot fully explain the apparent success that I and my friends had in constructing my Wolof identity. It is possible that I overestimate it to some extent; too many visitors would like to delude themselves into believing that they "truly belonged." However, this newly constructed identity also had visible effects on me as an individual. I found myself behaving at times in ways that are alien to the beliefs that I brought with me to Senegal. An important change in attitude concerned my own self-presentation. I firmly believe that fine clothes and physical beauty matter far less than other values. In Senegal, however, clothing "makes the (wo)man" in a very obvious way. Catherine Ndiaye notes that Senegalese fashion does not mark originality or individuality, but rather, personal dignity.

Ici, l'extravagance existe, mais pas comme acte isolé. J'opposerai volontiers une extravagance collective (permise, parfois encouragée) à une fantaisie individuelle (laquelle apparaît tout de suite comme suspecte). . . . C'est ainsi que dans le domaine très codé de l'élégance, du paraître extérieur, (1) il n'y a pas de recherche systématique de l'originalité, du fait singulier, ou de la distinction (dans les deux sens du mot) individuelle.

Here, extravagance exists, but not as an isolated act. I wish to oppose a collective extravagance (permitted, sometimes encouraged) to individual fantasy (which immediately appears suspicious). . . . This is why, in the highly codified field of elegance and of external appearance, (1) there is no systematic search for originality, nor for singularity nor for individual distinction (in both senses of the word).

(1) Chacun sait que l'accoutrement vestimentaire est un symptôme très éloquent sur la façon dont les individualités sont situées—et veulent se situer—dans le corps social. Ainsi, aux Etats-Unis (où la "démocratie" repose sur le culte de l'individu) la libéralité vestimentaire est telle que la mode ne se comprend plus qu'au sens très restreint. La mode c'est, tout au plus, le signe de reconnaissance d'un groupuscule ou d'une micro-société. . . . Quant aux pays très pauvres où être bien mis est synonyme de dignité—et où la garde-robe peut engloutir une large part d'un maigre budget—le vêtement est plus qu'un symptôme.[9]

Everyone knows that apparel is a very eloquent symptom of the way in which individualities are located—and want to locate themselves—in society. Therefore, in the United States (where "democracy" rests on the cult of the individual), fashion's liberalism is such that it can only be understood as fashion in a very restricted sense. Fashion is at best the sign for recognizing a small group or a micro-society. . . . As for very poor countries where being well dressed is synonymous with dignity—and where the wardrobe can swallow a large part of a meager budget—clothing is more than a symptom.

Although Ndiaye's rough schema simply gives the contours of the two systems, it readily describes the clash between my presentation of self when I first arrived, and the successive versions of self that emerged as I began to gain a social identity in Senegal. I had deliberately brought very few clothes, because I did not want to appear conspicuous; those that I did bring were very modest and schoolgirlish, for I hoped to show respect for Muslim values through my modest clothing. Little did I realize that Dakar is a fashion capital where women dress extravagantly, often in revealing, sexy fashions. I soon learned that my difficulties in gaining interviews—particularly at the National Theater—were at least in part caused by my clothing. Once I dressed in a "respectable" way, rather than in schoolgirl skirts and blouses, I obtained the appointments I needed.

By the end of my stay, I had internalized many Senegalese attitudes about extravagant clothing. *Sañse*, or dressing well, functions as a "means of communication" that "is tied directly to the material posses-sions at one's disposal, and thus to the varied social, historical processes that produce inequality."[10] This is true not only because of the unequal distribution of economic resources, but also because of the caste system. I first realized that I, too, had adopted *sañse* as a value when I criticized a friend's neighbor, who always wore the same *boubou*[11] to every event. My friend quickly defended her neighbor, saying that she attended events out of curiosity. Indeed, my friend would have liked to attend events more often, but did not wish to be embarrassed by her scanty wardrobe. I myself was shocked at my criticism; as I have said before, I attach little importance to appearance. In my attempts to deal with the problems of class and identity as they relate to my personal experiences, I take egalitarianism as a basic value. It was thus a shocking reversal for me to become aware that I could criticize someone on the basis of cloth-ing.

Although the example I have given may seem trivial, the many fem-inist critiques of women's slavery to fashion prove that appearance is never a trivial part of self-presentation. Often, it is impossible to distin-guish reality from appearance when it comes to questions of gender. Indeed, Judith Butler's discussion of gender suggests that nothing does distinguish the "real" sex from the masquerade, as "gender proves to be performative—that is, constituting the identity it is purported to be."[12]

My experiences in Senegal indicate that this is true, for I could very well have chosen to accept the "honorary male status" that many Sene-galese were prepared to give me as a foreign researcher. Many women doing field research have noted that they found it easier to contact men than women.[13] This is partly true because of language barriers—men are still more likely to benefit from a formal education that includes instruc-tion in European languages. However, I also suspect that many women researchers enjoy the unexpected chance to become "a user of signs, rather than a sign-object, an item of exchange,"[14] the position that they often hold in their own societies. As for myself, my research topic dic-tated that I opt for a feminine masquerade. Since this performance dif-fers from the one that I have been taught in my own culture, behaving like a woman in Senegal meant learning new modes of self-presenta-tion—including new fashions.

The great contrast between many of my American and Wolof sub-ject positions proves to me that the researching subject changes because of the research subject. Changes in self-presentation may seem superfi-cial, for anyone can decide to wear a different suit of clothes in order to fit into a different social setting. The important change, for me, involved attitudes toward self-presentation. During my research, for instance, I too judged clothing as a mark of dignity, rather than as the mark of individuality. Such shifts could be seen as further evidence of stable and coherent categories that can be used in order to determine the Same and the Other. On the other hand, they also highlight the important internal contradictions that all attempts to create an identity entail. How stable is an identity constructed over approximately thirty years if one year in another context leads to radical changes?

Clearly, we cannot conflate the experiences of an adult researcher with those of a child being socialized in its own community. Judith Okely makes this point sharply, arguing that

> the commonplace analogy between the anthropologist and a child learning another culture is misleading since the anthropologist is already formed and shaped by history. He or she has to change or superimpose new experience upon past embodied knowledge (Mauss 1938), and come to terms with a changing self embodied in new contexts.[15]

Changes provoked by field experiences may lead to deep internal conflicts and pose important ethical questions. Lila Abu-Lughod has even considered such fieldwork identities a form of dupery that could be seen as a lack of human respect for informants.[16] Although some may see the collective intersubjective construction of a culturally appropriate identity as mere hypocrisy, it is also questionable whether researchers in the field can indeed represent those identity positions that they occupy in other contexts. Perhaps they may be described, but I doubt that it is possible to *perform* them when the researcher already occupies other positions. Ethnographic researchers might even be said to resemble split-personality patients in that they cannot find a language to bridge the gap between two or more identities.

Although some reticences may be strategic, many of the silences that Abu-Lughod describes in her work seem also to stem from the fundamental gaps that lie between a newly constructed identity and an older set of identities that are irrelevant to the context. I do not wish to sidestep the very real ethical problems that Abu-Lughod raises. Even though my own attempts to "perform" a Wolof identity were always highly marked as performances because of the conflicting signs of race and self-presentation,[17] Abu-Lughod's questions interpellate my research experience as well. However, the fact that a griot, doubtful about my "true" identity, decided to call me Haïdara, indicates that such constructions are never entirely those of the individual researcher.

The ethical issues related to imposed and self-imposed constructions of identity provide both the starting-point and the end-point of the reflections that I offer in this study. In chapter 1, I examine the Western imposition of the ideology of individualism on African autobiography

and performance, arguing that this ideology does not exhaust the possibilities for theorizing the relationships that may exist between the individual agent and the community. In chapter 7, I return to the issue of
imposed identities in an analysis of the truth value of autobiographical
discourses that springs from my reading of a performance about one
woman's experiences as a refugee. The post-face, too, addresses the
issue of the ethics of cross-cultural scholarship. These reflections on ethical issues arise within a study focused on Senegalese women's self-representation in performance and text. Just as social identity presents us
with a complex interplay between self and society, self-representation
exists within its own framework. Since the forms of self-representation
available to women in Senegal vary enormously, I will attempt to
explain the choices I have made as a researcher in the following remarks.

AFRICAN AUTOBIOGRAPHY

This study is based on the premise that we cannot analyze particular
forms of self-representation without first considering broader discursive
constructions of self. These constructions depend upon speech genres
for meaning, as I argue in chapter 6. The genre that most obviously presents the process of self-construction for examination is autobiography.
Surprisingly, relatively few scholars have examined African autobiographical discourses, although many have given their attention to the
construction of social identity in Africa. Indeed, a certain blindness to
the great variety of autobiographical discourses has long removed
African autobiographical forms from critical discussion. In the field of
African literature, the first direct criticism of this limitation appeared in
Bernard Mouralis' short preface to a collection of essays entitled *Autobiographies et récits de vie en Afrique*.[18]

This study takes up Mouralis' challenge in that it seeks to present
an African form of autobiographical discourse that cannot be considered a mere tributary to the western autobiographical tradition, nor to
the western ideology of individualism. Opposing the widely accepted
ethnocentric definitions of autobiography as a *western* genre from an
ideological standpoint, as Mouralis did, marks the point of departure
for further studies of autobiography in Africa. However, purely ideological objections—especially if they intend to claim that African literary production is "just as good" as western literary production *because*
it is capable of producing similar genres—not only fail to convince us for
very long, but also lead to an ethnocentric trap, as Amadou Koné cau-
tions in an essay on the autobiographical novel.[19]

In spite, or even because of the dilemma Koné describes, critical interest in African autobiography has grown enormously since Mouralis presented his challenge. For proof, we might indicate the proceedings of the Sixth International Jahnheinz Jahn Symposium, published under the title *Genres autobiographiques en Afrique/Autobiographical Genres in Africa* (Berlin: Dietrich Reimer, 1996), or the 1994 Bordeaux conference proceedings, *Littératures autobiographiques de la francophonie* (ed. Martine Mathieu, Paris: L'Harmattan, 1996). Moreover, *Research in African Literatures* devoted a special issue (volume 28, number 2) to the topic in 1997.

Many of these studies are perhaps most original in that they question the importance of autobiography, as well as received definitions of the genre. In fact, life histories and autobiographies have long played a special role in African Studies, for scholars hope that these genres will allow the subaltern's voice to resound. In spite of these good intentions, we may reinscribe colonialist attitudes by focusing solely on works written in European languages or collected by western scholars. Edward Saïd has observed that heightened awareness of the devastating effects of imperialism and colonialism may unintentionally sustain imperialist views by presenting postcolonial societies as irredeemable. This is tantamount to arguing that nothing exists in the wake of colonialism but the West. However, recognizing colonialism's impact does not mean that all literatures everywhere derive from European traditions, but that analyses of local literary production require a broad, comparative framework. As Saïd suggests, "what is perhaps more relevant is the political willingness to take seriously the alternatives to imperialism, among them the existence of other cultures and societies."[20]

I have turned to the study of oral forms of autobiographical discourses in Senegal to show that alternatives to European autobiographical forms do indeed exist. I am not alone in seeking to describe African formulations of self that owe less to the encounter with Europe than to other influences. At the 1997 MLA meeting in Toronto, I found myself among like-minded researchers at the panel on "Masking and Unmasking the Subject: Biography and Autobiography in African Literatures." Oral poetry, rather than narrative genres, has proved to be fruitful terrain for our investigations. Several chapters of my study thus focus on the *taasu*, a form of declamatory poetry. I focus on performance contexts in chapter 2, on the performer in chapter 3, and on generic identity in chapter 4.

Although these forms of autobiographical discourse existed before Europeans arrived, they are not fossilized survivals emblematic of some pretended cultural purity, for they exist within a dynamic, changing "tradition," or framework. Such "alternatives" to colonialism do not ignore colonial history itself, but represent it within a radically different critical and poetic framework. Scholarship on oral performance not only debunks the colonialist trope of "primitive, oral man,"[21] but also offers a viable solution to the problem Saïd raises. Such work not only presents us with the words of the subaltern who contests colonialism, but also give, us theoretical alternatives to anticolonialist discourses that presume a western conceptual framework.[22]

That framework too often leads us to assume that "orality" and "writing" exist in separate spheres that never touch each other. However, research in literacy studies suggests that we might more fruitfully concentrate on linguistic practice, rather than relying on the narrow definitions of writing as alphabetic script that found the theory of a Great Divide between the written and the oral.[23] In fact, we do not need to privilege one form over another, as I argue in chapter 5. In affirming the importance of oral forms of autobiographical discourse, then, I do not wish to dismiss Senegalese women's reinventions of the self in texts written in French, for I share other scholars' conviction that "there is an unbroken continuity in African verbal art forms, from interacting oral genres to such literary productions as the novel and poetry."[24] In this context, we may see more clearly by focusing on the interplay between performance and document. Such an approach does not negate the very real differences between performance and written text, but evaluates them otherwise.

In my study of those discourses of the self that Senegalese women articulate through autobiographical practice, then, I do not focus exclusively on oral performances, but compare them to texts written in French. Consequently, I view the differences between oral and written discourses of the self quite differently than Alain Ricard, who has argued recently that oral forms of autobiographical discourse cannot exist.[25] Ricard's genuine respect for the difference between performance and writing leads to an unfortunate reinscription of the Great Divide based on the contrast between physical presence in performance and authorial representation in the text. Ricard assumes that physical presence means the same thing in all cultural contexts; however, the performer's presence does not play a predetermined role, but depends upon social constructions of the body, of the self, and of performance. Moreover, the notion of identity as a form of presence is highly problematic, as Jacques Derrida insists. The embodiment of a text or performance consequently becomes a question worth reconsidering.

In this study, I examine the problem of embodiment in various ways. Throughout the study, motherhood and the female body play an important role. However, I examine the issue of the body more directly in chapter 3, where I discuss the performer's identity as it relates to caste and the inherited professional roles that performers play. In chapter 6, I take up this issue again as it relates to Ken Bugul's struggles to understand her embodiment in the world and to make choices about the place she wishes to occupy. Ken Bugul is sharply aware of the need for choice—whether this means greater choice with regard to social identity and status or with regard to motherhood itself. An earlier generation of women, represented by Amina Mbaye and Nafissatou Diallo, believed that women could take a more active role in shaping their lives through the processes of modernization and nation-building that formal independence seemed to announce. In chapter 5, I examine these themes and the growing awareness of the gap between official rhetoric and women's aspirations that appear in the works of Mbaye and Diallo. Their questions are clearly related to Ken Bugul's interrogation of women's identity and agency.

I have chosen to compare various forms of autobiographical discourse, rather than viewing "written" and "oral" inscriptions of self in isolation. Although I do give some attention to the formal similarities between women's written and oral autobiographical forms in chapter 4, the primary bases for comparison in this study are thematic and contextual. In these reflections on the politics of women's self-expression, I do not attempt to defend African women's autobiographical discourses in contrast to other forms of autobiography. As Koné has argued, this would mean re-inscribing western dominance. However, awareness of this trap does not mean that we must give up all interest in comparative studies of the ethical, political, and social dimensions of self-expression. Indeed, studies of the interactions between many different forms of autobiographical practice provide the best source of convincing data to counter theories that would endow any particular tradition of autobiography with genetic purity and primacy. This comparative study of written and oral forms of autobiographical discourse in Senegal seeks to do just this.

CHAPTER 1

Autobiographical Subjects

Waay Gànnaar duma fa dox di dee	Oh, Mauritania, I will not go there to die
Ni siggi dee	If you raise your head, you die
Taxaw dee	Stand, you die
Gëstu dee	Look, you die
foo yëngu mu dig dee	Wherever you move, death promises to come
Dee gaanga Gànnaar	Death is in Mauritania
Gànnaar duma fa dox di dee	Mauritania! I will not go there to die

This fragment of a performance that I recorded in a Senegalese village in 1993[1] reflects the performer's experiences in 1989, when she and many others were forced to flee Mauritania. The "ethnic cleansing" that took place there occurred for many reasons; however, it was made possible only because collective identities erased individual identities. These erasures are never simple, given the complex identitarian politics of the region. Strategies for constructing identities in such a situation are just as complex. Anta Bouna Dieng's poem is but one example of such strategies, for in it, Dieng has made the blank space of an individual identity under erasure into the sign of a new identity that is at once individual and collective. She is now known as Mother Mauritania, a title that simultaneously refers us to the experiences that made of her an anonymous refugee and the *individual* creator of this poem.[2]

On one level, we can describe ethnic cleansing as a form of forced collectivization, for individuals are forced into identitarian categories that they may or may not accept. Forced collectivization occurs on a discursive level in some formulations of "Third World" literature as well:

> Even those [works] which are seemingly private . . . necessarily project a political dimension in the form of national allegory: *the story of the private individual destiny is always an allegory of the embattled situation of the public third-world culture and society.*[3]

I deliberately choose to contrast this extremely sympathetic and idealistic position to the horrors of an ideological collectivization that leads to ethnic cleansing in order to point out the logical error inherent in opposing a collectivist Third World to an individualist West. The positive form of collectivism that Fredric Jameson and others assume simply *exists* in the context of the "embattled Third World" is the product of hard work, just as the collective political consciousness that different groups in the West have sought to establish is the result of intense labor. If the "Third World individual" cannot choose such associations as a social agent, it is difficult to see the difference between the two types of collectivization. Jameson clearly sees the "Third World" individual as representative of the collectivity out of idealism; however, this idealism fails to recognize both the creativity of performers such as Mother Mauritania and the need to resist forced collectivization.

Social scientists face a similar problem, as Abu-Lughod explains very lucidly.

> What became for me the most troubling aspect of ethnographic description was that it, like other social scientific discourses, trafficked in generalizations. Whether "seeking" laws of human sociality or simply characterizing and interpreting ways of life, our goal as anthropologists is usually to use details and the particulars of individual lives to produce typifications.[4]

These typifications are analogous to the literary and literal collectivizations described above. They not only reconstruct or reinforce the exoticism of our Others, while robbing them of their individuality, but also feed the notion that these Others are somehow trapped within the coherent, fixed bounds of their "culture." The notion that Africans experience reality solely in terms of a collective identity belongs to the same problematic school of thought. In fact, observers frequently let the ideological category of western individualism blind them to the very possibility of varied sociocultural constructions of individuality.

Autobiography as a genre offers a solution to the dilemma. Few texts are as unique and full of particulars as an autobiography; however, autobiographies exist as part of a vast discursive project (culture, in other words) that provides the framework for the autobiographer's chosen subject position. In outlining the autobiographical functions of one highly particular form of autobiography (the Wolof *taasu*) in relationship to other discursive forms of self-representation in Senegal, I hope to find another answer to this dilemma, one that neither erases discursive articulations of individuality, nor ignores the wider network of relationships in which the individual is embedded.

INDIVIDUALITIES

Simplistic oppositions between individualist and collectivist societies obviously cannot describe the complex, shifting phenomena involved in the construction of identity, especially when such constructions become acts of resistance. A heavy emphasis on the life of the community and a corresponding lack of willingness to be separated from it as a singular member of society does not necessarily negate individuality as a category of experience. As Jacqueline Rabain argues in her study on early childhood in Wolof communities, every culture must negotiate the particular in relation to the general.[5] A myriad of different configurations of this relationship between the particular and the general is possible, but these possibilities remain invisible to us when we accept a model based on dichotomies opposing "individualist" and "collective" societies.

Autobiography offers us the most striking form of discursive articulation of the problem, for in this genre, the individual agent presents and actively creates a textual self. The autobiographer's fictional self[6] takes shape in relation to others, thus offering insight into the interaction between the individual and the community. Clearly, the autobiographical self shapes the community as well. This reciprocal relationship between autobiography and other cultural discourses has led some scholars to ask whether autobiography can be tied to particular cultures, as Georges Gusdorf does in his seminal essay on autobiography, "Conditions et limites de l'autobiographie."[7] In Gusdorf's view, autobiography is a purely western product,

> a late phenomenon in Western culture, coming at that moment when the Christian contribution was grafted onto classical traditions. Moreover, it would seem that autobiography is not to be found outside of our cultural area; one would say that it expresses a concern peculiar to Western man, a concern that has been of good use in his systematic conquest of the universe and that he has communicated to men of other cultures; but those men will thereby have been annexed by a sort of intellectual colonizing to a mentality that is not their own.[8]

Gusdorf's type of criticism clearly attempted to use the genre to anchor empire. Any further attempts to trace the autobiographical tradition in Africa that define autobiography solely within the rigid limits set by western examples risk reinscribing "self-writing" in an imperialist framework. Studies of African autobiography, then, must attempt to discern the specificities of "self-writing" in Africa.

Given the complexity of this task, it is easy enough to fall into overgeneralizations when seeking to define "African" autobiography. As a result, the few studies that specifically focus on African autobiographies often rely on simplistic cultural models that oppose western individualism to African collectivism. The only book-length study, James Olney's *Tell Me Africa: An Approach to African Literature*,[9] covers a remarkable number of autobiographies. Olney's sensitive readings of these autobiographies and his arguments for a distinctively African form of autobiography[10] constitute a major shift in critical practice, for he reveals Gusdorf's blindness to specifically African forms of autobiography. Nevertheless, his account of African autobiographical discourses suffers from a failure to question Gusdorf's foundational dichotomy. Olney presents that dichotomy differently, but accepts the basic premise that western societies are individualist, while African societies are collective.

Olney's attempt to reconcile the singular with the collective leads to an unfortunate conflation of the two. First, he assumes that cultural "reality" in Africa is a monolithic, unchanging, and ahistorical entity, and argues that African life "has about it an extraordinary unity and cohesion" made possible by a "single principle" that determines everything about life in Africa, including autobiography.[11] Eliding all differences among Africans in this way may simplify the task of the critic, faced with enormous diversity within the field of African autobiography; however, a simplistic criticism that flies in the face of substantial evidence is the result. Next, Olney accepts the premise that African identities are always and only collective, arguing that the lateral "unity of life and the communality of existence, as African autobiographies display it" means that "the individual is taken as essentially identical with the group and the group as identical with the individual."[12]

Only a few years after Olney's book on African autobiography was published, Honorat Aguessy argued for a different understanding of individuality in Africa.

> Dans tout mode de production culturelle, qu'il s'agisse de la scripturalité ou de l'oralité, aucune valeur ne surgit dans le champ de la consommation publique sans passer, ne serait-ce qu'un instant, par l'individu. Mais l'individu ne s'oppose pas à la collectivité, au groupe. . . . Il y a donc, entre l'individu et le groupe, mille liens tissés et qui demeurent indéchirables.[13]

> In any mode of cultural production, whether written or oral, no value emerges in the field of public consumption without passing, even if just for a moment, through the individual. But the individual is not opposed to the collectivity, to the group. . . . There are thus thousands of ties woven between the individual and the group that remain indestructible. (my translation)

Certainly one can argue that throughout most of Africa, the life of the community provides the framework for individual experience. Since this premise provides the basis for all of the human and social sciences, however, it appears to be a given. Indeed, the high degree of individualism that Olney and others point to as the defining characteristic of western societies follows the same logic. Individuals do not necessarily choose their relative degree of autonomy; western society provides a framework that values and encourages the western *ideology* of individualism, a specific configuration of the relationship between individual and community. Olney's otherwise laudable attempt to explain the discursive phenomenon of African self-representation thus founders upon an uncritical acceptance of a limited number of anthropological theories and exaggerated overgeneralizations.

In fact, the models used by Gusdorf and Olney do not give an accurate description of current autobiographical practices in the West any more than they do of African autobiographical discourses. As János Riesz claims, too many scholars have elevated the eighteenth-century confessional model of European autobiography to a definitive status.[14] Yet the confessional model does not explain the wide range of European autobiography, either, for it simply cannot account for experiments such as Sartre's *Les mots*, Roland Barthes' *Roland Barthes*, Michel Leiris' multivolume autobiographical experiment, or any number of other texts we might name. We must look elsewhere, then, for a theory that can cope with this genre's complexity and plasticity.

THE AUTOBIOGRAPHICAL PACT

The culturalist models outlined above disappoint us primarily because they assume that each culture presents essentially unchanging models of self. In contrast, more recent culturalist analyses of autobiography historicize and contextualize concepts of selfhood and identity. Poststructuralist ideas have played an important role in this shift. Although many theories of autobiography now take poststructuralism into account, few of them take up the notion of the individual's relationship to the community. Philippe Lejeune's theory is an exception, as it focuses on the relations between text and audience. Lejeune's work had a revolutionary impact on genre studies because he argued that generic identity depends upon the reader's interaction with the text. Obviously, cultural conventions of reading inform such a theory. One may ask what is so original about these propositions, since they are common to the schools of reader-response and reception theory. Unlike most reader-response critics, more interested in questions relevant to the psychological experience of the reader (Holland), the construction of a reading community (Fish, Jauss), or the hermeneutic problems involved in reading (Iser), Lejeune applied the concepts of reader-response theory to the formation of a genre and combined the theory with a "thick" contextualization.

The major problem addressed in *Le pacte autobiographique* is that of the seventeenth- and eighteenth-century philosophers: how and why did individuals give up the total freedom of autarchy and form a society or community? Lejeune's work stays well within the borders of the Enlightenment tradition of the social contract, since he chooses Rousseau's *Confessions* as the basis for his theory. Therefore, he accepts the legalistic definitions of the person that grounds the theory, including the notion that each individual possesses property rights in him or herself (the self being construed as the physical body as well as the intellectual capacities attached to the person). In addition, Rousseau defined individuals in terms of their personal interests, arguing that individuals choose to give up the unlimited freedom of the "state of nature" in order to gain a form of collective freedom that is limited but secures certain advantages. Because the community serves individuals' interests, the individuals are loyal to the interests of the community.[15]

Likewise, autobiographers sign a contract with their readers; the name on the title page corresponds to the name of a real person, who accepts the legal responsibility that any signatory to a contract holds. According to Lejeune, the key to the genre is the status of the proper name in relation to the text. Because the author is not a person, but a contractual function,

> the entire existence of the person we call the *author* is summed up by this name: the only mark in the text of an unquestionable world-beyond-the-text, referring to a real person . . . [whose] existence is beyond question: exceptions and breaches of trust serve only to emphasize the general credence accorded this type of social contract.[16]

This is a striking shift from the attempt to isolate the formal elements that distinguish the genre toward a relational model that understands autobiography as a form of social interaction.

Although Lejeune's theory thus offers a more flexible understanding of the relationships between the individual author and the community, it remains well within the bounds of European social contract theory, which provides the basis for the notion of the autobiographical pact. Most scholars of autobiography accepted the historical and cultural limits on the genre that this and other western theories imposed until the late 1980s. However, critics of social contract theory have multiplied since the poststructuralists first presented their reading of the Enlightenment project.[17] These critiques can be linked to increased interest in postcolonial studies, as well as to minority or ethnic studies and women's studies.

As western cultural observers note a growing fragmentation and anomie that trouble the positivist conceptualization of the individual as the agent of progress, the continuing struggle for self-determination in "postcolonial" regions has led to other formulations of the self that must inform our theories of the genre. The struggle for the "right" to self-determination has not only led to nominal independence in Africa, but has also brought western conceptions of subjectivity into doubt.

Nevertheless, many fairly recent attempts to conceptualize the right to self-determination still depend upon the theories of a social contract made by consenting individuals that found their strongest expression in the political thought of the Enlightenment. This is paradoxical, for social contract theory assumes that only those autonomous individuals who can in some way affect their conditions can demand the right to self-determination. Membership in a group conceived of as "natural"[18] thus precludes self-determination *as a member of that group*. For this reason, members of the groups excluded from the social contract protest the current centrifugal revisions of individual identity. For instance, bell hooks writes that it seems suspicious that elite theorists decided to erase the author's name[19] just as the voices of oppressed minority groups have begun to gain a measure of public influence. Henry Louis Gates, too, has rejected the "grandfather clause" of criticism that has removed the possibility of self-determination just as subaltern groups have gained public space to articulate their own identities legally, as well as privately and poetically.[20] Paradoxically, then, emancipatory movement has been caught in a conservative, centrifugal backlash because of the contractarian framework of the modern nation-state that initially made resistance possible.

The complexity of these problems does not do away with the need for self-determination. As Gates argues, "self-identification" is a prerequisite for agency, and, by extension, of liberatory action. Although such self-identifications clearly have no permanence, as philosophers from Heraclitus to Derrida have argued, this knowledge does not obviate the human need for names. Autobiography and praise poems, two ways of naming the self, voice this need clearly. Yet no one name can satisfy this desire forever; if it were to do so, we would have no need of history. This is as true of group identification as it is of individual identification (and partly explains the history of changing names for peoples of African descent in the Diaspora). This is just another way of saying what Derrida has already told us: the center (of interest, of power, or of any framework we care to build) constantly shifts, and constantly restructures the Law.

Although the rule of Law does imply coercion, anarchy—the absence of Law—does not preclude violence, according to Thomas Hobbes and other social contract theorists (life was "nasty, brutish, and short" before the social contract that instituted the reign of Law). Contractarians, then, perceive the subject as a hyperindividualistic, isolated outlaw who will participate in the life of the community only when constrained to do so. Poststructuralist critics who seek to end the reign of Law in order to achieve greater freedom must thus contest the contractarian notion of subjectivity. Either "outlaw" subjectivity must be redefined in positive terms, or the subject itself must be redefined. Typically, poststructuralists have chosen the latter option, proclaiming the fictionality of the subject. Those accounts focused on the individual subject have offered few explanations for the relationships formed between the individual and the community, signaling a contradictory acceptance of social contract theory's insistence that individuals alone can claim the right to self-determination.

Other critics of social contract theory target this very problem from various standpoints. Feminists such as Carole Pateman now argue that the contractarians' thesis that each individual owns himself as one might own a piece of property not only leads to absurd contradictions, but also excludes women from the field of subjectivity. She states that the patriarchal contract establishes a fraternal form of male power and a dual system that structures society in private and public spheres. Since women are part of the private sphere, they are excluded from civil society. "Women both are and are not part of the civil order. Women are not incorporated as 'individuals' but as women" (Pateman, 181). Race, too, has operated to exclude individuals from the social contract. Patricia Williams argues, along Pateman's lines, that African-Americans cannot obtain the right of self-ownership crucial to the social contract in the discursive order that establishes them as a separate group.[21] These problems heighten our awareness of the difficulties of using social contract theory to explain the relationships between individual agents and communities.

In fact, the social contract offers and simultaneously removes the individual's freedom of choice in the matter of social relationships. We might wish to argue that agency disappears with choice in this context. To do so would mean accepting the model of power relationships that Hobbes presented in *Leviathan* in the seventeenth century. If we accept, for the moment, the notion of a global system much like a leviathan that swallows all in its path, we might associate the beast with European colonization. In the wake of decolonization, Africa does not seem to have emerged whole from the neocolonial leviathan, which also appears to leave monstrous young in its wake. Many postindependence African states have established an internal dual system to distinguish the remainders of precolonial civil society from postcolonial civil society.[22] In other words, the modern state's structure both requires the concept of the individual as owner and excludes or gives limited recognition to individuals who participate in the local civil society.

AGENCY AND HUMAN RIGHTS

These problems of theory are directly related to ethical and human rights issues of great urgency. Whether they focus on the same issue or not, human rights activists must struggle with the same need to redefine relationships between the singular and the plural, the individual and the community. Autobiographical discourses thus play a larger role than that of mere testimonies to human rights abuses. Indeed, they may offer new answers to old problems—such as the difference between African and western conceptualizations of human rights in a broad sense. Western notions of human rights have been predicated on contractarian theories of the individual that many African (and Asian) commentators and theorists dispute, claiming that collective rights subsume those of individuals. Here the importance of autobiography theory may seem clearer, as I have presented it as a debate on the construction of identity. The recent, postmodernist interrogation of identity seems to obviate the need to discuss yet again these conflicts between western and African or Asian definitions of human rights, for postmodernists accept the radical contingency of identity.

Autobiographical genres seem most unlikely to disprove postmodernist theories of constructed subjectivities, since they are the record and indeed the very process of self-construction laid out for readers to share. Although some may have taken the postmodernist exposure of the "illusion" of individual identity to mean that studies of the genre (in the sense of studies of an individual's life) are futile, others regard autobiography as the fascinating site of the collapse of concepts of subject, self, and author.[23] As John Eakin argues, the constructed nature of the autobiographical self may make the discursive articulation of such constructions—in other words, autobiography—more precious, rather than less so.[24] In arguing that individuality has falsely been identified with individualism, and that individuality exists in Africa as well as in the West, I do not dispute these theories. Indeed, the fact that a performer such as Mother Mauritania presents the agony of castration endured by male prisoners in Mauritania as if it were her own points in the opposite direction (see the full version of the poem in chapter 7). Rather, I wish to stress that specifically African articulations of individuality have been virtually ignored in the past. In spite of western attempts to reject the heritage of Cartesianism in the twentieth century, this continues to be true, mocking all efforts to escape the prisonhouse of language and the subjects it creates.

Concomitant essentialism rehabilitates the form of individualism that "has ruthlessly excluded countless numbers of our people."[25] Any further discussion of subjectivity or the relationship between the one and the many thus requires some consideration of human rights. I could easily avoid the real difficulties of the problem by simply arguing that all language is social, thus individuals exist as sociolinguistic creations. This glib answer, however, avoids the problems of human rights and responsibilities that Mother Mauritania's performance emphasizes. What if someone assigns me an identity that I do not accept? What if my social identity is reduced to that of the pariah who must be destroyed for fascists and ethnic "cleansers" to achieve their political goals?

If we wish to take the victims' pain into account, human rights must take center stage. Collectively distributed, human rights do not resolve the problems under discussion. Indeed, the argument for a specifically African, collective basis for human rights legislation was rejected in Dakar in 1967, when francophone legal experts claimed in their "Declaration de Dakar" that "il ne pouvait y avoir différentes interprétations de la dignité de l'homme . . . les exigences fondamentales de la primauté de droit ne sont pas différentes en Afrique de ce qu'elles sont ailleurs" [Different interpretations of human dignity could not exist . . . the fundamental demands for the primacy of law are no different in Africa than they are elsewhere].[26] Although the theoretical battles about collective versus individual rights continue, this conference demonstrates that the people who must make legal decisions reject a purely relativist standpoint in the matter.

Yet purely individualistic notions of human rights ignore the possibility of conceptions of individuality other than that of the social contract theorists. If my rights end where another individual's begin, where do we set the limits of individual space? The Senegalese judge Kéba Mbaye claims that precolonial African societies resolved the dilemma in a very practical way, by linking individuals' rights to others' responsibilities. "Il s'agit d'affirmer ces droits indirectement sous la forme de devoirs des autres. Cette conception des droits de l'homme nous paraît beaucoup plus efficace que celle qui se contente d'énoncer des droits sans prévoir la manière de les faire respecter" [This involves affirming rights indirectly in the form of others' duties. This conception of human rights seems much more effective to us than that which is satisfied by proclaiming rights without foreseeing a way of enforcing them.][27]

Blending the rights of the community and the rights of the individual in such a way reflects a conception of individuality that always puts the individual subject in a social framework. Since individuality only appears within such constructed frameworks, the battles over whether a notion of constructed identity erases the empirical reality of the individual or not seem unanswerable. Moreover, the individual agent can only be observed with regard to other agents.

> The acting subject or agent is . . . a pivot of relationships. I do not mean one who is an assemblage of or locus of relationships—that is the 'person,' the form of their objectification. By agent, I mean one who *from his or her own vantage point acts with another's in mind.*[28]

This definition of agency implies that agency and responsibility for others are tied to each other, thus supporting Mbaye's description of a practicable form of human rights.

CHAPTER 2

The Gift of Praise

As I have argued in chapter 1, identities become visible primarily through the individual's active negotiation of her relations to the whole community. Autobiography offers a public space for just this sort of negotiation of identities. Indeed, many observers have noted that autobiographers frequently choose the genre in order to gain prestige or rectify misunderstandings. This is true of the oral autobiographical discourses performed in Wolof communities as well. The *taasu*, a form of praise poetry that women perform at family events, provides the most striking example. *Taasu* mark the subject positions of an individual agent, but also provide a discursive space for negotiating relationships between participants at these events during and through the exchange of gifts. Examples of the very special subgenre of autobiographical *taasu* are the fruit of many years of verbal and material exchanges between performer and audience members. Indeed, autobiographical discourse becomes autobiographical *exchange* within the *géew*, or ring formed by audience and participants in the *taasu* performance.

These rings evoke another circle—the hermeneutic circle. This circle bedevils critics dealing with panegyric genres, perhaps even more so than other critics, because the relationships between the whole and the parts that make up the text are so unstable. Praise poetry as a genre defies definition, for it is a fluid, yet circumscribed literary genre. We cannot interpret praise poems satisfactorily in a New Critical style that seeks to describe each poem as an autonomous entity. Rather, these are richly allusive, context-specific works that can best be understood if we consider their social function as well as their internal textual tools for creating meaning.

This is the approach that Leslie Kurke has taken toward Pindar's odes, which have received relatively little critical attention simply because few scholars considered their functions as praise poems. In contrast, Kurke's analysis focuses on the odes as praise poems deliberately composed for gain, thus revealing the literary wealth of the genre. Kurke argues that these poems were of great significance in ancient Greek society, for they provided the measure of a household's reputation, much as the praise of Wolof performers insures the reputation of compounds today. The Greeks depended on praise from poets such as Pindar, not only because boasting of one's own accomplishments was disdained, but also because performances of praise poetry created a symbolic arena for social competition. Kurke's innovative interpretation of praise poetry in terms of exchange thus opens up new possibilities for the scholarly study of Pindar's oeuvre and of other forms of praise poetry that this chapter explores in light of Wolof women's performances of praise poems known as *taasu*.[1]

PRAISE NAMES

The Wolof say that "Teraanga moo dox sunu diggante, nde du lu ñaaw"—literally, "It is gift-giving[2] that brings us together, for it is not ugly." The proverb suggests that *teraanga* not only brings people together, but is necessary for relationships to function, since *dox* also means "to function." The reciprocity expressed in the proverb threads through many Wolof social interactions. Praises such as "she has *teraanga*," are subtly reciprocal, since the giver is honorable *because* she honors others. In fact, all praise is reciprocal in a sense, for praise too is a form of gift that joins people. Research on the *taasu* undertaken outside of the circle of reciprocal exchanges would thus ignore the essence of the genre. Indeed, such work would be "ugly," for the concept of *teraanga* excludes the ugly and the unpleasant. The circular esthetic of *taasu* subsists only within the round of gift exchanges.

The word *taasu* itself refers us to the idea of *teraanga*. According to Arame Fall, linguist at IFAN (Institut Fondamental de l'Afrique Noire), *taas* roughly means to bless someone. More precisely, she says, it means the act of associating Allah's *baraka*, or blessings, with someone [through praise] in hopes that the person will receive those blessings (personal communication, Dakar 11/25/93). In the Wolof-French dictionary that she and her collaborators produced, *taas* and *taasu* receive the following definitions:

> **taas,** v. associer, faire participer [to associate, cause to participate]. Utilisé, en général, dans des expressions du type: *Na nu Yàlla taas ci barke nit kooku!* Que Dieu fasse que nous ayons notre part de la bénédiction de cet homme! [Used, in general, in expressions of the type: May God give us a share of the blessings due to that person (mentioned in the sentence)].
>
> **taas w-,** n. devise déclamée par le danseur [praise name declaimed by a dancer].
>
> **taasu,** v. chanter sa devise avant de danser [to sing one's slogan or associated praises before dancing].[3]

Saxiir Caam, renowned not only for his work as a mathematician, but also for his knowledge of Wolof culture and language, gives a definition more closely related to the idea that the verb means to associate someone with something pleasurable or profitable. In his view, *taas* means "de faire goûter à quelqu'un," or to give someone a taste of something. He adds that *taasu* means "se faire goûter," or "to give oneself a taste" [of something]. As an example, he mentioned the blessing, "Yàlla na Yàlla taas ci barkaam," which he translated into French during our interview, as "Que Dieu me fasse goûter une partie de son *baraka*." [May God give me a taste of part of his blessings] (Interview, Liberté V, Dakar 11/12/93).

If we accept these definitions of the word *taas* and *taasu*, it is clear that we are dealing with a panegyric genre.[4] *Taas* clearly means something close to "to bless," or "to praise," but suggests nuances of meaning that no specific English word can capture. In addition, the definition given above does not distinguish between praises directed at others and self-referential praise. The reflexive use of the verb *taas*, however, opens up the possibility not only for "auto-louange," or self-praise, but also for autobiographical enunciations. Indeed, the reflexive form implies that the speaker attempts to gain part of whatever blessings she may bring to the subject of praise, or even speaks in order to gain blessings for herself alone. Furthermore, in my informants' usage, the reflexive form was much more common than the first form, *taas*. Rather than saying "Dafa ko-y taas" [She is praising her/him], informants most often said "Dafa-y taas" [She is performing a taasu/blessing], or "Dafa-y taasu" [She is praising (for herself)].

NAMING THE DAY

Although these are useful definitions, they have meaning only in context. Context also appears indissociable from the production of meaning in *taasu* performance. Indeed, the most sophisticated definition of the *taasu* available to date focuses on the boundaries demarcating the *taasu* from other events and from everyday linguistic practice. As Cherif Thiam's entire study revolves around defining the genre, it is difficult to extract a brief and simplistic definition of the genre. The title itself, "Introduction à l'étude d'un genre satirico-laudatif: Le taasu wolof" [Mémoire de maîtrise, UCAD, 1979] provides the best brief description of the genre, for the genre is both praise poetry and satire. Thiam defines the *taasu* contextually, then formally. In terms of context, he insists on two particularly interesting points: first, that every Wolof can expect "her" day to arrive, and thus that events belong to individuals; second, that the audience complements the chorus (which complements the *taasukat*) during performance. According to Thiam, "chez les Wolof, les jours se suivent mais ne se ressemblent pas. Chaque personne a son jour, et l'expression est connue de tous qui dit 'SAMA BIS BI' pour signifier 'c'est mon jour'" [Among the Wolof, the days follow each other, but do not resemble each other. Each person has his/her day, and everyone knows the expression "SAMA BIS BI," which means, "It's my day"].[5] Although Thiam restricts his discussion to family events, his explanation of the importance of "sama bis bi" is enlightening. If a particular woman can claim the day as her own, then the event is necessarily personalized. Thiam adds that these "days" mark the different stages of the life cycle of the individual.

Although these points may seem banal at first sight, they are vital when placed in the context of Western discourses on Africa that de-individualize and depersonalize such events. Anthropologists long focused on an abstract life-cycle in their attempts to arrive at general truths about African societies, thus losing sight of the intensely individual, particular character of the events marking the different stages.[6] It is in literature and in the life histories of individuals that the intensely personal character of "sama bis bi" has appeared. For example, Thiam quotes Camara Laye's *L'enfant noir* to support his argument, reminding us that autobiographical discourses counterbalance the anthropological bias in favor of impersonal accounts of the "typical" life-cycle.

The event, as well as the *taasu*, depends upon the interaction between the individual performer and her audience, whose "contribution se situe dans leur reconversion en chorale, par la reprise du refrain" [Their contribution converts them into a chorus, [as they] repeat the refrain].[7] This description defines the role of the audience clearly, if briefly; however, Thiam merely suggests the importance of the audience, without revealing that it is the key to *taasu*. The *taasu* is so highly contextual that it only exists in relation to a specific audience. The audience not only repeats the refrain and interprets the meaning of the poem, but also assists in the creation of the poem through the exchange mechanisms that inform my analysis of this genre as a form of autobiographical expression.

Most *taasu* are improvised on the spur of the moment. Some of them are two or three lines long and completely circumstantial, as Mariama Ndoye and Abdoulaye Kéïta remark;[8] others are much longer. The duration of a performance depends on many factors; among the Wolof, as in Kpelle communities in Liberia, performance time is expandable. According to Ruth Stone, Kpelle time "may be characterized by expandable 'moments' or 'presents.' Within these presents, people . . . [are] constantly negotiating, fitting, and adjusting to one another, making past experiences fit into the present."[9] This describes the *taasu* performance perfectly. Once a performer enters the ring formed by spectators, she negotiates the temporal order as well as the content of her performance with the audience. Poems are of highly variable duration, as performers add new lines to the poem in a seemingly effortless flow, improvising and extending the poem for as long as they can hold their audience. On the other hand, the audience and other potential performers also give cues when the performer should end her poem. This fits Stone's description of Kpelle music events as well.

The conception of time as expandable is enlightening not only in terms of *taasu* performance, but also with respect to the way many Wolof conceptualize experience itself. If time is perceived as a non-linear series of expandable moments that involve constant negotiations with others, surely this conception will affect not only forms of self-expression, but also the content of that expression. In fact, discursive time and space interact in the *taasu*. The "same" poem fulfills an entirely different function and takes on a new meaning in various contexts. This might explain the disagreements among scholars and informants concerning the appropriate contexts for the performance of *taasu*.

In general, most *taasu* performances take place during family ceremonies such as naming ceremonies (*ngente*) and *ceet* (the ceremony that marks the bride's departure from her family home), at women's dance parties (*sabar*), and at the social meetings of women's credit associations (*túr* and *nàtt*). These contexts favor non-professional performances by family members and friends, but do not exclude performers who have a primarily professional, client relationship with the family. Nevertheless, women may perform *taasu* on almost any occasion in order to express themselves. For instance, one woman punctuated the end of our interview with a *taasu* in order to express her pleasure at our meeting. Young girls often perform *taasu* when they play together, as well. These informal performances offer a chance for young girls to hone their skills as performers. They also prove the continuing importance of this genre. Many informants tended to view the formal events as the most important space for *taasu* performances; however, informal, spontaneous performances create the backdrop and the anticipation necessary to the relatively more important performances at naming ceremonies and other formal events.

In other settings, performances lose their spontaneity and take on other qualities that are linked to the professional status of the performers. Purely professional performances take place at political rallies, the Théâtre National Daniel Sorano, on radio and television, and even in nightclubs these days. Although some informants exclude the *taasu* per-

formed in contemporary urban settings as well as the purely professional forms from their definitions of the genre, my findings contradict
the notion that we should relegate the *taasu* solely to village events.
Doing so simultaneously romanticizes and dehistoricizes Wolof culture.
Ignoring urban *taasu* not only means relegating the genre to the margins, but also blinding oneself to the contemporary realities of *taasu* performance. As Deborah Heath writes, "It [*taasu*] is a dynamic tradition;
new *taasu* appear regularly, spreading quickly from city to city and from
town to village, with many variants emerging in the process"[10] (Heath,
93).

Given the wide variety of contexts favorable to *taasu* performances,
contextualizing the genre is an extraordinarily difficult task. Other
scholars' efforts reinforce this impression, for the available studies
examine only a few of the possible performance contexts. Ndoye
remarks that "le taasu est une sorte de melting-pot, de genre à tout-
faire . . . [qui] révèle les valeurs culturelles de l'ethnie, de par la diversité
de ses thèmes" ["The taasu is a sort of melting pot, an all-purpose
genre . . . that reveals the cultural values of the ethnic group through the
diversity of its themes],[11] emphasizing the *diversity* of the genre. For this
reason, we may frame *taasu* performance in many different ways. These
may be overlapping or even contradictory, depending on which aspect
we choose to examine. These shifts in perspective may be seen as an
inescapable problem, but they can also be seen as a source of new and
rich insight into the same phenomena.

We cannot ever master the whole, but perhaps we can glimpse a bit
of it if we squint to bring the overlapping circles of interpretation
together. Just as when we try to bring a kaleidoscope into focus, we may
see more possibilities in the moment before the frame snaps into place
than we do afterwards. One way of studying overlapping spheres
involves "what Barber and Farias advocate in the study of oral texts,
that is, the capacity of a performance, any performance, 'to activate
spheres beyond the confines of its own textuality, and be implicated in
social and political action.'"[12] I have attempted to bring these spheres of
taasu performance into focus by examining the exchanges that take
place within the performance context; now we must turn to the socioeconomic context in order to better understand these overlapping
spheres.

GIFTS AND GAIN

In Senegal, informal gift exchanges unfold within an official political
economy whose representatives periodically condemn the informal gift

economy, frequently by passing laws against ostentatious celebrations,[13] even though they, too, are implicated in the gift economy. Leonardo Villalón notes that these exchanges distinguish the independent state of Senegal sharply from the former colonial administration. This is true, but the colonial administration could not ignore the gift economy either. According to colonial circulars on celebrations, the official budgets for festivities usually specified payment for the oral performers known as griots, or *géwël*.[14] Other evidence indicates that the gift economy is an almost unavoidable part of life in Senegal.

Theoretically, modernization and development do away with the need for this gift economy, often equated with premodern or "archaic" culture.[15] However, attempts to develop Senegal according to the "rational" model often stumble against the Wolof notion that investments in relationships are safer than investments in objects. The experiences of the CHODAK project in Grand-Yoff (a suburb of Dakar) financed by the non-governmental organization ENDA provide great insight into the workings of this "silent partner" of the formal economy. The CHODAK group participants offered loans and technical assistance to various groups with the goal of establishing a more egalitarian society through "un modèle de gestion transparent, démocratique et égalitaire" [a transparent, democratic, and egalitarian model of management].[16]

This model failed. Each time that the group attempted to set up a savings account, they found that the women involved emptied it in order to use the money for their different needs. "A leurs yeux, 'un dépôt d'argent n'a pas de sens.' Ce qui compte c'est la 'circulation' de l'argent au sein des quartiers ou des réseaux sous divers prétextes" [In their eyes, 'a warehouse for money has no sense.' What counts is the 'circulation' of the money within the neighborhoods or networks, under different circumstances].[17] When the group's participants attempted to influence the women to follow a different model, the women pretended to agree, but continued to act according to their own economic model. Indeed, they attempted to persuade the CHODAK workers to accept their model, and participate in their exchange networks.

"The Wolof have a fairly sophisticated understanding of many of the economic problems which confront them," as the anthropologist David Ames has noted with reference to Wolof villagers in the Gambia.[18] Senegalese women, urban and rural, certainly show just as much, if not more, sophistication in their analyses of their economic situation. In any case, they clearly had a more sophisticated understanding of their economic situation than these development workers realized. The economic decisions that the CHODAK group saw as problems were actually very reasonable in light of the women's situation and the foreseeable economic changes. Since many of the women involved in the project were used to highly unstable and irregular sources of income, they argued that "Wut nit moo gën wut alal" [It's better to seek people than wealth].[19] In their experience, the loyalty of friends and family lasts longer than the profit they might gain from any purely economic activity. Since they belong to multiple and diverse networks, they do not depend on any one relationship. Emmanuel Ndione concludes that "l'activité économique n'est pas le seul moyen de survie. Au contraire, tabler exclusivement sur elle conduit à une rupture avec le réseau de solidarité existant, à un isolement et donc à l'inertie ou à une impasse" [Economic activities are not the only means of survival. Conversely, counting exclusively on them leads to a break with the existing network of solidarity, to isolation, and thus to inertia or to an impasse].[20] Following the development team's plan would have meant giving up the safe investments of a lifetime for the uncertain rewards of a new economic activity within the framework of a fluctuating, uncertain local economy. If the CHODAK project in Grand-Yoff had succeeded, its success would have been mitigated by the many problems such a success would create.

The problem with the women's model is that it rests on the practice of "Rey bukki, suul bukki"—killing one hyena in order to bury another. When speaking French, many Wolof simply call this practice "faire bukki"—doing a hyena. Doing a hyena means borrowing from one place in order to pay another debt. It can even involve buying a product and selling it at less than cost. Women will do this when desperate, and are forced to sell at less than cost because they have no other way of attracting customers, who would otherwise go to one of the many stores that give credit. Wolof look down on "doing a hyena" as a dishonorable practice in general, but the practice has grown widespread as economic conditions worsen. Clearly, this practice does not improve a woman's situation; however, it does allow her to keep a credit line at the local store, making it possible to feed the family.

"Doing a hyena" is the desperate act of a consumer who has lost the power of economic agency. As Arjun Appadurai argues in light of global capitalism,

> the consumer has been transformed, through commodity flows (and the mediascapes, especially of advertising, that accompany them), into a sign, both in Baudrillard's sense of a simulacrum which only asymptotically approaches the form of a real social agent; and in the sense of a mask for the real seat of agency, which is not the consumer but the producer and the many forces that constitute production.[21]

The only way in which these women can approach the status of economic actors consists in building networks on the basis of the gift.

Although many of them do produce goods, few can be considered economic actors as a result. Indeed, most economically powerful women are market traders, rather than producers of goods. Historically, trade has been the source of wealth in the region, rather than production. In other words, the ability to *distribute* goods has been the source of power. Studies of precolonial political structures in Senegambia confirm this point.[22]

For most women, unable to achieve this status, membership in rotating credit associations known as *nàtt*, or "tontines," *mbootaay* (cooperatives), and even *túr* all function as attempts to turn an impersonal and fluctuating economy to the agent's ends. *Nàtt* literally means contribution. Members give a specified sum each month, and at the end of a certain period, someone receives the amount saved. All members are assured that they will receive a large sum at some point in time. *Mbootaay* are associations based on some economic activity, such as tie-dying or preparing fish for sale. *Túr* are seen as parties; the word comes from the French word "tour," or turn. Each month, one of the group's members invites the entire group to her home for a party. The women eat a meal, or snacks, talk, dance, and sometimes add *taasu* to the event. At the end of the event, gifts will be distributed to some of the women whose "turn" it is. Each month, each member gives a contribution, and each can be sure that she will receive one of the gifts at some time in the coming months. At one *túr* I attended in a Dakar suburb (Liberté II, March 1993), women received special headties, as well as incense. *Túr* essentially help women pay for the cosmetics and accessories that they need in order to be properly dressed. The demands of the *sañse* system pose real problems for women with a meager income. In contrast, the sums that women gain from *nàtt* are far more important, and allow them to consider long-term economic projects. Unfortunately, these organizations are not infallible sources of credit; many women accuse the managers of these funds of corruption and mismanagement.

THE TRAFFIC IN PRAISE

In the past, anthropologists and other scholars have focused heavily on the systematic exchange of *material* gifts; however, the exchange of symbolic gifts such as praise poems has received far less attention. Nevertheless, one can explain the importance of such poems in an economic fashion.[23] Public reputation is a precious good in many communities, for it is the key to the mutual assistance upon which individuals depend. Praise poems fit into this economy of exchange, as they serve to reinforce alliances. If a woman's friends support her by performing laudatory praise poems at family ceremonies, her public reputation improves. She will exchange the favor at the next opportunity. The obligations toward family members and friends that determine formal gift exchanges at events such as baptisms and *ceet* (the public ceremony during which a bride moves to her husband's home), as well as the underlying conflicts or alliances among women, often form the basis for the content of praise poems that are performed during celebrations. As a result, praise poetry offers a public space for the expression of experiences and sentiments that would otherwise remain hidden to those outside of the family circle.[24] If this blurring of the lines between the public and the private is essential to autobiographical discourse, as some would argue, then this category of *taasu* performance clearly performs an autobiographical function. Professional performances differ markedly, for the performer expects an immediate material reward; however, some professionals still use their art to reinforce long-standing relationships to their patrons, in accordance with older client-patron patterns.[25] For the moment, I wish rather to focus on amateur performers of praise poetry.

Because public reputation matters so much, public performances of praise poetry offer a useful strategy for negotiating social relationships. If a woman stingily refuses to share food with her husband's sisters, they will surely allude to the situation during her child's naming ceremony, or *ngente*, in order to humiliate her and effectively force her to behave correctly. The following example, performed at a baptism in Louga 5/26/93, highlights exactly this situation.

Faatu J.	Faatu J. (name of the child's mother)
Jabar ju la xàllal sa kër	The woman who clears [tidies] her house
ba sa njaboot dëkk	So that her family [has room to] live there
moo ma gënal	Pleases me more
ku la xàllal sa kër	Than she who clears her house
ba sa njaboot tuxu	of her family [so that her family moves out]
Chorus:	
Faatu J.	Faatu J.
Jabar ju la xàllal sa kër	The woman who clears her house
ba sa njaboot dëkk	To make room for her family
kooka jarna fas u Naar	That one is worth an Arab horse
jar na naaru góor	She's worth a stallion
jar na oto	And deserves a car
Waaye, jabar ju la xàllal sa kër	But a woman who clears her house

Ba sa njaboot tuxu	So that the family leaves—
Kooku jarna yat u kel	That one deserves a wooden club;[26]
Jar na dóor ba dee	She deserves to be beaten to death

Chorus:

Ewaay jabar na la jig	Oh, may you have a wife who brings you luck
jabar bu la jigee	With the woman who suits your destiny
Loo yóotu jot ko	Whatever you attempt will succeed
Jabar na la jig	May your wife improve your fate
Jabar bu la jigul	If your wife brings you no luck
Loo sàkket ca la	Whatever you build will fall
jabar na la jig	May your wife bring you luck

The head of the household had forbidden all *taasu* performances, ostensibly because he is a *sëriñ*, or religious guide. The *taasu*, with its trivial and even scandalous connotations, does not fit his public image. The only sanctioned entertainment at this event was provided by a group of men who sang religious songs in the courtyard in the morning, and later by a group of Bàay Fall,[27] who sang religious songs, danced, and flagellated themselves out of religious fervor that afternoon. The women's striking disobedience of this order emphasizes the urgency of their need to settle affairs with their sister-in-law Fatou. On the surface, this *taasu* didactically outlines the behavior of a model wife: she welcomes her in-laws and offers such generous hospitality that they feel at home in her house. The comparisons made with the wife who "selfishly" attempts to "keep her husband for herself" are menacing. The beating that the *taasukat* recommends for such a spouse would be fatal.

Several other poems performed at this event criticized avaricious spouses just as harshly. Clearly, Fatou was having problems with her in-laws. No one would say much about these problems, but they were so serious that her sisters-in-law refused to care for her children while she worked. Fatou worked at Sotexca, the clothing company that was the major source of salaried employment for women in Louga at the time of my research. The company received most of its contracts from foreign companies, and employed local women at exploitative wages to sew in a production-line system. Each day before Fatou went to the Sotexca factory, she was obliged to take her two children to her mother's home on the other side of town. Another poem made it clear that her mother was unwelcome as well. Fatou's family was much wealthier than that of her in-laws, and the in-laws did not appreciate the snobbish attitude of Fatou's mother and other relatives. However, the conflict obviously went much deeper.

My suspicion is that she had attempted to create a separate *oikos* within the family compound. Since she had access to her family's resources, she probably wished to reserve these economic advantages for herself, her husband, and her children. Although Wolof women control their own income by right, they cannot be said to control that income in reality. Men are ostensibly responsible for their family's basic needs,[28] but most women need to earn their own income in order to provide for basic needs such as food. In fact, no one I met during my field research—including relatively well-to-do male members of Dakar society—had complete economic autonomy. Their many unavoidable social obligations meant that they often had little real control over their expenditures. Nevertheless, more and more young people refuse to accept the head of the household's right to pool and distribute all household members' finances, because many heads of household do not manage household finances impartially and fairly. According to A. B. Diop (1985), the extended family is in crisis because of these conflicts. Nevertheless, Wolof proudly uphold the idea of solidarity within the extended family, even if they do not always enjoy the tremendous burdens of such solidarity. Indeed, the economic crisis makes it extremely difficult for most members of Wolof society to survive outside of these links. The system of exchanges that I have been describing is of course most visible within the family compound. Fatou, then, had sinned against the very foundations of the family compound.[29]

Highly integrated in this web of exchanges, couples form nodes within the larger pattern, rather than independent webs of relations. Fatou's efforts to create a separate network challenged the notion of a lineage-based system of exchanges as well as the related notions of conjugal life. Since sisters-in-law often play an important role in the relations between a man and his wife, their criticism holds more weight than that of other women. Indeed, a man usually chooses a number of *njëkke*[30] among his sisters and female friends when he marries. Socially, they have the same status as the husband, for they are his representatives and mediate between man and wife. Women often make extraordinary efforts to please them, but they also benefit from their advice when problems arise. Indeed, a woman will normally discuss delicate or intimate problems—especially those concerning her sexual relations with her husband—not with her husband, but with her *njëkke*. Discussing such problems directly with her husband would be embarrassing and indelicate. These counsellors thus help the couple preserve the mutual respect and *fula* [dignity] considered necessary to maintain conjugal peace.

This structure contextualizes the *taasu* performed at the naming ceremony, for a few of Fatou's sisters-in-law warned her of the coming storm with the first *taasu*. They welcomed her again into their house, and told her that correcting her behavior was an unpleasant duty. Clearly, the *taasukat* who performed the following poem still had great liking for her.

Wara mëna takk	You should [be able to] marry,
Wara waane	Be clever (rusé, habile),
Wara wacce	Be alert,
Jeeg ji dellusi ak ñoom	Woman who returns with them[31]
Bu la neexoon dëngël	When the one who pleased you takes a crooked path
Da la neex nga jubal	You won't enjoy putting [her] straight[32]
Ne xam nga ne	Say, you know that
Kër goroom du ko yàq de	You didn't harm your in-laws' house
Kër gi yaa ko moom	This house is yours
Faatu kër goroom du ko yàq	Faatu, you didn't harm your in-laws' house
Ne kër gi yaa moom	This house is yours

This performer later softened the others' criticism again, by declaiming:

Ewaay baax bari bañ	Oh, many refuse goodness
	Oh the good have many enemies
Faatu sama waaja	Faatu, my friend
taxula sa bañ yi ree	Your enemies won't laugh because of you (at you)
Chorus:	
Ewaay taxula sa bañ yi ree	Oh, Your enemies won't laugh at you
Ewaay taxula sa bañ ree	Oh yes, your enemies won't laugh at you
Ni keng keng ni keng ni keng ni mbas	Say keng keng say keng say keng,[33] say enough!
taxula sa bañ yi ree	Your enemies won't laugh at you
Chorus	

Critical or satirical poems not only teach the recipient a humiliating lesson, but also offer the performers a chance to express otherwise hidden sentiments publicly. In that sense, they allow us to sketch the tensions affecting the relationships between the women in the household. In addition, the poems present another aspect of the circle of exchanges we have been examining. Exchanging goods and services ties people together, and cements family bonds. Those who fail to fulfill their duties in this circle of exchange will be humiliated or punished in some way if they do not "take the straight path." Justice can be harsh, as the woman who declaims "jabar ju la xàllal sa kër/Ba sa njaboot tuxu/Kooku jarna yat u kel/Jar na dóor ba dee" [A woman who clears her house/So that the family leaves—/That one deserves a wooden club/She deserves to be beaten to death] warns. It bears repeating that public opinion of an individual is vital, for it is the key to the mutual assistance upon which Wolof depend. No one can survive alone.

Nevertheless, a purely economic analysis of the force of *gaaruwaale*, the form of *taasu* that satirizes or criticizes addressees[34] can only give us part of the picture. Fatou could have survived on her salary, and her own family is well-to-do; therefore, one's economic well-being is not the only reason for wishing to avoid such situations. Cultural and symbolic exchanges cross-cut each other and material exchanges on many different levels. Performances of praise poetry, for example, unite many different forms of exchange in space and time, offering a unique intersection of social exchanges. As one Wolof woman stated at a naming ceremony, "Jom rekk amna solo" [Honor alone is important] (Castors, Dakar; 1/93). No one wishes her moments of humiliation to dominate her public image. Indeed, the purely economic punishment for failing to participate in the circle of exchange may be less difficult to accept than public humiliation. Purely economic evaluations ignore the basic insight of thinkers such as Karl Polanyi; that is, that individuals value goods only insofar as they insure their social standing and increase their social prestige.[35]

Taasu performances thus form an integral part of the elaborate system of exchanges that forms a frame for negotiating relationships in Wolof society. However, *taasu* are not simply the tokens of that exchange, nor are they the signs of a symbolic exchange that takes place concurrently with the exchange of material goods, for they also exist within a system of textual exchanges. As tokens of the material exchange, *taasu* are commodities, just as the other gifts are, or as a book is. Patrons offer gifts to the performers for their praise. If we see the poem within the frame of symbolic exchange, it becomes the sign of the multiple exchanges and negotiations taking place among social actors. Without the poem as public marker of exchange, the negotiations crucial to developing or maintaining relationships are displaced or deferred. This is why a family event that does not include this symbolic exchange is "unthinkable," according to Bonnie Wright.[36]

Apart from the socioeconomic layer of exchange, we can observe another level of exchange that takes place between the text of the poem and the context. The poem exists only within a specific event, and acquires its meaning in the context of the *ngenté, ceet, nàtt,* or other appropriate context. Yet the *taasu* also produces the event or context, for *taasukat* interpret the events for their audience members (who in turn interpret the *taasu*). Textual exchange also occurs during these performances. One woman's *taasu* usually provokes another woman to respond with a *taasu* that will receive its own response, and so on. This exchange of *taasu* belongs to a long chain of such exchanges stretching from the past into the future. *Taasu* are thus gifts that must be returned, in either verbal or material form.

CHAPTER 3

Panegyrics

The gift economy that provides the basis for the articulation of individual and collective identities in performances of *taasu* makes an important distinction that western economic systems generally ignore. The gift exchanges I have described actualize personal relationships that give exchange meaning. In other words, the individual persons involved in the exchange matter as much if not more than the exchange itself, which becomes a means for creating a relationship. Praise names signal this very clearly, for they anchor individual identities in public discourse. In contrast, modern economies that make exchange itself the goal minimize the value of the individuals involved, to the point that they are equated with account numbers. This depersonalization remains alien to those who understand themselves as participants in a gift exchange that depends on them as individuals for its existence.

The popular belief in the oral performer's anonymity thus ignores the social framework of the performance itself. In Wolof communities, performers gain a certain fame that precludes anonymity. In addition, the notion of gift exchange itself focuses attention on the individual. The individual performer's identity also implies the existence of community, as exchange networks induce individuals to articulate their identities as members of particular groups. In Wolof communities, gender, age, class, and caste all serve to define these exchanges. Although Wolof caste systems define the professional status of oral performers, smiths, leatherworkers, and other groups to varying extent, professional status alone does not explain the ideology behind the system that this chapter explores in relation to *taasu* performance. I will not attempt to add to the large number of studies of caste that social scientists have produced; rather, I choose to describe frameworks for the competitive interactions between individual and group identities that engender self-representation. My understanding of the *taasu* as a means for articulating the relationships between individual and community will also guide my attempts to place the genre into the larger context of studies on panegyric genres in Africa.

41

CASTING PERFORMERS

Gender plays an important role in the Wolof taxonomy of oral genres. Although male performers such as the *mbàndkatt*[1] have long performed *taasu* for comic effect, the genre has almost exclusively been defined as a women's genre. It has been trivialized for that reason as well. Since the *taasu* is a popular form of entertainment, conceived of in opposition to forms such as the *tàgget*—praise for an individual that consists in a recitation of the family's lineage with appropriate laudatory epithets— few observers had noted at the time of my research that the *taasu* has grown in importance, while the *tàgget* and other "high" art forms have declined. According to Ami Guèye, "Taasu dafa-y yokku léegi" [*Taasu* is increasingly important now] (Dakar interview, November 1993). However, this resurgence of the *taasu* can hardly escape attention now that young musicians have begun promoting the *taasu* as a local form of rap. Indeed, even in the early 1990s, the popular group Lemzo Diamono regularly performed *taasu* as part of its nightclub act.

This development also demonstrates that gender roles are more fluid than accepted wisdom might imply. Although Wolof proverbs alone present a formidable array of regulations for women's behavior, discursive constructions of gender roles are not as monolithic as they might appear at first. I will explore gender issues in greater detail in chapter 4; however, I wish to note here that the highly gendered definition of *taasu* actually promotes a playful attitude toward sexuality. Lemzo Diamono effectively highlighted this in a 1997 music video that humorously deconstructs gender roles, as the male musicians, dressed as women, performed *taasu*. This carnivalesque use of cross-dressing for comic effect seems very similar to the traditional farce of the *mbàndkatt*, yet it may also signal a shift in perceptions about gender roles that warrants further research on male *taasu* performers. My own analysis focuses almost entirely on women, as I defined the project in terms of women's self-representation from the outset.

In spite of my choice to limit the research to women's performances, I learned that *taasu* performers constitute a highly varied group. Age, as well as gender, is relevant to performance. Most *taasukat* that I encountered ranged in age from thirty to fifty. Younger, more recently married women are expected to make a place for themselves in their husband's family by behaving in a submissive, proper way. Even the sauciest girls and women often bend under social pressure to "behave." However, in the 1980s, one of the most popular radio performers was a young girl just entering puberty. As they are assumed to be innocent of sexual experience, young girls' public performances of erotic *taasu* are accepted as comic entertainment. Young girls between the ages of nine and fifteen often perform scandalously erotic poems, to the amusement of their elders. Abdoulaziz Diaw, a researcher at the Centre de Linguistique Appliquée of the University of Dakar, concurs that these erotic *taasu* may once have served as a form of sex education (personal communication, 7/93). Since Wolof society has no form of initiation school for girls analogous to the training boys receive prior to and after circumcision, *taasu* appears to be the only medium in which women can openly share sexual information. Erotic *taasu* definitely provide a much-needed outlet for sexual tensions, as well as for the stress women experience in marriage. *Taasukat* have never mentioned sex education as one of the functions of the genre, but they do insist that the poems are often didactic.

Professional status is another useful criterion for distinguishing among performers. Among the amateurs, one can find brilliant performers who exercise their skills only in family events and informal settings. However, *taasu* performance has grown increasingly professionalized over the last few decades. This means that caste plays an increasingly important role in the performance of *taasu*, even as it seems to be diminishing in importance in the official rhetorics of politics and economics. For the purposes of this discussion, I refer to caste primarily as a system for assigning social and professional roles according to descent. Caste status is inherited, thus it appears to be immutable to Wright; however, the caste system itself is subject to historical change, as is any other social institution. In other words, the caste system plays a role in the production of meaning, and the meanings that it produces change over time.

The historical depth of the system informs the anthropologist Abdoulaye Bara Diop's account of the Wolof caste system and his theory that a system of binary oppositions defines the institution of caste. For Diop, the crucial distinction separates nobles (*géer*) from their clients (*ñéeño*), the artisans and oral performers. Binary oppositions also operate to distinguish different categories within the casted, or *ñéeño* group. The *jëf-lekk*, (literally those who make in order to eat), or artisans, are distinguished from the *sàbb-lekk*, those who eat words, or speak to eat. The *sàbb-lekk*, better known as *griots*, or bards, live from their verbal artistry. *Griot* is a term that came into usage after contact with Europeans; in Wolof, oral performers are more generally known as *géwël*. During the period of the Wolof empires, *géwël* belonged to various subgroups depending on their special branch of expertise. Many of these terms seem to have fallen into disuse; it is possible that patrons cannot support all of these forms of entertainment as well as newer forms such as amplified, popular music.

Although this and other descriptions of the elaborate hierarchies of caste and relative social status in Wolof society—and in other West

African societies—might give a falsely static image of these societies, we must remember that caste is an historical phenomenon. The relative importance of caste changes with time. Currently, caste is far more important socially than professionally for most Wolof (Fatou Sow, personal communication, 11/93). For example, many Wolof continue to follow the guidelines of caste endogamy that Judith Irvine and Abdoulaye Bara Diop describe (Fatou Sow, personal communication, 11/93). Even young people follow these codes quite strictly. However, the continuing social importance of caste does not imply unquestioning acceptance of all traditions in Senegal. The Wolof social theory of caste described here is one that many Senegalese condemn. Saxiir Caam and Penda M'Bow, both professors at the University of Dakar, have spearheaded efforts to promote a more democratic form of social organization.

In spite of these developments, caste remains highly relevant to discussions of *taasu* performance. Indeed, it seems to be taking on greater significance with the increased professionalization of *taasu* performance. Saxiir Caam categorically denies that women of noble caste ever perform *taasu*, and argues that the genre was always reserved for *ñeeño*, or casted, women alone (12/11/93). My research suggests that this is not entirely true. Women of noble caste often deny any knowledge of *taasu* or any ability to perform them; however, some of them are quite capable performers. Relative status appears more relevant than caste in these cases. Experience also varies; rural women sometimes have more performance experience than urban women. During a visit to her relatives in the Dakar suburb of Usine, one woman of noble caste from a village near Louga amused all of us during a *túr* by performing at least twenty short *taasu*. A few other women half-heartedly performed as well, but they clearly had little experience. All of the women refused to perform in the courtyard, as too many people were about. They protected their status by declaiming their poems in the privacy of Ami D.'s room.

This discrepancy between my experience and the statements of informants who denied the very possibility that women of noble caste might occasionally perform *taasu* is a telling one. In Wolof society, those of higher status distinguish themselves through speech and action. According to Judith Irvine and Abdoulaye Bara Diop,[2] Wolof of noble caste are relatively silent when compared to the *ñeeño,* or casted members of society.

> It is one of the most fundamental Wolof cultural assumptions that speech, especially in quantity, is dangerous and demeaning; it is likely to be false or at least frivolous. The tongue is "dangerous as a lion"— out of respect for others and for himself, a noble must not speak too much.[3]

In order to preserve their status, village leaders speak through intermediaries—usually *géwël* (Irvine 1973, 151). In addition, a stately, slower
pace is associated with high status; rushing about is considered indicative of lower status. These differences, however, are *relative*. As Irvine
adds, a Wolof "monitors his speech level . . . not only according to his
own caste but also taking into account the rank of other persons present
and their relation to himself" (Irvine, 1973, 149). Since Ami D. had only
invited women of noble caste, they did not feel the need to distinguish
themselves in terms of caste. Instead, the visiting villager performed the
most actively. Clearly, she simply knew more *taasu* than her hosts, born
and educated in the capital; however, her use of speech may also indicate that she held a relatively lower status than the other women. Dakar
residents often refer to villagers mockingly as *kaw-kaw*, or hicks. In the
presence of women of caste, however, she, too, would probably have
claimed total ignorance of *taasu*.

In general, women of caste are more likely to perform *taasu* openly,
and are thus usually better performers. Although they are the most
expert of *taasukat*, the *géwël* and Laobé (woodworkers and traders) are
not the only performers. Women of the metal-workers' (*tëgg*), and
leather-workers' (*wuude*) castes often perform *taasu* as well, especially
at family ceremonies. As Irvine and Diop explain, the hierarchical relationships between the casted and the noble obligate nobles to provide
gifts for casted people associated with their family. In response, even the
artisans may praise their patrons verbally.

Further distinctions among oral performers are made on the basis
of the client's relationship to patrons. According to Ami Guèye, there
are two types: those who praise a few patrons, and accompany them to
all events in order to represent and praise them, and those who praise
almost any guest at the events they attend (Dakar, interview, 11/93).
The first model of behavior has a longer history than the second. *Géwël*
and noble families are often linked through several generations, so
géwël were expected to represent a patron and his/her family exclusively. These performers are known as *géwël u juddu*. Although no one
has dated the rise of the second model, nobles have long complained
about the mobile performers who do not even know them, yet expect
payment for praise. In general, *taasu* performed for a well-known
patron tend to be longer and more complex than those performed for
less familiar patrons. Obviously, the poem will be much richer in biographical detail as well. The second type of professional *taasu* more
often embroiders on a well-known proverb, or employs the trite, well-
worn stereotypes of the "good" woman, rather than presenting praise
that describes the individual, because the performer may know very little about the subject of her poem.

Only highly skilled performers are able to weave such *taasu* into verbal works of art; however, *taasukat* must do so more and more often. Many nobles condemn the roving performer who seeks new patrons at various events, rather than offering her services exclusively to the family that can claim her as its *géwël u juddu*.[4] Understandably, nobles dislike the phenomenon, for they wish to restrict the number of their clients. It is to the advantage of *géwël*, however, to widen their patronage base. In villages, traditional lineage alliances restrict *géwël* to a small pool of patrons. In urban areas, however, performers have been able to choose from a much wider pool of nobles. Even village performers now travel in order to gain new patrons and to take advantage of new sources of revenue. Television and radio also broaden the pool of patrons.

Critics of the contemporary professionalization of the *taasu* claim that the poems of itinerant performers are a deformation of the genre. *Taasu* broadcast on television or radio programs fit the model set by the "roving" performer, rather than that of the more stable *géwël u juddu*. Since the relationship between the performer and her audience shapes her performance, the *taasukat* who must perform to a faceless television or radio audience recasts the genre to meet the demands of the medium. The demands and new possibilities of these media lead to changes in performance styles; however, such innovations do not necessarily deform oral performance, as some purists would argue, but represent changes in a living tradition.

Shifting ethnic identity also provides an index to the changing status of groups within the hierarchy of castes. The example of the Laobé, a third important class of professional *taasukat*, clarifies this point. The Laobé form a tiny Fulßé minority within Wolof society. Although "Laobé" is a caste term in Fulßé communities, the performers we are considering here are extremely Wolofized. These Laobé now form a relatively new caste among the Wolof. Few of them speak more than a few words of Pulaar, the language of their ancestors. Nevertheless, this group has yet to be fully accepted, and prejudice against the Laobé is widespread. Indeed, even Cheikh Anta Diop's short excursus on the Laobé in *Nations nègres* represents Wolof prejudice, rather than an objective description of this minority group's subculture.[5] Irvine bases her brief description of the Laobé on Wolof informants' opinions, stating that the Laobé "are a gypsy-like, semi-nomadic people whom the Wolof sometimes characterize as a separate ethnic group, unlike other *Nyenyo* [people of caste], who are thought to be true Wolof" (Irvine, 1973, 77). Ethnicity thus affects performers' status. Although both Laobé and *géwël* performers are considered *sàbb-lekk*, the *géwël taasukat* may claim higher status as a "Wolof bu piir," or "pure Wolof."

The research that I conducted among the Laobé leads me to view earlier descriptions with a critical eye, for they present Wolof views without comparing them to Laobé perspectives. As in all cases of conflict, both parties tell the story differently. Wolof stories of Laobé trickery are not completely groundless, yet the recent Laobé claims that they are an oppressed minority group has validity too.[6] Given this imperfect integration of Laobé into Wolof society, it is interesting that the binary system regulating caste status in Wolof communities also plays a definitive role in theirs. Laobé too divide themselves into two separate categories—*Laobé yétt* (woodworkers) and *Laobé jula* (traders).[7] The Laobé *jula* are among the most successful taasukat, and one of the most famous performers of recent years, Fatou Tacko Thioune, is Laobé.

Indeed, some observers give Laobé pride of place in *taasu* performance. Ndoye even argues that the Laobé actually introduced the *taasu* to Wolof society. This assumption is questionable, given that my Wolof *géwël* informants claim this honor for their own and distinguish the *géwël* style of *taasu* performance from that of the Laobé. Furthermore, Ndoye gives no evidence for her belief that the genre is of Laobé origins. She simply notes that a woman of another ethnic group who "pratiqueraient ce langage licencieux [celui du *taasu*] serait assimilée péjorativement à une laobé" [Any woman of another ethnic group who "might practice this licentious language would be pejoratively associated with a Laobé woman."][8] Rather than offering proof of the genre's Laobé origins, this remark illustrates the tenuous position of the Laobé in Wolof society.

In fact, many *taasukat* delight in "salty" *taasu*. Often, when praising a *taasu*, informants would say "Dafa am xorom" [It's salty], meaning that the poem is witty, and possibly a bit licentious or even frankly erotic in tone. Wolof women as well as Laobé women perform and enjoy these "salty" poems; however, Laobé women are considered the experts in this genre. One Wolof informant criticized Laobé women for this reason, saying that they have total verbal freedom and "waxñañu lépp"[9] [They tell all]. I too noticed that Laobé women excel in performing *taasu;* however, the attempt to define the cultural boundaries between Wolof and Laobé *taasukat* appears conflicted. After one afternoon of interviews and performances at the house of a Laobé family in St. Louis (Pikine), as a final question I asked what the difference between Laobé and Wolof (*géwël*) *taasu* might be. A *géwël* informant promptly replied that Wolof *géwël* are proper, and respect moral codes; therefore, they do not perform erotic *taasu*, but didactic or panegyric poems.[10] As a result, my hosts were extremely embarrassed, and preferred not to perform any *taasu* in the presence of the *géwël* women. The *géwël* women had in effect affirmed the superiority of Wolof culture by sexualizing the Laobé women's performance before it even occurred. In light of this incident, I view the identification of Laobé women with erotic or licentious behavior as problematic.

Laobé women take pride in their reputation for beauty, and capitalize on their reputation for excelling in the erotic arts (Mamadou Diouf, personal communication, April 1993). Many Laobé women sell incense, waist-beads, and wrappers (*sér,* or *pagnes*) embroidered with suggestive phrases or with strategic holes at events that commonly include *taasu* performances. However, they are clearly aware of the way that Wolof use their reputation for erotic skill in order to denigrate them. In her book *Black Looks: Race and Representation,* bell hooks provides an enlightening analysis of the multiple ways in which African-American women have been denigrated and controlled through a similar reductionist logic.[11] Clearly, representations of Laobé sexuality fit the political model that hooks describes. *Géwël* criticism of Laobé sexual appetite merely repeats Wolof nobles' criticism of *géwël* appetite for meat and good food. The rhetorical justification for the lower status of both groups is that their excessive appetite—for food or sex—is ignoble. This critique of the two castes is twofold. If one's behavior determines one's status, members of these groups are themselves to blame for their lower status if they behave poorly—for instance, by showing excessive appetite. On the other hand, members of these groups are stereotyped, so that all Laobé or *géwël* are assumed to be greedy for meat or sex, regardless of actual behavior. If greediness is hereditary and innate,[12] members of these groups can never change their status. Discrimination against Laobé and *géwël* can thus be explained as a just condemnation of bad behavior, even though they cannot change this behavior, according to the theory that their appetite is hereditary. According to Irvine, "the negative stereotype of the nyenyo outlines the nobles' own moral superiority and justifies their political supremacy to their own moral consciences."[13]

These stereotypes affect *taasu* performance in many ways. The performer of *taasu* takes on client status in relation to a patron of relatively higher status. The social hierarchy defines the performance context according to gender, age, caste, ethnicity, and professional status. In other words, performance highlights social competition between different social groups.[14] This explains the great power of the praisesinger; she may laud her patron, but if dissatisfied, might also choose to vilify the noble. For this reason, nobles often fear *géwël,* who are masters of the word not only because they are skilled artists, but also because they may forge verbal weapons when necessary.

COMPETING SELVES

Translated into discourse, social competition makes the consciousness of individual agency possible, according to Mikhail Bakhtin. His sociological definition of competing voices (heteroglossia) leads him to conclude that "consciousness awakens to independent ideological life precisely in a world of alien discourses surrounding it, and from which it cannot initially separate itself."[15] The various idiolects represented by the heterogeneous voices (heteroglossia) present in any text compete and negotiate for space within the text, in a fashion analagous to the class competitions that take place in society. Dialogic discourse cannot be neutral, as dialogic forms constitute themselves through *competitive* discursive exchanges. This exchange takes place very literally in *taasu* performances through the call-and-response mode of exchange between performer and chorus. *Taasu*, then, create a discursive space for articulating the relationships between the individual and the group.

The genre thus offers performers a space for self-referential discourse. In fact, most of the *taasu* performances that I have recorded contain allusions to the performer. Some of these are abbreviated or encoded in the conventions of *taasu* performance; others are extended autobiographical texts. Most performers insert themselves in the genre by marking themselves as *speakers*. Frequently, a *taasukat* opens her performance by saying, "Maa ne," or "I say." Since Wolof verbal constructions emphasize different aspects of the action, Wolof speakers may emphasize the status of the action (complete or incomplete), the predicate, or the speaker. In all instances that I have recorded, the *taasukat* uses the verbal construction that emphasizes the speaker when she says "Maa ne."[16] No performer ever chose another type of verbal construction. In addition, the professional performers usually work their own name into the performance in some way. Sometimes she will do so rapidly—"Man Ami Guèye, dama ne" [I, Ami Guèye, I say]—at other times, she will do so in a more extended fashion. For instance, Aby Ngana Diop's most famous *taasu*, "Liital," takes the form of a series of questions and answers. The chorus asks *her* opinions of various women, and she responds. The entire structure of this *taasu* focuses on the performer, who literally judges a wide spectrum of society through her performance.

Other performers produce more overtly self-referential *taasu*. Ngoné Mbaay, probably the most famous *taasukat* of the past twenty years, earned her fame through such a *taasu*. Although she is deceased, I was able to find recordings of many of her *taasu* in the now defunct Archives Culturelles du Sénégal and in the Archives of Radio-Télévision Sénégal. The personnel of the Archives Culturelles recorded the

taasu that catapulted Mbaay to national fame in her village, Colom
Fall, on April 4, 1969. I owe the following transcription to Mamadou
Chérif Thiam.[17]

> Ngòòne Mbaay, loo làkle?

Li ma làkle bari na
—Ngòòne Mbaay loo làkle?
Dama ne Maget Silla! Rëkël ma jiin gi, gis nga gàn yi ma am
Gàn yu tol ne gàn yi am am, kuy fo ak ñoom
War nga wax bu baax. *Lërwa*!
Dama ne yëguloo ne damaa làklee?
—Ngòòne Mbaay loo làkle?
Ngòòne Mbaay, La ma làkle bari na
—Ngòòne Mbaay loo làkle?
Lërwa yëguloo ne dama làkle?
—Ngòòne Mbaay loo làkle?
Màn Ngòòne Mbaay la ma làkle bari na
—Ngòòne Mbaay loo làkle?
Ma ne laaw la cat, ca ba mu la dalagul
—Ngòòne Mbaay loo làkle?
Moone dey, maa ka raagal sawara
—Ngòòne Mbaay loo làkle?
Lërwa! buma masaa taal, bala maa nelaw taal ba dafa fey
Man daa na taal ba wara dem fey, ndax wut lu wóór
Moo Ngòòne Mbaay, la ma làkle bari na
—Ngòòne Mbaay loo làkle?
Waay laaw la cat, ca ba mu la dalagul
—Ngòòne Mbaay loo làkle?
Ma ne Lërwa! ak ñi mu aandal kenn du ci como
Duñu wën deng, ba tax tiis ji ma dal, ñoom laa ko bëgga diis
—Ngòòne Mbaay loo làkle?
Ngòòne kañ la ma làkle bari na
—Ngòòne Mbaay loo làkle?
Moo Ngòòne Mbaay kay ko xam kako xam, kooka sax yëram na ma
—Ngòòne Mbaay loo làkle?
Moo Ngòòne Mbaay lamu làkle bari na
—Ngòòne Mbaay loo làkle?
Seetal ñetti sëru njor
Ñaari sër u dënk
Ak ñaari jare
Ñaari garan-mbubbu
Ñaari simis
Ak ñaari bagaan
Ñaari beñuwaar
Ñaari aset

Juróom ñetti bóóli
Ñeenti supeer
Fukki kopp ak juróóm ñaar
Ndeysaan ma ka saf ab neek
  —Ngòòne Mbaay loo làkle?
Cey waay maa ka wodduwoon kaar
  —Ngòòne Mbaay loo làkle?
Ngòòne Mbaay kay ku xam kako xam, kooka sax yëram na ko
  —Ngòòne Mbaay loo làkle?
Peeri jare, oru Ngalam
Ñaari peer-u jaaro
Paaka ginaar
Ak cuuraayal màkka
Ak sama lam ya
Sama jaara ya, sama ceen u wurus ga
Ma rax ca sama gongo ga Lërwa!
Saa jaaro baaraam ba daa seey
Màn lama làkle bari na
  —Ngòòne Mbaay loo làkle?
Waay seetal juróóm-ñetti néék
Yaari waañ ak ñaari wëru wërmbañuk singwaay
Ak bañuy sàngoo. Ngoone kañ la mu làkle bari na.
  —Ngòòne Mbaay loo làkle?
Juroom ñetti simis u dubal maas u sama jëkar
Ñaari mbaxanay laafaam, ak ñaa ci mbaxanay jaraaf
Ak dolli marakiisam ak tengaadeem bu baax bu rëy ba ñu ëw
Man lama làkle bari na
  —Ngòòne Mbaay loo làkle?
Moo Lërwa yëguloone damaa làkle
  —Ngòòne Mbaay loo làkle?
Yow daal maa ngi ne dungg ni jommi; léégi yoratuma dara
Ndax awmas kumba, yoruma kamisol, amatuma mbub mu baax.
Te leegi ag musóór sax sawara da ma ko xañ
  —Ngòòne Mbaay loo làkle?
Ngòòne Mbaay la mu lakle bari na
  —Ngòòne Mbaay loo làkle?
Lérwa sama taabal ja ni rëpp, sama kafceer ba ne farr
Fanweri kaas-ak-ñaar yééw ko. La ma làkle bari na.
  —Ngòòne Mbaay loo làkle?
Seetal juróóm-ñetti neek
Yaari waañ ak ñaari wurmbañuk singwaay ak bañuy sàngoo
Ndeysaan maa ka jagoon kaar
Te Lërwa dama doon jeema baax
wut juróóm-ñaari barigo ak gennwall, akub paan
Ma def ca ndexum daaw, ma reer ca reerub ceeb
Jënd jaaro, jaaro ya reer, ma yobub séét

Ñu joxmab séét, Lërwa,
Ma jóngal sama caat ma
Ñu may ma wujj.
Xam nga ne yooya barina
   —Ngòòne Mbaay loo làkle?
Lërwa! Xanaa yëram ngéén ma?
   —Ngòòne Mbaay loo làkle?
Ma ngi ne dung ni jommi, leegi yooratuma dara
Moo Ngòòne Mbaay loo làkle (Thiam, 114–122)?

Ngoone Mbaay, What Has Burned?

   —Ngone Mbaay, What has burned?
   Ngone Mbaay, What has burned in your fire?

N.M.   I lost so much!
   Maget Silla! Beat the welcome; see the guests I have.
   Whoever enjoys the company of such guests
   Must speak well.
   Don't you know about the fire?

   —Ngone Mbaay, What burned in your fire?

N.M.   Leroi, don't you know about my fire?
   I lost so much!

   —Ngone Mbaay, What burned in your fire?

N.M.   Spare me from evil tongues,
   Don't let them touch my guests!

   —Ngone Mbaay, What burned in your fire?

N.M.   Leroi! When I lit the fire, before I slept
   I put it out.
   I always put out the fire
   Before I left, in order to be safe.
   I, Ngone Mbaay, I've lost a lot.

   —Ngone Mbaay, What burned in your fire?

N.M.   Oh, stop the wicked tongues
   Before they touch you!

   —Ngone Mbaay, What burned in your fire?

N.M.   Leroi! And those with him are no ignorant children
   They are trustworthy, that's why
   I want to share this worry with them

   —Ngone Mbaay, What burned in your fire?

N.M.   This Ngone Mbaay, whoever just knows
Someone who knows her,
Even that person will pity her

—Ngone Mbaay, What burned in your fire?

N.M.   I, Ngone Mbaay, I have lost a lot

—Ngone Mbaay, What burned in your fire?

N.M.   Look—Three wrappers of Njor cloth
Two wrappers of dënk cloth[18]
Two boubous
Two shirts
And two calabashes
Two basins
Two plates
Eight platters
Four tureens
Seventeen cups
Oh, my room was full!

—Ngone Mbaay, What burned in your fire?

N.M.   How well dressed I was! Kaar!

—Ngone Mbaay, What burned in your fire?

N.M.   Whoever knows someone who knows
Ngone Mbaay must pity her

—Ngone Mbaay, What burned in your fire?

N.M.   A pair of wigs
Gold from Ngalam
Two pairs of earrings
A knife for gutting chickens
And incense from Mecca!
And my bracelets
And my rings, my gold chains too
I've lost a lot

—Ngone Mbaay, What burned in your fire?

N.M.   Oh, look! Seven rooms burnt
Two kitchens and two sitting rooms
And two bathrooms
Poor Ngone lost a lot

—Ngone Mbaay, What burned in your fire?

N.M.   My husband's eight double-sleeved shirts
Two wool hats, official's caps

His Moroccan shoes and big leather cap
Oh, what I've lost!

—Ngone Mbaay, What burned in your fire?

N.M. Leroi, don't you know about the fire?

—Ngone Mbaay, What burned in your fire?

N.M. You know, I'm dazed
As if I'd seen a ghost;
Now I can do nothing,
Because I have nothing,
Not even a camisole or a good dress.
And now the fire has deprived me
Even of a headtie.

—Ngone Mbaay, What burned in your fire?

N.M. Ngone Mbaay has lost a lot

—Ngone Mbaay, What burned in your fire?

N.M. Leroi, my table broke,
My coffee pot too
Thirty-two cups also.
How much I've lost!

—Ngone Mbaay, What burned in your fire?

N.M. Look! Seven rooms
Two kitchens
Two sitting rooms and bathrooms
Oh how well built they were! Kaar![19]
And Leroi, I tried to make the house complete
I looked for seven and a half cauldrons
And a pan
Put in last year's water[20]
Took from there the water for today's dinner
Sold earrings, but they disappeared
Brought a co-wife home for the wedding
Gave her a wedding feast, Leroi!
I circumcised my last child,
And they presented me with a co-wife
You know, all of that's too much

—Ngone Mbaay, What burned in your fire?

N.M. Leroi! Don't you pity me?

—Ngone Mbaay, What burned in your fire?

N.M. Leroi! Help me to cover myself
      I'm overcome, as if I'd seen a ghost—
      Now I can do nothing.
      I, Ngone Mbaay, what has burnt me?

Mbaay probably performed this *taasu* at a naming ceremony at some time; however, the only recording of the poem available to me was made during a session with personnel of the now defunct Archives Culturelles du Sénégal.

Clearly, Ngone Mbaay created this *taasu* out of need; she wished to make her crisis known so that her hearers would sympathize and offer her gifts to replace what she lost. Indeed, most listeners do believe that she lost her goods in a fire. There is now no way of interviewing Mbaay to find out the truth, but the structure of the text reveals that Mbaay may have been referring to another crisis as well. Although it is possible that the fire never took place in reality, some devastating loss did take place. Current descriptions of the Wolof institution of marriage offer us another interpretive framework. About half of all Wolof compounds are polygamous, and the main source of conflicts between co-wives is economic injustice.[21] Husbands are rarely completely fair when distributing wealth among their wives; often, a favorite spouse receives more than her co-wives. The proverb that Abdoulaye Bara Diop quotes to describe these conflicts literally means "A woman's satisfaction is her co-wife's death in the harvest season."[22] The fire thus functions as a metaphor for marital problems. The fire that destroyed her house is analogous to the passion for another woman that led her husband to remarry, "destroying her house," or marriage.

This interpretation puts the poem into the context of competition that is the basis for all *taasu* performance. Clearly, the poem serves to elevate Mbaay above her rival. The list of goods lost in the fire proves her blamelessness and details her many virtues. According to her *taasu*, she was an excellent wife, ready to work in order to make the household as "complete" as possible. She also provided her husband with sons, as her last child was circumcised shortly before the wedding of her co-wife. In short, Mbaay did everything that Wolof society expects of the model wife, yet her husband presented her with a co-wife. Her response is that "You know, that's too much!"

Clearly, Mbaay cannot share such sentiments openly. In addition, performing such a self-referential *taasu* can be highly dangerous. Her frequent exclamations of phrases believed to ward off evil, such as "Laaw la cat! Kaar!" [Avaunt!] prove this well enough. The structure of the *taasu*, however, allows her to express herself openly. The chorus plays a highly active role, continually repeating the question, "Ngone

Mbaay, what did you lose in your fire?" The performance thus consists of a dialogue, and reflects the circular dynamic of exchange that often structures formal communication in Wolof society. Rather than putting herself forward and providing us with an autonomous autobiographical statement that could leave her vulnerable to criticism for expressing herself so openly, Mbaay responds to the chorus. This structure provides a formal justification for making such a self-referential statement.

As I have argued in the Introduction, identities become visible primarily through the individual's active negotiation of her relations to the whole community. Autobiography offers a public space for just this sort of negotiation of identities. Indeed, many observers have noted that autobiographers choose the genre in order to gain prestige or rectify misunderstandings. This is true of the oral autobiographical discourses performed in Wolof communities as well. *Taasu* mark the subject positions of an individual agent, but also provide a discursive space for negotiating relationships between participants at these events through the exchange of gifts. Indeed, examples of the very special subgenre of autobiographical *taasu* are the fruit of many years of verbal and material exchanges between performer and audience members. Autobiographical discourse thus becomes autobiographical *exchange* within the *géew*, or ring formed by audience and participants in the *taasu* performance.

PANEGYRICS

In attempting to link text and context, performer and audience, I have presented a modified theory of the autobiographical pact between reader and text. This modified model seems all the more appropriate because the study of genres such as the proverb or the praisesong demonstrate that textual meaning depends in large part upon context, even though texts deploy many strategies for making sense. The model differs from theoretically untenable homologies between economic and literary production[23] in that the performance gives rise to the exchange, while the exchange engenders the performance. This dynamic relationship differentiates the autobiographical exchange from totalizing models, for it does not assume that one form of exchange alone shapes Wolof articulations of self and community in a deterministic fashion. This model thus offers definite advantages over earlier culturalist models that relied on static notions of culture and autobiography.

Although these modifications reflect Wolof cultural models, I believe that a flexible notion of autobiographical exchange could fruitfully be applied to other forms of self-representation in African literatures. The *taasu* is not the sole form of self-referential panegyric. Indeed, much of the African poetry we describe as panegyric also plays a self-referential function. Ruth Finnegan noted early that "Self-praises, created and performed by the subject himself, are not uncommon."[24] Isidore Okpewho's findings also back this assertion.[25] Indeed, the contestatory, carnivalesque nature of panegyric genres such as the *taasu* lends itself perfectly to the process leading to a self-conscious construction of identity described by Bakhtin. The *taasu* is only one of the many types of panegyric that offer a space for discursive contruction of the self. Although the self-referential aspects of African panegyric have been neglected in scholarly analyses of panegyric, self-referential praise poetry seems to be the norm in some areas, rather than the exception.

A brief review of the scholarship on praise poetry in Africa proves that much of it is self-referential, but few scholars have shown an interest in this aspect of the poetry. Although scholars acknowledge the importance of self-referential praise poetry, they tend to neglect it. Damane and Sanders agree with E. Casalis' early statement (1833) that "the hero of the piece is almost always the author of it,"[26] adding that "in most praise poems the hero is the author," but they choose to focus on those poems that are not self-referential, because "the exceptions, however, are particularly important, for they are the praises of certain chiefs."[27] This choice seems extraordinary, in light of the remark of the Sotho chief reported by Damane and Sanders: "'Nowadays the chiefs of the Sotho are praised just like cattle,' one chief remarked to us, with obvious contempt: 'but,' he added, with equally obvious approval, 'Chief Maama and Chief Lerotholi used to praise themselves.'"[28]

Other scholars too have noted the self-referential tendency in praise poetry from southern Africa. G. P. Lestrade noted that "persons of but modest rank in Bantu society usually compose their own praise-poem . . . while those of higher status have theirs composed by professional bards."[29] I. Schapera, on the other hand, refers to Demane and Sanders' work as well as to his own data to refute the notion that only persons of modest rank compose their own praises in southern Africa.[30] More recent work focusing on women supports the notion that much of the praise poetry performed in southern Africa is self-referential. Elizabeth Gunner's work on Zulu women's *izibongo* shows that tendency. However, the textual relationship between the performer and the performed persona does not play a role in determining the analytical categories she uses. As a result, she does not comment upon the highly self-referential character of the poems she presents.[31]

Self-referential praise poems are not geographically limited to southern Africa; scholars working in Central, East and West Africa provide ample data to back this point. Joseph Nsengimana argues that the

Rwandan *ukwivuga* (speaking of oneself) includes lyric odes and heroic poetry that are "profoundly" autobiographical.[32] In his book on kiHaya *ebyebugo*, the Tanzanian scholar Y. I. Rubanza also makes the autobiographical functions of this panegyric genre explicit. "Tukichunguza mfano mwingine wa mwisho wa mazingira tofauti na yale tuliyotaja, tutaona kuwa mtu aliweza kujigamba binafsi kuhsu ukoo wake na matendo yake yeye (mtambaji) binafsi" [Finally, if we analyze another example of the context [of *ebyebugo*], unlike those we have mentioned, we will observe that one can praise oneself, one's lineage and one's own actions (the praise singer), oneself].[33]

A specific form of the Yoruba *oriki* appears to be self-referential as well. In her study of Yoruba *oriki*, Karin Barber presents a variety of types of praise. The *oriki* performed on the occasion of the *faaji iyawo* (the bride's enjoyment) clearly perform a self-referential function. Since Barber was not deliberately seeking autobiographical praise poems, as I was, the autobiographical content of these particular texts make for important evidence of the autobiographical exchange. According to Barber, the bride adorns herself and stays at home to receive visitors. In the afternoon, she tours her family compound and the town, performing *rara*. As "the day of the bride's enjoyment is exactly at the turning point of the protected process by which a woman born into one lineage is incorporated as wife into another" (Barber, 106), this performance marks an important change in the woman's identity. Since she is not yet married, the girl must construct a new identity for herself during the period before she marries officially. Thus she "begins a series of symbolic acts demonstrating her willingness to contribute her labour and her property to her husband's people" (108), in these acts demonstrating what sort of wife she will be, that is, constructing a new identity as wife.

"Everything the bride says in *rara iyawo* is intended to direct attention back to herself. The genre, in fact, is a long reflection and dramatisation of, the bride's change of status" (Barber, 113). Therefore, the examples that Barber gives are all self-referential in content. The bride may sing

> I'm going to my new home now
> I'm going to my home to have money
> I'm going to my new home now
> I'm going to my home to bear children
> If you say your good luck will escort me
> It will escort me right to my room
> May good luck attend me today
> I've left the stage of "Come in the evening"
> I've left the stage of "Drop in on your way back"

I've joined the club of mothers of new-born babies
Mother of a new-born baby that is a boy
May good luck attend me today
I would have liked to be a hunter, but I have no quiver
I would have liked to be a blacksmith, but I have no bellows
When I would have liked to go on living in my father's house
I, Abike Omotanbaje
Child of the Okin people, I did not turn into a man
May good luck attend me today.[34]

Barber does not indicate to what degree the *rara iyawo* are formalized, set pieces. I assume that, like the other *oriki* she describes, these combine familiar texts and yet give space for individual innovation. Even if new brides do not improvise new *oriki* reflecting explicit personal details that go beyond self-identification (here, "I, Abike Omotanbaje/Child of the Okin people), the context and function of the performance clearly include self-referential aspects.

Often viewed as a minor genre in the past, praise poetry clearly plays a highly significant role in many sub-Saharan African societies, even if we judge from a merely quantitative standpoint. Indeed, some have even argued that other genres, such as epic, grow out of extended praise poems (John Johnson, personal communication, 1/1994). In spite of the weight that praise poetry has as a literary form with important social functions, Barber reminds us that we cannot forget the literary nature of panegyric.

> In Africa there are numerous genres of "praise-poetry" that resemble *oriki* in their fluidity and internal indeterminacy. All of these forms are radically unlike the kind of "literary text" which critics educated in the mainstream Euro-American literary tradition are used to dealing with—and this includes, at least in certain respects, most African literary scholars. Perhaps this is why there really has been no adequate poetics of such forms. Instead, genre after genre has been documented, described, and placed against a social 'background." Interesting and informative as these presentations are, they do not allow us to get to grips with the textuality of these poetic forms: how they work as texts and hence how they constitute meaning. (Barber 21)

Barber's work represents a breakthrough in the study of praise poetry as a genre. My own study of the autobiographical functions of *taasu* marks an attempt to put her theoretical remarks into practice and come "to grips with the textuality of these poetic forms."

The constitution of meaning, however, depends on interpretive contexts and frameworks, as reader response theories prove. In focusing on the implications of self-reference in praise poetry, I have thus chosen a particular critical framework. I have found that this delimitation of the genre has opened new interpretive spaces to me. Seen in this way, pan-egyric not only disqualifies earlier attempts to "collectivize" African identity to the point of denying individuality to Africans, but also offers scholars a mine of data about the construction of identity in the per-former's cultural context. In addition, self-referential panegyric genres provide new data about the nature of self-representation in public dis-course. In other words, they open up a space for re-thinking our theo-retical conceptions of autobiography.

CHAPTER 4

Genre and Gender in the Autobiographical Exchange

The concept of *teraanga*, or gift-giving[1] "est l'élément de référence de morale sociale wolof-sénégalaise" [is the element of moral reference in Wolof-Senegalese society][2] that regulates all relations between groups and individuals. It also regulates discourse. Furthermore, it regulates the taxonomy of discourse genres, for these genres are determined by the performance context—which exists because of exchanges. These exchanges exist within the framework of international trade with other African communities, as well as with European societies; for this reason, any analysis of the *taasu*, or, indeed, of any literary texts from Senegal, must take a wide range of influences into account through intertextual analysis. Genre questions, then, do not escape the larger questions of influence and politics. Naming the autobiographical *taasu* involves naming the subjectivities and identities that this type of discourse constructs in the context of gift exchanges. In this chapter, then, I will examine the problems and politics involved in naming discourses.

GENDER AND GENRE

The Wolof system of genres defines performance contexts according to gender and gendered performances. Thus, the *taasu* is widely considered a feminine genre because the genre is performed at events associated with women: baptisms, weddings, and women's *túr*. Obviously, this strict opposition of male and female spheres does not reflect the whole social reality, any more than rigid oppositions between masculinity and femininity do anywhere else. Some men do perform *taasu*; however, the community's definition of the genres as feminine and masculine determines the reception of their *taasu* performances.[3] Questions concerning the construction of identity and individuality—and thus of the construction of civil society and human rights—cannot escape sex, given the Wolof taxonomy of performance genres.

The same can be said of autobiography as a genre. In the past, women's writing has been scorned as "merely" autobiographical; how-

ever, when the genre has high status, women's autobiographical discourses have also been denied the status of autobiography because they
do not resemble male autobiographies.[4] For these and other reasons,
Celeste Schenck argues cogently that the generic hierarchy supports the
gender hierarchy. Indeed, some feminist critics have rejected the term
autobiography itself, seeing it as an inescapable link in the patriarchal
chain-letter that Schenck takes the critical tradition of autobiography as
a genre to be. Some have renamed autobiography "autogynography,"
for instance.[5] More fruitfully, perhaps, Leigh Gilmore examines the
"autobiographics" of self-referential texts. Briefly, autobiographics consists in the interruptions and gaps that allow women to invent and represent selves that cross the bar of gender that, say, Augustine's conception of the self raises before them.

These gaps are formal, as well as social. "There is an implicit identification . . . of identity and truth with formal integrity, which upholds
our Western prejudice in favor of generic purity and perhaps even a
transcendental metaphysics of genre."[6] On this basis, women's texts
were again disqualified. This situation has changed a great deal in the
last twenty years of autobiography studies. Although critics once
described the genre as narrative, rather than as poetic, current critical
discussion of the genre accepts a huge range of texts under the rubric of
autobiography. Not only life histories or autobiographical essays, but
also diaries, letters, works in the third person, poems, and even photo-
journals have been considered forms of autobiography. Although most
readers still tend to think of autobiographies as narrative texts, the conventions that shape the reading of autobiography are gradually shifting.[7]

The changing assessments of poetry's relationship to autobiography
offer an interesting measure of that shift. Critics have compared autobiography and poetry in the past to elevate the status of autobiography,
or to legitimize fragmentary or experimental texts, as well as to explore
the theoretical implications of autobiographical poetry/poetic autobiography. Influential critics such as James Olney, William Howarth, and
William Spengemann have all noted similarities between autobiography
and poetry. Olney uses the "poetic-autobiographic metaphor" in order
to argue that "art, both autobiographic and poetic, mediates between
the transient world of sensation and feeling, or event and emotion, and
a constant, stable realm of pattern and significance."[8] Olney's essay
"Some Versions of Memory/Some Versions of *Bios*: The Ontology of
Autobiography" is one of the most convincing attempts to deal with the
hybridity of autobiographies in poetic form to date. Olney deals
squarely with the main problem: the *bios*. If we consider autobiography
only as the expression of the *course of a life*, very few poems can be
termed more than autobiographical. Olney argues that we often mis-

takenly assume that "life" means "course of a life" when in fact, "Life . . . does not stretch back across time but extends down to the roots of individual being; it is atemporal, committed to a vertical thrust from consciousness down into the unconscious rather than to a horizontal thrust from the present into the past."[9] Olney sees *bios* as process, rather than as a rigidly linear chronicle of events.

The "expandable moment" of *taasu* performance clearly fits this processual definition more closely than the standard linear notion of time that some critics expect to find in autobiography. Clearly Anta Bouna Dieng or Ngoné Mbaay did not present life histories through *taasu*, but important moments of consciousness that shaped their current definitions of self. If we accept Olney's premises, self-representation in *taasu* thus can be seen as a valid form of autobiography. The poetic form does not disqualify a text or performance from being categorized as autobiography. As Olney remarks, "if we accept that a legitimate definition of life . . . can be 'consciousness' . . . then we will be the less disinclined to call [the] work 'autobiography,' even if, within the confines and categories of literary genre, it is classified as lyric poetry."[10]

The structuring of consciousness thus occurs within various structures, which are in turn defined by a variety of factors, such as gender and culture. Focusing on gender, Leigh Gilmore argues that characteristic women's autobiographies follow a non-linear mode. Her notion of autobiographics parallels that of the Wolof *taasu* with an important difference: autobiographics relies on the jagged interruptions of hegemony performed by critical texts, while the criticisms made by *taasukat* take place in a performance time that expands like a bubble (to use Stone's metaphor) as performer and chorus/audience interact within *taasu*.

This performance time exists within a separate, feminine sphere. Although western feminists have often theorized a utopian woman's world separate from the patriarchal present, this sphere either remains in the domain of the unknowable *chora*, in Julia Kristeva's terms, or in some future world of feminist science fiction.[11] Wolof women, on the other hand, arguably do share experiences within a loosely woven "women's world." Family ceremonies such as *ceet* (final stage of the wedding ceremonies) and *ngente* (naming ceremony) offer the clearest examples of what I mean by a women's sphere, simply because women organize, run, and attend these ceremonies for other women. Only closely associated men (a father or brothers) will attend an *ngente* in most cases. Indeed, men protest the expenditures that they are forced to make in order to support this women's sphere of activity. This sphere is temporally bounded not just by Wolof convention, but also by the rhythms of performances (whether of *taasu, xaxaar,* or other genres) specific to these settings.

This sphere and the exchanges that occur among women play a fundamental role in shaping self-representation. In any case, we cannot ignore the circumstances under which women produce texts as we examine the possibilities for such self-representation. *Taasu* may provide most women with the only available discursive space for self-representation. Women elsewhere, too, have tended more often to represent themselves in lyric texts than in long narratives, simply because they lacked the time for writing such long narratives. According to Schenck,

> poetry as autobiography constitutes a potential space in which a subject may be repeatedly and repeat*ably* present to herself during the act of utterance, in a genre that, Audre Lorde reminds us, is economical; having been the refuge of women and the poor in this century, she argues, poetry has been an underprivileged genre itself.[12]

THE TRAFFIC BETWEEN THE SEXES

Our chosen reference point—exchange—also regulates male-female relations. Since most *taasu* performers are women, but most *boróom-xew* (who literally "own" the event because they finance it) are men, *taasu* performances offer a window onto male-female relations and the construction of gendered identities in contemporary Senegal. The most common context for *taasu* performances—naming ceremonies—serves to name and celebrate sexual difference. Wolof names distinguish the sex of the person, and so do naming ceremonies. The birth of the first child, whether male or female, is the occasion for celebration; however, the most lavish naming ceremonies are organized for first-born male children. These events introduce the child to the community. In addition, they mark the woman's new status as mother.[13] At least in part, the naming ceremony's function is to name sex. They make the sex of the child known to the public, but also affirm the mother's sex as a woman.

The performance circle recreates the system of exchanges that once eased precolonial inequalities. According to Dorothy Davis Wills,[14] Senegalese women are "finding that, in the modern situation of aggressive economic violence, the traditional system of compensatory status guarantees them neither the respect of their husbands, nor food for the family." Although some women may be lucky enough to have salaried positions or to become important traders, most do not have these opportunities. Given this context, most women must engage even more intensely than usual in building exchange relationships *with other women* in order to survive. Although this is so, relationships among women are also articulated within a system that defines women by contrasting them with men. Cross-gender relationships thus dominate my analysis of the construction of women's social and discursive identities.

Although some women achieve significant economic success, most of my informants were economically dependent upon men.[15] The independent and well-to-do women I encountered were nationally famous performers such as Fatou Géwël and Ami Guèye. Senegalese women's growing dependency on men reflects developments elsewhere in Islamic Africa, where Hausa women have only accepted purdah since colonialism, and Sudanese women "have become more economically dependent upon men as the village has become integrated into the regional and international economy. Men's incomes are now the major determinant of family well-being, overshadowing the importance of women's domestic labor contributions."[16]

This applies to Senegalese women as well. Although Islam gives men the responsibility for taking care of the basic material needs of the family, many men in Senegal fail to do so. Indeed, Barbara Callaway and Lucy Creevey argue that religious belief has little impact in determining who assumes family expenses.[17] According to Marie-Denise Riss, retirement, age, sickness, unemployment or cultural values may make women's expectations that men will provide unrealistic.[18] Polygyny may also be a factor that makes it difficult for men to take care of all of their family's expenses in a monetary economy. In addition, many couples live separately for professional reasons, making it more likely that men's financial contributions will be uneven. At the same time, women's dependency on men has also grown, because "as men's horizons and occupational choices widen, women's remain comparatively narrow."[19] Long-term labor migration creates another source of conflict between men and women, for as it provides more and more men with wider opportunities, it locks women into long-distance marriages that seldom offer much satisfaction.

For these and other reasons, relationships among women thus seem to endure, while marriages are often short-lived. According to some studies, divorce rates are as high as 62 percent for male heads of household. (Since women often remarry, the male divorce rate provides more accurate data.)[20] The most frequently cited reason for divorce is that the husband refused or was unable to satisfy the material needs of the family. Riss' research shows that urban women receive a greater part of their income from their husbands than do rural women.[21] Urban women are thus more dependent on men and more likely to divorce than rural women when the man fails to provide. Economic relations between men and women alone cannot elucidate the complex indexicalization of sex in Wolof communities; however, they do provide a crucial context for activating a "virtual sexuality," in Strathern's terms, and have reshaped urban *taasu* performances. Naming ceremonies in particular not only offer a space for the discursive and symbolic construction of mother-hood, but also offer women opportunities to negotiate their economic relationship with the child's father.

Motherhood decisively shapes the relations between most spouses in Wolof communities, for it legitimates marriage. Until a woman proves her fertility, her marriage may be put into question. Although barrenness does not automatically lead to divorce, most women will receive a co-wife upon confirmation of infertility. Competition between co-wives also tends to be expressed through children. Rabain's work on early childhood in two Wolof communities presents further evidence that motherhood is a key index for sexual identity in Wolof communities; in one household, informants said that their barren co-wife was a man ("*Kii góor la*").[22] Motherhood offers access to the status of womanhood, for childless women are often considered less mature than mothers. F.D., of Louga, was often mistakenly identified as the younger sister when people met her and her sister M.D., primarily because, at age thirty-eight, she had never married and had no children. This angered her, for visitors thus denied her her "rightful" status as the older sister. According to Kate Modic, motherhood also offers West African women access to power.[23] Since motherhood confers adult status on Wolof women, who do not undergo any other organized initiation, it clearly allows them to enter into the social ring and fight to gain power.

The naming ceremony takes the mother as its axis, even though she remains invisible in her room during most of the event. "La femme est le maillon autour duquel s'organise cette trame socio-économique. Elle est au coeur du rapport de l'être à autrui. Elle est la source de la production, de la circulation, de l'échange et de la consommation sociale du bien-objet" [The woman is the center around which this socioeconomic framework is organized. She is at the heart of the relationship between one being and others. She is the source of the production, circulation, exchange and social consumption of goods],[24] according to Fatou Sow.

The woman of whom Sow speaks can only be a mother. The fact that she only stays with her guests during the exchange of *teraanga* during her child's naming ceremony supports the argument that women are central to these exchanges. The mother presents herself publicly three times during the naming ceremony; each time, she wears different clothing, if possible. Otherwise, she receives guests privately, in her room. That is when most guests, other than her family and in-laws, present their gifts. In 1993, when I conducted my research, the standard gift was 500 CFA. However, friends give according to the closeness of their relationship. Relatives' gifts are calculated according to a strict protocol. The paternal aunt (*bàjjan*) takes on an important role as director of protocol, but also as a major contributor to the event. The most important rule of etiquette demands that the recipient double the sum when the woman who gave it to her organizes an event.[25] The paternal aunt, or the woman chosen to fill her role, however, must sometimes pay up to five times the sum she receives. This is why some *diriyànke*—society beauties known for opulent wealth and generosity—now refuse the honor of playing the *bàjjan*'s role when asked. Since a woman may decide to give the *bàjjan*'s role to an important *diriyànke*, the exchange does not necessarily reinforce family ties. By choosing an important patron, however, the woman may gain social prestige and enrich herself. Such women are motivated not only by the desire for social prestige, but also by economic interest.

Men thus argue that, for women, "toute cérémonie est occasion de s'enrichir au détriment, bien sûr, des copines et amies" [any ceremony is an occasion to enrich oneself to the detriment, of course, of one's friends and acquaintances].[26] Men's vehement opposition to these events does not add up if this represents the whole truth. In fact, they oppose these events because they usually finance these exchanges among women.

Although women dominate naming ceremonies, men finance the exchanges. According to Heath, "such prestations make a public statement, along with other visible ceremonial expenditures, about what the woman's suitor or husband has and who he is. He will, therefore, make every effort to use his own ties to patrons, friends, and kin to meet these costs."[27] Apart from the father of the child and close male relatives, few adult male guests stay long at these events; however, these guests are very important. As members of the father's exchange network, they have assisted him in meeting his obligations. At least part of the time, financing naming ceremonies preoccupies male exchange groups among the Wolof, as among the Toucouleur.[28] The father is responsible for the cost of his wife's new clothing and her visit to the hairdresser; he must also rent chairs, large cooking pots, and a canvas pavilion, and pay for the food and beverages distributed to all guests. These normally include at least two meals—the *laax u sóow* (millet porridge and yogurt) distributed after the actual naming, and the noon meal. Usually, guests also receive a small plastic bag filled with *bissap* (a juice made from the leaves of a local plant) or *buy* (a yellow drink made from soaking the seeds of the baobab). In addition, the father must rent the services of a D.J. and his equipment for the entertainment of the guests. Since naming ceremonies cost from 20,000 CFA to 250,000 CFA (in 1993, this was the equivalent of approximately US$80 to $1,000), men have great difficulty paying for these lavish events. Not surprisingly, they frequently condemn extravagance and try to abolish the practice of organizing lavish family ceremonies.

In contrast, women oppose male attempts to reduce the importance of naming ceremonies. The naming ceremony has become a major site for women's gift exchanges. Since husbands finance the entertainment and food, the goods and funds distributed among women remain in their hands. When a woman hosts a *túr*, on the other hand, she must finance the event itself. The naming ceremony gift exchanges, then, operate much as other rotating credit organizations do, with the exception that male wealth is transferred to women at little or no expense to the women.

In reference to male exchange networks' financing of Toucouleur naming ceremonies, I. Wane argues that no surplus remains after the ceremony.[29] This fits the classic anthropological descriptions of exchanges on the Northwest Coast (potlatch) or in Oceania (*kula*). For Marcel Mauss, the gift is "un fait social total" [a total social fact]. This succinct description not only stresses that the gift is a social construct, but also universalizes the phenomenon. As a universal, total phenomenon, it holds the key to all social structures. According to Mauss's theory, the processes of gift-giving bind the concerned society together as a whole; indeed, such a "total" social phenomenon mirrors the entire society in miniature. In light of the phenomenon of *lekk u ndey* (the mother's part), however, this analysis presents a glaring defect: Mauss ignores the sexual identities of the agents involved in exchange. Wane, too, appears to focus exclusively on exchanges among men. Nevertheless, the roles assigned to men and women in the exchanges at naming ceremonies clearly differ; men gain prestige by expenditure, but women appear to gain wealth as well as prestige by building profitable ties to other women.

SEXUAL PERFORMANCES

Although these material exchanges shape the construction and performance of gendered identities, the performance mode is no less important as a defining factor. The representational *taasu* performance takes place within the context of another mode, one that is expressive and celebratory, rather than mimetic.[30] The mode of ceremonial parade in celebration of motherhood parallels the *taasu* performance of sexuality, but does so by transforming the "'play' of private and individual agents into a public ceremonial event. As in language itself, it is the certainty of an underlying grammar of mask and parody, of . . . the evasion of verisimilitude in the parados, that makes it possible to posit meaning to nonverbal events."[31] In contrast, the *taasu* itself often employs the mimetic mode. The "meaning" of motherhood in Wolof communities cannot be reduced to one single performance expression of that profoundly important role; however, such expressions illuminate some of the meanings of motherhood and women's identity.

The ceremonial performances of motherhood that I observed during my research only became visible to me as my research drew to an end, for only then was I able to attend naming ceremonies as a friend and guest, rather than as a researcher.[32] Ironically, these experiences revealed new aspects of the naming ceremony to me simply because I was not seeking further information on a specific issue. When I went to the naming ceremony for the second child of my friend and neighbor Besse, I waited with the other guests until the honored mother arrived, freshly coifed, from the beauty salon. Besse was unrecognizable. She had been heavily made up in a highly stylized manner, with eyeliner and eye shadow curling to her temples, powder masking her natural complexion, and the traces of a lip pencil and red lipstick changing the normal curve of her lips. A complex, glossy new hairstyle kept in place with a great deal of gel also changed her appearance. What struck me was not the makeup itself, for I had seen Besse wear makeup before; however, I suddenly realized that almost every mother I had seen at an naming ceremony had worn the same stylized mask of motherhood. One does not need to know the mother in order to recognize her as the woman whose child is being presented to the community, for she presents an ideal image of motherhood, rather than herself. On the day that her child is to receive a name that will distinguish it from all other children forever, she recedes into the mask of maternity.

Mimetic *taasu* performed in honor of motherhood not only complement this expressive mode of performance, but also take on elements of it at times. For example, several *taasu* that I collected at various naming ceremonies focused on the theme of the archetypical "good mother." This ideal figure reflects the context discussed in the section above, on material exchanges between men and women. None of these *taasu* discusses the woman's parenting abilities. Instead, the *taasukat* praises the woman who knows how to please her husband and in-laws, and who maintains good relations with her own family. The latter was clearly the case in the following *taasu*, performed in honor of Tanor Dieng's daughter Fatou Sarr Dieng.

Jii yaay mat na yaay	This mother meets motherhood's challenges
yaay su mate yaay	If a mother's worthy of motherhood,
bëccëg lay jóg	She goes out at daylight
Géwël yi di ko dar	The griots escort her
Waaye yaay su matul yaay nag	But if a mother does not meet the challenge, then

guddi la-y dox	She walks at night
Rekk xaj ya di ko bów	Only the dogs bark at her

Chorus

Faat Saar Jeng	Faat Saar Jeng
Mat nga yaay	You are worthy of motherhood
Tanor ay sama baay	Tanor oh my father
Waay doy na Kajoor	Oh, he suffices Kajoor
Faat Jeng ay sama yaay	Faat Jeng, oh my mother
kooku doy na Kajoor	That one suffices Kajoor
Faat Jeng ay sama yaay	Faat Jeng, oh my mother
kooku doy na Kajoor	That one suffices Kajoor
Faat Kinne sa ndey ak sa baay	Faat Kinne, your mother and your father
doomu yëkk ak doomu wëll	Child of a bull and child of a cow
Nga dëkk Kajoor	You live in Kajoor
Tanoor ay sama baay	Tanoor, oh my father
Waay doy na lu ne	That is enough
Dama ne Kinne	I say, Kinne!
Ndey bu mate ndey kat	A mother who meets the challenge of motherhood, indeed
bëccëg lay jóg	She goes out at daylight
Géwël yi di ko dar	The griots court her
Waaye ndey su matul ndey nag	But the mother who's not worthy of the name mother
guddi lay dox	Walks in the night
Muus ya di ko ñeew	Cats yowl after her

Chorus

Faat Saaro	Faat Saaro
Ne wu ma muus	I did not say cat
Dama ne ñeew rekk nga ne ma ale	I only said [unclear] and you told me to leave

Chorus

Dama ne Kinne	I say Kinne
Ne wo ma muus	You did not call a cat
nga ne ma sipp	You cried "Sipp!"[33] at me.

Chorus

Kinne jal bi Yàlla jal	Kinne, the pile that God made
soo ko jale mu jal-jali[34]	If you add to it, it will grow
Soo ko jalul mu jal-jali	If you don't, it will still grow
Dama ne Faat Saar	I say Faat Saar
Yëkk gu gas ci diggu Manding	The bull who digs in the ready field[35]

ba yoor-yoor fees	Until mid-morning passes
Ganaar gu jóg jaar ci digg jal ba	A hen goes out, passes in the middle of the heap
Gay Demba la cay jële	Gay Demba took it there
Faatu Kinne	Faatu Kinne
Mat nga yaay	You are a true mother
Waay yaay su mate yaay daal	Oh, a worthy mother, well
bëccëg la jóg	She goes out in daylight
Géwël ña di ko dar	Griots accompany her
waaye yaay su matul yaay	But the mother who does not deserve the name
guddi lay dox	Walks at night
Xaj ya di ko bow	The dogs bark at her

Chorus

Dama ko ne ajul	I say to her, [find a] perch
Ajul ba ca kaw	But do not perch on high
Yàlla ko aj-ajal	God put her on high
Abdu ca kow	Abdu on high
Elisabet ca kow	Elisabeth on high
Abib Caam ca kow	Habib Thiam on high[36]
kon jàllal ba ca kow	So pass until you are on high
Yàlla mi la aj	God himself elevated you
moo la aj-ajal	He lifted you on high
Maysa Buri Dégén Koddu ma ca Gille	Maysa Buri Dégén Koddu from Guilé
Tanoor ay sa baay	Tanoor is your father
doyna Kajoor	And suffices Kajoor
Faat Jeng	Faat Jeng
Jal bu Yàlla jal	The pile that God made
te jal ko	Add to it
te jal ko jal a jal	And adding to it, heaping it up
jal bi Yàlla jal	The heap that God made
Soo ko jàle mu jal-jali	If you add to it, it will grow
Soo ko jalul mu jal-jali	If you don't, it will increase
Yaay Bàmba[37]	You are Bamba.
Ku la lebbal kér	Whoever offers you shade
Nga feyee ko guddi	You pay him back at night
Kii yaay Bàmba	This is you, Bamba

Chorus

Xoolal	Look!
doomu Tanoor bi moo-y yaay Bàmba	The daughter of Tanoor is Bamba
ku ko lebal kér	Whoever lends you shade

| mu feyee ko guddi | He pays him back at night |
| kooku mooy Bàmba[38] | That one is Bamba |

Chorus

This *taasu* highlights the relational character of individual identity central to Irène D'Alméïda's (1994) conception of female identity. Fatou Sarr Dieng's role as a mother depends in part on her conduct as a wife, but only in part. If the honored wife appears only in daylight, this proves that her life is open to public observation, as she has nothing to hide. She takes no lovers, for instance. On the other hand, the *taasu* extends the proverbial wisdom that a mother must please her husband in order to assure her children a prosperous childhood to encompass the entire network of clients and patrons who might assist her children. She should help increase her father's status, and thus her family's and her own; however, she should also behave as Cheikh Amadou Bamba did, by showing generosity and fairness to her numerous clients.

As another *taasu* would put it, the mother should be a great tree whose wide-spreading branches offer shade to all. The mother is a giver of gifts. This highly popular *taasu* that I recorded at a naming ceremony in St. Louis (July 10, 1993) reflects that role.

Ku ci am ndey ju réy	Whoever has a great mother
Dinga am bés bu réy	Will have a big day
Ku ci am ndey ju sew	Whoever has an insignificant mother
Dinga am bés bu sew ruuc	Will have a teeny-tiny event
Danga yëndu ak jantam	You will spend the day [alone] with the sun

This *taasu* was repeated several times with zest and energy. At the end of the performance, the performer gave several gifts to the women who had organized the event. They first protested, "Déedéet, danga ñów bëggee baleese[39] rekk, waaye ñun loolu taxuñoo jóg. Déét, bul def loolu!" [No, you came just to beat us, but we didn't come for that. No, don't do that!] before accepting the gifts with evident pleasure. Clearly, gift-giving allows the giver to gain prestige. The *taasukat* gave the gift of her performance, in addition to material gifts.

The text itself supports the notion that motherhood is a challenge in building networks that will later assure the child's future. The "ndey ju réy" is a big woman because she has many friends and allies who will help her organize an important and memorable event to celebrate the birth of her grandchild. A woman who has failed in establishing such a network, however, will be unable to assist her daughter. In addition, very few people will attend the event. Most guests join the family at the naming ceremony in the afternoon, so the last phrase is a telling one. If one's mother has few or no allies, mother and daughter will spend the day in the sun alone. Since Wolof avoid the heat of the sun, seeking shade, this metaphor aptly expresses the notion that such women must face difficulties on their own.

Although naming ceremonies are privileged contexts for the performance of *taasu*, relatively few of them address the issue of motherhood so directly. More frequently, the *taasukat* will praise the mother's ability to manage her interpersonal relations with her husband, in-laws, and other family members. She may also praise those qualities that promote harmonious family relations. One short *taasu* presents the notion that this is the source of all lasting happiness.

Njaboot jàmm ay mbokkam[40]	Peace is the family's friend
Bu ko amee moom la bëgg	If you have it, it's what you want
Bu ko amul moom la bëgg	If you don't, it's what you want
Njaboot jàmm ay mbokkam	Peace is the family's friend

If the mother promotes family harmony, then her child's happiness and success are almost assured. Clearly, choosing the "right" wife is crucial according to this ideological construction of motherhood;[41] not only must the woman be fertile, but she must have good social skills and an established network that will assist her child in later years. However, exaggerating the importance of marriage choices proportionately diminishes the role of the mother as a social agent. Even if the "right" wife is found, she must *choose* to promote harmony. As Obioma Nnaemeka writes, few African women writers and performers accept the western feminist notion that yokes motherhood and victimhood; rather, they often present motherhood as an activity.[42]

Naming ceremonies and other events also allow Wolof to stage and perform sexual identities that subvert as well as reinforce the apparently hegemonic sexual order. At a naming ceremony I attended in Colobane, cross-dressing highlighted the issue of gender. One female guest chose to dress in khaki shorts, men's socks and shoes, a vest and a shirt stuffed to simulate a pot-belly, and the red fez-like hat favored by older men. Her makeup was intended to allow her to present a caricatural figure of the colonial *Tubaab* (the common term for Caucasians), for she painted white circles on her cheeks and chin. She strutted, blew a whistle, then danced, to the laughter of her audience. At the same event, a homosexual man performed a female role. (Since he confided the fact to me and my research assistants, I know that he is homosexual. On many other occasions, I observed other men playing similar roles, but I can only guess at their sexual preferences.) He attempted to speak in a feminine way, mimicking the talk of wealthy, upper-class Dakar women, danced without displaying any of the more clearly masculine moves,[43] and helped women prepare and serve food. These playful performances of sexual identity contrast sharply with the stylized image of the mother, but they also fit the performance mode described above that I contrasted to the mimetic *taasu*, for they represent similar forms of expressive, celebratory and parodic performances of sexuality.

In fact, gender can be interpreted as a form of aesthetic whose performance fits under the broad rubric of aesthetics as "all constraints of form."[44] In other words, social identities can be seen as performances because individual agents operate within social systems that constrain them to a restricted set of meaningful codes. This is particularly true of the social interaction that takes place at the *ngente*, or naming ceremony, for it is a context in which agents actively create and perform sexual identities. These performances have meaning insofar as others can recognize and interpret them in light of social codes. It follows that sexual identities remain virtual until an agent takes action in relation to another agent, for the social significance of sexual identity thus depends on interaction.

The very broad use of the metaphor of dramatic performance to describe social action may lead us to ask whether it is indeed possible to distinguish social drama from performance in the more limited sense of artistic or musical performance.[45] Clearly, *taasu* performances partake of both. The dilemma arises because of naïve use of the metaphor, rather than through the metaphor itself. We need to heed Fabian's warning that static definitions of performance lead to stale and ethnocentric conclusions because of the many connotations that the metaphor bears. He contrasts earlier theories of social action as drama that assume that actors are guided by a set of transcendent cultural values with the view that social praxis/performance is "making, fashioning, creating."[46] This view links theories of social drama with theories of social constructivism in dynamic fashion.

Similarly, the search for some essential reality behind sexed performances exemplifies the "drive to isolate and identify the boundaries of situations so as to contain and control them, thereby preventing slippages and keeping the really real distinguishable from play, the serious from the unserious."[47] However, play and praxis intersect in such a way that our attempts to see them as discrete depend upon pretense as well. Wolof theories of metaphor make this much clear, for when someone tells you that a person actually embodies the thing with which she is equated in a *taasu* (whether this is a tree, animal, or other object), or with her family "totem," they do not fail to recognize metaphor as a literary device. On the contrary, they choose to stress the connections between the woman and the world.[48]

THE AUTOBIOGRAPHICAL EXCHANGE

The material and symbolic exchanges that I have described above suggest that anthropological and feminist theories of gender and exchange present important "horizons of interpretation" for the study of *taasu* performance. Many of these theories focus on the competitive aspects of gender and its performance. Feminist anthropologists have focused on marriage as the site of the "traffic in women,"[49] while other analyses of exchange have concentrated on the notion of male-female complementarity. A strictly complementary distribution of roles automatically locks both sexes into particular spheres of activity, hence feminist critique of this theory of sex roles. Complementary distribution parallels the gift economy's operational mechanisms in certain ways, since women are exchanged in marriage. Both forms of cross-gender exchange demand reciprocation—either of women, or of women's work. Reciprocation, the rule of all exchange, thus would seem to found women's subordination. In part, this explains Jacques Derrida's understanding of the gift as an essential element of the Master/Slave relationship.[50]

Although this interpretation of Marcel Mauss' theory of the gift relies on Heidegger and, more broadly, on modernist thought, Derrida's description of the gift that founds the Master/Slave relationship also seems to re-inscribe his earlier critiques of the social contract theory that founds competitive western possessive individualism. Again, we find ourselves on the horns of the dilemma described in the introduction, for Derrida explains that subjectivity itself is constructed in the very moment of the competitive exchange that simultaneously offers and withholds the gift.

> One would even be tempted to say that a subject as such never gives or receives a gift. It is constituted, on the contrary, in view of dominating, through calculation and exchange, the mastery of this *hubris* or of this impossibility that is announced in the promise of the gift. There where there is subject and object, the gift would be excluded. . . . But the subject and the object are arrested effects of the gift, arrests of the gift. At the zero or infinite speed of the circle.[51]

The gift, then, represents the always impossible erasure of the difference between Subject and Object, Self and Other, Master and Slave. Although Derrida has conceded elsewhere that this is an unattainable ideal, the essay teasingly suggests that the gift could embody it, then demonstrates that the gift can never deliver the promised gratuity. It could only do so by abolishing the giving subject, and thus the act of gift-giving itself.

This critique is highly relevant to the gift exchanges I have described, for these exchanges expose the political economy of sex in Senegal. Events that include gift exchanges highlight the importance of caste as well, showcasing both the power of nobles (who show their power through their generosity) and the power of the *ñeeño*, or casted members of society, who can make or destroy a noble's public reputation through speech. If Irvine and Wright are correct in analyzing these power relationships in terms of discourse and "the power of articulation," however, speech offers a space not only for fixing status, but also for negotiating power. Verbal exchange, then, simultaneously anchors the system and gives it a limited flexibility. Wolof women obviously do compete for goods and prestige, as the *taasu* prove; however, the exchanges that base their relationships also preclude the kind of *total* dominance and objectification of others that the western ideology of individualism seems inevitably to promote.

Sex does make a difference that Derrida seems to ignore in his essay on the gift. Other poststructuralist thinkers, however, have taken this issue to be central to their long-standing intellectual engagement with the gift. Hélène Cixous, for instance, addressed the issue in early essays such as *La jeune née* (Paris: UGE, 1975). In her more recent work, she describes the gift of the self quite differently from Derrida. Her conceptualization of a shared subjectivity, or of "séparéunion" [separate-dunion][52] seems particularly pertinent to *taasu* that emphasize motherhood, for pregnancy, as we will see in chapter 6, interrupts the possessive form of individualism that Derrida apparently considers fundamental to subjectivity itself. Since the relationship between mother and embryo does not entail simply dissolving the self into the other—the necessary condition of the gift exchange, in Derrida's theory—it renews the promise of the gift. Certainly, women do not experience exchange relationships as men do, given the patriarchal relationships that frame exchanges.

Furthermore, we might extend the notion beyond this very specific relationship, as few members of Wolof society experience the kind of economic autonomy that this western model takes for granted. It follows that the effects of the cycle of gift-giving will differ as well. The notion of expansible time also radically alters the process of exchange. The time between the gift and its reciprocation, as Derrida notes, tends to erase the gratuity of the present, for it too easily becomes a synonym for the duration of a loan that accrues interest. In this chapter, I have outlined the way in which that time operates as a form of credit between the sexes; obviously, such given time stands in opposition to Derrida's notion of the gift. Yet Derrida ignores the truly gratuitous result of the time of the cycle of exchange—the time spent *together*. If exchange serves to build and cement human relationships, the time that partners in exchange spend together, regardless of motivation or intention, takes place beyond the limits of calculation and ruse.

Although many of these relationships may not fit our notion of disinterested "friendship," any more than the gift cycle fits our notion of the disinterested "gift," the gift of time spent in cameradery does indeed fit our notions of the gift. Perhaps this is why the best part of the day among the Wolof is the afternoon, which is almost always spent drinking tea (*àttaya*) with visitors. Although coming up with the money for tea and sugar may be painful, this aspect rarely touches the enjoyment of this gift of time shared.

The gift of common time accompanies many other gifts. One of these is the name. We can hardly conceive of personal identity outside of this common time, for identity is constructed through the process of dialogic exchange within the community. Panegyric genres give great weight to this claim. In her study of Yoruba *oriki*, Karin Barber shows that *oriki* have an onomastic as well as a laudatory function. As a result, they provide highly convincing proof for her theory of dialogically constructed identities. In addition, they reinforce the basis for a notion of autobiography as a system of symbolic exchange.

> When a performer utters *oriki*, she attains special access to the subject. She is felt to have touched the heart of the subject's identity. At the same time, she constructs her own identity, as the interlocutor personified. . . . It can involve—indeed at one level always does involve—a merging of identities or the subsumption of one identity by another. . . . Individual subjects thus share with others the components that make up their innermost identity, and recognise fragments of it in other people wherever they go.[53]

If we attempt to diagram the relationships Barber describes, we almost inevitably draft some kind of circle. Indeed, the sign of the circle figures prominently in more than a few theories of identity. According to Eakin, the circularity of the theory that the individual self and culture mutually engender each other "seems to vitiate [its] value as explanation, but some observers now point to this circularity as a clue to the dynamic reciprocity that structures any exchange between self and culture."[54]

This dynamic reciprocity is precisely what I wish to indicate by the term exchange. These circular models of identity thus re-present the problem of the hermeneutic circle. We cannot understand the whole without the individual elements, nor the individual elements without understanding the whole, just as we cannot understand a *taasu* out of context, nor an event's significance without *taasu*. Here, I wish to suggest that we must also examine the ring as a process of textual exchange. Indeed, my fieldwork experience leads me to envision the hermeneutic circle as a form of the *kula* ring of exchanges that joins the Trobriand islanders in B. Malinowski's account.[55] Knowledge of *taasu* can only be received if one gives. If a *taasu* does not invite you to join the ring of exchanges on one level or another, it is impossible to actually receive the gift-poem.

Interpretation also depends upon some code that regulates the exchange between author and reader, performer and audience-member, speaker and addressee. The *kula* ring is a dynamic circle, rather than a static exchange of gifts; it encourages participants to add to the quantity of goods produced and exchanged in order to gain prestige and honor. By attempting to do the same in our analyses—patching new elements (supplements[56]) onto our notion of the autobiographical exchange—perhaps we can enlarge the hermeneutic circle and our understanding of performance and autobiography.

CHAPTER 5

The Politics of Praise

Paradoxically, exchange holds the promise of freedom within community, but it also presents the threat of a political order based on the subordination of women. Women's autobiographical discourses represent a special response to this fundamental paradox, as Carole Boyce Davies suggests by defining women's autobiography as the act of inserting the private self into public life. Davies thus defines African women's autobiographical acts primarily as political acts. She observes that African women's autobiographies are generally "not a statement on a 'self' after a success but an insertion of a 'self' within a historical and social framework which accepts her invisibility or silence. Within such a context, her autobiography also becomes political statement."[1] This resistance to exclusionary hegemony takes place in both written and in oral discourses.

Although much scholarly attention has been directed toward the political uses of oral performance in Africa, relatively few scholars have focused on women's political expression. According to Molara Ogundipe-Leslie and Carole Boyce-Davies, the emphasis on epic and other male-centered performance genres in the scholarly literature on oral performance in Africa reflects the biases of researchers.

> Even in the formulation of the language surrounding the study of African oral literature, the absence of women is taken as a given. In other words, the assumption is that the "griot" is always male or that there are no women to whom attention needs to be paid.[2]

They argue further that scholarly erasure of women's words complies with colonial policies that actively curbed women's political and economic roles in order to impose western models on African societies.[3] Postcolonial states have attempted to redress the situation by reserving certain ministries for women or by creating ministries of women's affairs; however, they also continue to implement many policies inherited from the colonial era that negatively affect women. According to Boyce Davies and Ogundipe-Leslie, then, we cannot attempt to understand women's performance genres without reference to women's general conditions. Those conditions are determined not only by internal affairs, but also by the global relations that affect the country as a whole. Although I can only touch upon these general conditions in a study focused on autobiographical discourses, I seek to provide these underpinnings through my discussion of the history of women's education and its implications for women's political involvement.

MINOR POLITICS

In the past, observers of global politics assigned Senegal and other African states the status of peripheral satellites to the multiple centers of power in the world today, diminishing their ability to negotiate in the political arena. For this reason, politics in a small state such as Senegal are considered minor, unimportant in the global scheme of things. Moreover, most of the postcolonial states in the world today are considered "minors," that is, as immature, developing entities. In official discourse, most of the world is infantilized by these metaphors. Ironically, many of the postcolonial communities treated as minors have longer histories than the linguistic communities using these metaphors of development.

These metaphors reflect the dual system of global inequalities (nations that are "haves" and "have-nots"). Senegal's civil society mimics this structure in certain ways, as do other postcolonial societies. In this context, the center is the modern state that takes its members from the francophone elite, while the remaining precolonial social institutions and the rest of the population remain far from power, in the periphery. Following this world-systems model, Peter Ekeh has argued that civil society in postcolonial Africa is thus marked by a "dual public." The modern nation state co-exists with Wolof civic society, but lacks the means to create the relationship of mutual dependence and moral accountability that one might find at the local level or village public sphere. Consequently, elites attempt to legitimize themselves in both spheres in different ways.[4]

This dual structure repeats itself on yet another level, for the private, or domestic sphere, is subordinated to the public sphere in national politics and in civil society. This neglect long played a role in the allocation of resources, both at the level of the Senegalese government and at the level of international development agencies. In response, feminist political theory and action often focus on the neglected connections between the political sphere and the domestic sphere. Although few women's groups in Senegal label themselves as feminists, apart from Yéwwu Yéwwi, many women's groups have clear political agendas (such as protecting women from spousal violence), and many of them produce their own discourses on feminist agency.[5] Erasing women's words and the sphere that was drawn around them by patriarchal authorities, many observers have ignored these discourses until recently. In part, this neglect can be attributed to the fact that such discourses often function in unexpected ways. Forms of self-expression that are considered minor, or unimportant, may take on a new importance, however, when we re-evaluate them in light of their political functions.

Although some scholars have noted the political uses of oral performance genres, attention has been directed almost exclusively toward a few specific genres of oral performance. As the epic form often represents and upholds the status quo, it has been singled out as the most powerful political vehicle; indeed, Julien claims that "this hierarchic form is tied to nationalistic agendas and military might, which have been and continue to be, for the most part, provinces of patriarchy."[6] The emphasis on nationalistic agendas and on epic as a nationalistic genre, then, has tended to devalue or even deny women's political and literary contributions, for the generic hierarchy replicates the social hierarchy[7] that subordinates women to men. *Taasu* and other panegyric forms have been trivialized as a result. Despite this trivialization, *taasu* is in fact an important vehicle of popular political expression in Senegal today, on the national as well as on the regional level.

In spite of the fact that women are now cast in the role of "keepers of tradition" in Senegal and in other postcolonial African states, this has not given them the power on the national level that their male counterparts enjoy. Often, it has served to relegate them to the margins of public life, for current interpretations of that role often suggest that they must uphold some form of static cultural "authenticity." In other words, an official discourse that runs counter to the highly politicized dynamics of Senegalese verbal arts seeks to immobilize these "mothers of the nation." This is particularly true of *taasukat* who perform praises to the nation at the Daniel Sorano National Theatre or on television. Nevertheless, this development indicates that women's performances have increased in importance, as they are now portrayed as emblematic of national identity.

This type of *taasu* performance often reaches the public through the mass media. Some Wolof argue that such performances are not *taasu*, because of the patron's absence. When the *taasukat* stands with her chorus and drummers on a stage, the context differs so dramatically from the familiar open competition for patronage or praise that these observers do not see them as *taasu* at all. In contrast, performers know very well that the state represents the absent patron. They respond by devoting most of these *taasu* to the nation. They frequently interject phrases such as, "Senegaal déggal!" [Listen, Senegal!] or "Senegaal gépp ko xam" [All Senegal knows about it]. These performances represent an invisible state, rather than the rural civil society that the state seeks to incorporate.

Political *taasu* also allow women to use the topos associating patri-archal authority with the state to criticize the state's shortcomings. As a genre, the *taasu* is tied to women and to events closely associated with women—weddings, baptisms, and *túr*—so women's *taasu* performances at political rallies highlight the gap between the public and the private. Because the genre floats between the domestic sphere and that of national politics, it disrupts the otherwise clear demarcations between the sexes, the public and the private, the individual and the community.

This is possible because those who wield the state apparatus must of necessity gain some measure of legitimacy among the large numbers of Senegalese who use other idioms of political and social expression than the francophone elite. The "sursaut national" [national leap] that marked Diouf's accession to power also marked a renewed effort to bridge the gap between voters who use oral forms of expression and political elites.[8] As a result, oral performance genres such as the *taasu* play an important role at political rallies. Moustapha Kâ, a Parti Social-iste [Socialist Party] careerist, clearly takes such performances seriously. Defending the factionalism that his party promotes, he remarked:

> These tendencies animate the life of the Party. It is a colourful, throb-bing, and noisy life which unfortunately is often subjected to tensions, conflict, and violence. They even awaken artistic activity. I am think-ing, for example, of the songs, *baks* and *tassous* [*taasus*] composed by the artists of the various tendencies to the glory of their leaders.[9]

Although Kâ mentioned the *taasu* in order to defend their political use, it is worth noting that he considers them part of the activity necessary to the life of the party.

The lively political rallies that I observed in 1993 during the presi-dential and legislative electoral campaigns[10] relied heavily on *taasukat*, as well as on musicians and dancers, in order to drum up support for the candidates. Panegyric has always had a privileged placed in Wolof polit-ical life, for the *géwël* not only speaks for the ruler, but also constructs the ruler's popular image and cultivates his power base through praise. In the past, the scholarship on praise poetry has almost exclusively focused on this aspect of the poetry. Most scholars have thus neglected the use of panegyric to voice popular concerns,[11] seeking information concerning popular political sentiment from other sources. The electoral rallies of 1993, however, demonstrated the potential of praise poetry as a vehicle for political expression.

In 1993, rising popular dissatisfaction with the status quo made it difficult for the party functionaries to continue repeating the same speeches, yet they could not innovate without risking party sanctions. At the meeting I attended in Sancaba, Louga on April 25, 1993, I found out by chance that the party follows its members' actions very closely. The man sitting next to me was scribbling notes as fast as I was. I took him to be a journalist, but he told me that he worked for the ruling party, when I asked. According to other members of the audience, his task was to report on party members' actions and speeches. In other words, he was a party "spy." Because of party spies, Parti Socialiste (P.S.) officials say little that is of interest at party rallies. They rely on *taasukat* and other entertainers to drum up enthusiasm. As a result of the banality of official political discourse, then, *taasu*'s political importance has increased.

As an example, I would like to share a *taasu* in which women in Louga expressed their opinion of the aid to refugees from Mauritania in a subtle fashion that both praised and criticized the ruling party and its government.

Ne Abdu Juuf	I say Abdou Diouf!
Bu dul woon nag doomu Kumba	If it weren't for that Kumba
Dem ja	Dem's child,
Deñuy dee ca Gànnaar	We'd have died in Mauritania
Kenn duñu jëli	No one took us in
Chorus	
Mane Abdu Juuf	I say Abdou Diouf!
Budul woonag moom	If it weren't for him
Deñuy dee ba jeex tàkk	We'd have died, all of us
Kenn duñu sowe	No one saved us
Ne Abdu Juuf sowetaas	Oh, Abdou Diouf—rescue!
Abdu Juuf	Abdou Diouf
Yaa ma gënal Ould Taay	I prefer you to Ould Taay[12]
muy dox di reye	Who walks and kills
Chorus	
Mane Abdu Juuf	I say Abdou Diouf
Wuuteenga ag Ould Taay	You are different from Ould Taay
muy dox di reye	Who walks and kills

This *taasu* requires some knowledge of the crisis that erupted in 1989, when Mauritanian authorities detained, tortured, or expulsed many black residents and citizens. Given the close historical and family ties between many Senegalese and Mauritanian communities, many of those who suffered were indeed Senegalese. Others were granted asylum in Senegal. Momar Coumba Diop and Mamadou Diouf briefly explain the historical and economic context of the 1989 conflict in chapter 14 of *Le Sénégal sous Abdou Diouf*.[13] According to Diop and Diouf, "durant la dernière semaine du mois d'avril, plusieurs centaines de Sénégalais furent tués et/ou mutilés dans les principales villes de Mauritanie avec une complicité évidente des forces de sécurité" [During the last week of April, several hundred Senegalese were killed and/or mutilated in the main cities of Mauritania with the obvious complicity of the police and of the army.][14] Senegal retaliated, and indeed, hooligans pillaged Mauritanian businessmen's shops in Dakar April 21–24, 1989. The two governments have re-established diplomatic relations, but the problems behind the crisis have yet to be resolved, as do the claims of thousands of dispossessed Mauritanians and Senegalese. Indeed, outbreaks of violence in villages near the Senegal River in 1998 make it clear that the conflict is far from being resolved.

Since the performance took place at a political rally, the women praise Diouf, the "Father of the Nation," for giving them and other refugees from Mauritania a safe haven. However, their praise has a subdued tone, for they simply say that Diouf is better than Ould Taaya because he does not kill. Although Wolof often express compliments in this indirect, understated fashion, this *taasu* presents a striking contrast to Diouf's campaign slogan—"Abdoo ñoo doy" [Abdou satisfies us/Abdou is enough for us]. The women's performance, on the other hand, implies that Diouf should do something positive to help them, rather than simply refraining from massive repression. In other words, women subtly refashion political slogans into a vehicle for popular political expression through the *taasu*. In addition, they present their own social vision, even if they must do so in a veiled and partial manner in the context of political rallies.

Recontextualizing a genre such as the *taasu*, as Wolof women do in political meetings, signifies that women are taking an authority otherwise denied to them in postcolonial civil society. Strikingly, women tend to do this by linking the personal to the political through *taasu* such as the one quoted above. Since the gap between the private and the public sectors erases women's discourse, women often bridge that gap by revealing it to be a politically motivated fiction. This attempt to bridge gaps and thus blur boundaries affects other aspects of women's lives that are of interest to us here.

"WRITING" POLITICS

Another dual system encourages women's silence by identifying women with oral traditions, then opposing these to the privileged technology of writing. Stereotyping women as "mothers of tradition" potentially bars them from the new sphere of power. Since Senegal is at least formally a democratic republic, however, postcolonial elites must win credibility in the public sphere that they consider "traditional," or "oral."[15] This necessity opens a breach that some women use to their advantage, indicating that the form or medium that the performer uses matters less than whether s/he has an audience.

This defines the political nature of the "great divide" demarcating oral from written texts rather precisely, for it means that we can only speak of "writing" in tandem with reception. A *taasukat* who gains an audience can inscribe meaning on reality because she has received the audience's attention. Similarly, those who wish to "write" in French must first gain an audience. At a very basic level, writing only occurs when the reader engages in textual exchange and reciprocates by offering the text attention or commentary. Succinctly put, the relevant difference between Senegalese writing in French and the performed "writing" of *taasu* is political. This difference founds a *habitus*, or structuring structure (Bourdieu), that shapes practice, experience, and power in Senegal.

In Senegal, writing signifies exclusion from politics for the greater part of the population. Less than 30 percent of all Senegalese can read and write in French, but ongoing efforts to spread literacy in national languages have as yet had a relatively small impact on the politics that tie power to literacy in French. In this context, Africanist research can, and often does exclude informants from the (written) discussion.[16] Idealistic attempts to overcome the obstacle of the written word as replacement for a woman's own words have not succeeded in changing this power differential. The many oral life histories produced by researchers determined to create a literate space for those who do not write have even been described as unwitting acts of linguistic colonialism, for

> access to autobiography, for whole groups of people, has only been possible through the dominant mediation of an investigator or fieldworker . . . [fostering] the various alibis that the dominant subject-position gives itself as it constructs the subordinate as other.[17]

This frustrating dilemma leads some critics to a new formulation of older theories of a "great divide" between oral and literate communities. In the past, scholars described the great divide in cognitive terms, focusing primarily on memory to distinguish oral from literate modes of expression and evaluate their cognitive effects.[18] More recently, attention has shifted to the ideological significance of orality and literacy. Brian Street, for example (1984, 1995), has argued that the distinctions made between those who use writing and those who do not are fundamentally political. Writing means power. Therefore, practical and discursive limits to Senegalese women's coming to voice define the "essential boundary between orality and literacy as a political and economic fact that cannot long be ignored,"[19] according to Christopher Miller.

Acceptance of theories of a Great Divide depends on the unexamined assumption that purely oral and purely literate situations exist. Although few would contest that oral and chirographic modes differ, little evidence exists to suggest that any society is "purely oral." Even those scholars once most convinced of the essential differences between written and oral modes now agree that no great, unbridgeable gap separates the two. Jack Goody writes of the "interface" between oral and written modes,[20] and John Miles Foley states that

> the old model of the Great Divide between orality and literacy has given way in most quarters, pointing toward the accompanying demise of the absolutist dichotomy of performance versus document . . . the question becomes not whether but how performance and document speak to one another.[21]

Current research on literacy thus focuses on the social meanings of writing or of literacy, rather than on proving the essential differences between the two categories.

Furthermore, we can no longer assume that verbal arts follow the familiar path from oral to written described in so many studies. My research shows that written documents and modern media influence oral performance, just as oral arts influence writers. At a *ceet* [final wedding ceremony] that took place in Usine, one *taasukat* compared a woman to Bocandé, a famous Senegalese soccer player.

Awa, yaay Bookande	Awa, you are Bocandé
Futbal boo fekee am nga ca bi	When you're at a soccer match, you score a goal
Yaay Bookande	You are Bocandé

These women know about Bocandé primarily through national television broadcasts. Although they do not communicate in French, they do incorporate French as a sign of literate culture in their performances. They do this in two ways: first, they enlist the aid of women who do know how to write in order to produce written records of the gifts exchanged at family events such as the *ceet* or the *ngente*. Second, they inscribe it in their performances, as in the following example.

Maa roy sa jikko	I'll follow your model
Doo sàcc, doo fen	You don't steal, you don't lie
Tëye nga sa làmmiñ	You hold your tongue[22]

Sa tànk guddul	You don't run around[23]
Ne Ken, yaw, ñetti "fuu" yu dalu la	Say Ken, the three "fuu"[24] don't touch you
Ñetti fuu yu dalu la (3 times)	The three "fuu" don't touch you
Ñetti fuu yu dalu la	The three "fuu" don't touch you
Je m'en fous ci goro yi	I don't care about my in-laws
Je m'en fous ci mag ñi	I don't care about my elders
Je m'en fous ci jabar yi	I don't care about my sisters-in-law
Ken Seen, ñetti fuu yu dalu la	Ken Seen, the three "fuu" don't touch you
(Chorus)	
Ñetti fuu yu dalu la	The three "fuu" don't touch you

The performer skillfully uses the near-homonymy between the Wolof word "fuy" [to disrespect] and the French "fou" [crazy] to explain what constitutes poor behavior, condemn it, and praise Ken for avoiding such bad behavior. In addition, she persistently inscribes the performance in the realm of writing in French. She uses the adjective "fou" and the idiomatic "je m'en fous" [I don't give a damn] as nouns, for Wolof verbs retain the infinitive form as gerunds, just as English verbs do. This sophisticated and elaborate inscription of French literacy in a Wolof performance allowed the performer to mesh two disparate spheres of experience.

Just as the interruptions or gaps between experience and ideological constructions of gender allow women to invent and represent autobiographical selves,[25] similar gaps between oral and written discourses offer a space for social action. If we choose to view one of these media as a more authentic representation of reality than any other, we fall automatically into the ideological trap set by the *habitus* discussed above. Writing then becomes a sophisticated, civilized product, oral performance an artless, or even primitive, image of reality. Political fictions that associate the oral with authenticity thus present a "prescription for mystification," as Eileen Julien argues so persuasively.[26]

The widespread view that francophone African women must break their silence with the written word[27] assumes that chirographic writing and liberation are linked in the inert and causal fashion refuted above. If we accept the argument that the written word alone offers a space for women's empowerment, it follows that writing alone can validate women's social visions.[28] We would then have to accept the notion that women have failed to develop any coherent social vision, as they are latecomers in the world of African letters. Celebrating women's entry

into the world of francophone belles lettres as the only possible "coming to voice" thus has the effect of erasing their voices when lifted in
song or declamatory poetry. In contrast, the evidence indicates that
Senegalese women not only have social visions of their own, but also the
means to express them in performance. Furthermore, *taasu* do not simply mirror experience—they shape it, too. The genre thus remains an
eminently *useful* form of discourse. In this sense, *taasukat* are "writers,"
for they, too, inscribe reality. The new importance of the *taasu* in the
generic hierarchy, then, would seemingly evoke a concomitant recognition of the importance of women's social visions, for generic tendencies
"do not offer the trace of authenticity but are more nearly a tool of
social vision."[29]

THE RE-EDUCATION OF DESIRE:
RECASTING WOMEN'S ROLES

The exclusion of women from the public sphere is a colonial legacy, in
many respects. In some ways, this dual system is analogous to the dual
system that polarized colonial society. The dual colonial system certainly reshaped male-female relations, as colonial debates about
women's education prove. Indeed, the construction of various forms of
sexuality was vital to the workings of the colonial order. Sexuality as I
define it here does not consist of innate instincts that society represses,
as Freud would have it; rather, discursive deployments of sex are used
to discipline and control populations. In other words, desire does not
originate with the individual, but elsewhere. As Foucault puts it, this discourse underpins the biopolitics of the population.[30] Education, then,
includes the education of desire.

Colonial literature became the primary vehicle for this form of education. Most studies on colonial literature have concentrated on attack-
ing the racist depictions of Africans that pervade these works; apart
from Fanon's *Peau noire, masques blancs*, few studies examine the profound effects they had on the construction of colonial subjects' identities. Literary and administrative evidence, however, shows that colonial
literature did indeed influence the young intellectual elite. Hans-Jürgen
Lüsebrink writes that teachers were encouraged to use works of colonial
literature in the classroom as part of the new, Africanized curriculum
linked to the policy of association.[31] Many Senegalese writers drew upon
that literature, for works about Africa written by Africans were practically unavailable to them until the 1950s. Lüsebrink's study of the
importance of "book culture" to these writers thus examines their relationship to colonial literature by necessity. His reading of Ousmane

Socé's novel *Karim* (1935) emphasizes the importance of colonial literature as the motor of a new education of desire. The title character's
friendship with a graduate of the elite school for francophone Africans
of the period, the École William Ponty, marks the beginning of a new life
for him. As he reads novels such as *Le roman d'un spahi* (1881), *La ran-
donnée de Samba Diouf* (1922), and *Batouala* (1921), he gradually
adopts a western lifestyle. Indeed, almost all of Karim's tastes change
because of his encounter with colonial literature.[32]

Colonial literature also introduced a new discourse on sexuality to
colonial subjects (as did pornographic postcards, another of the erotic
discourses of the colonial order). It played an important role in fabri-
cating African sexualities for African *évolués*, who had received a French
education and accepted French values, as well as for Europeans interested in the "exotic." Socé's descriptions of Senegalese women's charms,
for example, differ little from those of authors such as Pierre Loti or
Ernest Psischari, who "ont fourni le modèle de telles évocations" [fur-
nished the model for such evocations].[33] These evocations, in turn, took
earlier nineteenth-century formulations of racial difference as models,
for "racial thinking in the nineteenth century frequently expressed itself
in sexual terms."[34]

Africans' concerns about the "woman question" paralleled those of
Europeans. In various publications across francophone Africa during the
colonial period, contributors raised the question of marriage's effects on
évolué status.[35] Writers eager to maintain and improve their social status
argued that *évolués* required suitably educated partners for political and
professional reasons, as well as for personal reasons.[36] Ironically, these
arguments reproduce the colonialist discourse that most of them decried.
Anticolonial protest thus originated from within the sexualized racist
colonial discourse that had formed colonized subjects. Perhaps as a
result of that discursive model, anticolonialist male writers frequently
used images of women to represent the continent. Expressing a new
national identity through images of black women marked a rupture with
Marianne, the French symbol of the nation; however, the trope of
Mother Africa in male writers' works reproduced the colonial model for
gender politics.

That model defined women primarily as mothers. As mothers,
women were considered the key to the success of assimilation.[37] Colonial
administrators promoted female education as a major part of the *mission civilisatrice* [civilizing mission], as they were convinced that women
educated in the French manner would spread the French language and
culture more rapidly than men simply because they would influence their
children.[38] Their role in colonial discourse parallels the role assigned to
European women to a surprising degree, with an important difference:

just as European women were supposed to uphold the colonial mission by rearing their children to become future colonial masters, Senegalese women were to educate France's docile colonial subjects of the future. Nevertheless, both African and European women were defined primarily as mothers who could transfer the values of a particular society on to the next generation.

Women's education, then, was intended to train them to accept, and even desire, this role in the *mission civilisatrice*. In spite of the fact that the number of women educated in French colonial schools never matched that of their brothers,[39] many women did acquire the desire to mother a new nation. More women of the writer Nafissatou Diallo's age-group, for example,[40] attended French schools than any previous generation. In most cases, fathers made it possible for these women to attend French colonial schools.[41] These men represent the generation depicted in *Karim*. Like that fictional character, they attempted to gain the privileges of *évolué* status, which, for some, included French citizenship, yet retain their cultural and religious heritage. According to Diane Barthel, they, too, believed that educated mothers would ensure their children's success in the French colonial system. They wished to anchor their class privilege by educating their daughters, but did not foresee any real changes in gender relations.[42]

This reluctance to imagine changed gender relations seems a bit odd, since writers of this generation such as Ousmane Socé and Abdoulaye Sadji describe young women as dangerous to men in their novels. This depiction represents a repetition of a theme common in colonial novels; in many of these works, young and naïve colonial recruits meet African seductresses who exploit them. Ironically, the same women were often useful to Frenchmen as intermediaries between the French and the local populations. However, African women who contracted *mariages à la mode du pays* [customary marriages] with Frenchmen came to be seen as a threat to French hegemony after the collection of commercial outposts representing French interests in the region was transformed into a handful of major population centers in a colony.[43] Such marriages had once consolidated alliances between French traders and the local elite. However, the children of these unions had a privileged relationship to African clients, as well as to their fathers' compatriots. As a result, succeeding generations of French entrepreneurs felt threatened by Creole competition. These marriages threatened the patriarchal hegemony in Senegal as well, for the women who thus became *signares* gained economic and social status surpassing that of African men through these marriages.

In texts of the day, women's moral status was inversely related to their power relative to men. The French tied relationships with powerful Senegalese women to the "decline" in Europeans' morality and efficiency in the tropics. Colonial novels such as Loti's *Le roman d'un spahi*, for example, described this decline in detail. African writers of the period, all male, shared the suspicion that women represented a trap. Women who adopted western ways were criticized as traitors who sought favors from the colonizer to the detriment of their community, or as unfit mothers. Those who did not go to colonial schools did not escape criticism, as they were supposedly capable of inducing a man to squander his salary on their frivolous whims. These fictional tensions parallel those present in French colonial literature of the time to a startling degree. As Arlette Chemain-Degrange argues, the portrait of women to be found in these works "recouvre une idéologie conservatrice" [dissimulates a conservative ideology].[44]

At a later period, women whose training was to fit them to play a role in the *mission civilisatrice* were also perceived as dangerous. Women educated in the colonial system did not passively accept the roles assigned them, according to Barthel, but actively worked to transform their place in society. She explains historical changes in attitudes about women's education on the basis of age-group affiliation. "Women's education has been determined by a generational progression, a process in which women as mothers, role models, and students have been actors rather than simply subjects."[45] The first generation combated widespread suspicion of French education for women. During the second stage, women like Nafissatou Diallo and Amina Mbaye dealt with the difficulties of fulfilling familial and professional duties and expectations. At the third stage, women's own expectations of their opportunities outpace those of previous generations.

The generation that I examine in this chapter was part of the second wave that Barthel describes. As students at the *École normale des jeunes filles* (founded in 1938), these women had a higher vision of their role than did either their male counterparts or the French administrators. "Their example now inspires younger women to demand that women's role in development be a larger and more varied one, not only that of educated wives and mothers, but also that of citizens and workers."[46] In light of the conflicts and suspicions generated by colonial discourses on sexuality, the success of educated women of the period in recasting their social roles seems all the more remarkable.

Women's autobiographical responses to this situation vary a great deal, and present various ambiguities. The decision to write an autobiography is not the least of these. I have chosen to accept the ambiguities for the moment, for this chapter focuses on the coming to voice of Senegalese women, rather than on the purely discursive features of their voices. Although such an approach has its dangers, most of the critics writing about African autobiographies have been forced to accept a certain blurring of genre distinctions. Maurice Le Rouzic writes that "on pourra aisément conclure qu'il n'y a pas d'écriture autobiographique sans sa part d'ambiguïtés, simplement parce que le projet de parler de soi, de se livrer au public, n'est pas un projet innocent" [one could easily conclude that there is no autobiographical writing without its share of ambiguities, simply because the project of speaking of oneself, surrendering oneself to the public, is not an ingenuous project]. The blurring of genres observed in the *taasu* has written counterparts quite simply because no autobiographical practice can be naive, given the genre's political overtones.

In the first work that we will examine, *Mademoiselle*, the author still understands her role from the perspective of assimilationist policies designed to modernize Senegal. *Mademoiselle*, Amina Sow Mbaye's autobiographical novel, portrays the many pitfalls that young professional women of her generation faced. Although the paratext does not indicate that this is an autobiography, she has admitted that it is an autobiographical work to Beverley Ormerod and Jean-Marie Volet.[47] In addition, the author claims at the end of her text:

> Si l'histoire d'Aïda et Ardo était un conte de fée, elle aurait pu se terminer par la conclusion de routine: ils vécurent heureux et eurent beaucoup d'enfants. Mais elle est bien réelle et un cortège de joies et de peines venait souvent dissiper de longues périodes de sérénité.[48]

> If the story of Aïda and Ardo was a fairy-tale, it could have ended with a routine conclusion: they lived happily ever after and had many children. But it is very real, and a cortege of joys and problems frequently broke long periods of serenity.

These and other clues have persuaded this reader to view the work as a thinly veiled autobiography.

This narrative of the first years in a young schoolteacher's career shows that women educated in colonial schools often did accept the role first assigned to them by the colonial administration. Aïda, the character who clearly represents Mbaye, views herself as a modern woman who sees further than the women of Dagana. Not only does she have a French education, but she also comes from the capital city of the time, St. Louis. As a result, she presents herself as the agent of progress in Dagana, "ville ou gros village qui n'était pas desservi par le chemin de fer et qu'on n'atteignait que par bateau ou par automobile après cent cinquante kilomètres de piste cahoteuse et poussiéreuse" [town or big village that was not on the rail line and that one reached only by boat or by car after one-hundred and fifty kilometers of a bumpy and dusty route] (6). Although *Mademoiselle* offers brief glimpses of another side of Aïda's character, the work as a whole presents her in roles more often assigned to French administrators or teachers. Aïda perceives herself as a modern woman who can disabuse credulous people of their superstitious, ignorant ways. She not only presents a new vision of womanhood, but also reveals a marabout as a fraud and criticizes school administrators' corruption. Contrasting herself with male authorities, she describes herself as so punctual and hard-working that her students give her the nickname "*Rabou École*" [*Ràbb u lekool*, the school spirit].

Mbaye first presents the people of Dagana with an alien model of womanhood when she decides to play basketball with the men. This is a radical action, for she plays with the men and dresses in a short miniskirt and "une culotte à dentelles que le moindre geste ou le moindre vent découvrit au public réellement admiratif" [lace lingerie that the slightest gesture or breeze uncovered to a genuinely admiring audience] (55). The scandalized women of the town treat her with hostility, and tell her students to do so as well. "L'hostilité que la population de Dagana voua à Aïda laissa la jeune femme d'abord indifférente puis la chagrina un peu à cause du travail de sape que certains parents opéraient en essayant de monter les élèves contre leur maîtresse. . . . Une révolution, c'en était une hélas!" [The hostility that the population of Dagana offered Aïda first left the young woman indifferent, then upset her a little because certain parents worked to undermine her by trying to turn the pupils against their teacher. . . . It was, alas, a revolution!] (58).

Aïda's reaction proves that she believes she must participate in the *mission civilisatrice*. She does so by redefining basketball as a progressive activity. "Elle avait maintenant un autre rôle à jouer à Dagana: faire évoluer et convertir les mentalités" [She now had another role to play in Dagana: that of converting attitudes and making them evolve] (56). In order to do so, she starts a women's basketball team in Dagana. Since this incident takes place just before independence, we must situate it within a colonialist discourse that sexualized racial difference. Aïda's actions almost certainly were interpreted as an attempt to gain the status of a French woman. This seems rather plausible in light of the fact that she came from St. Louis. Residents of four communes in Senegal (Dakar, Gorée, Rufisque, and St. Louis) automatically gained French citizenship, yet they did not enjoy all of the benefits of this status. They did not hide their ambition to gain the privileges that had been denied to them in spite of their actual citizenship.

Women like Aïda, then, took the assimilationist model and fashioned another type of "modern" womanhood from it, one that might allow them satisfactions other than those that motherhood offers. This clearly posed some difficulties; in a biographical note, we read, "mère d'une famille nombreuse, Amina Sow Mbaye essaye de concilier ses

devoirs de femme et d'enseignante avec l'aide d'une foi religieuse profonde" [mother of a large family, Amina Sow Mbaye tries to reconcile
her duties as a woman and as an educator with the help of a profound
religious faith]. Although we learn about Aïda's fiancé and the other
men who court her, she presents herself as a professional above all.
Indeed, she closes her text with the following regrets: "Et bien souvent,
Aïda ou Madame la directrice, seule à son bureau, dans l'obscurité qui
envahissait peu à peu son école déserte jusqu'au lendemain, songeait
avec mélancolie à l'heureux temps de Dagana où elle était encore 'Mademoiselle'" [And quite often, Aïda or Madam the Principal, alone in her
office, in the darkness that, little by little, invaded her deserted school
until the next day, reflected with melancholy on the happy times in
Dagana, when she was still "Mademoiselle"] (158). Perhaps Aïda simply regrets her youth; however, the fact that she is so nostalgic about the
position she abhorred because of the location (Dagana) indicates that
she also wishes to define herself primarily as a professional woman.

In contrast, Nafissatou Diallo intertwines the personal and the public in her works for adults, all of which address issues of women's representation and their roles in public life. Her novels criticize women's
subordination as subtly as her autobiography does—so subtly, in fact,
that many readers assume that she supported the status quo. Unlike
openly rebellious women, such as Mbaye's autobiographical figure
Aïda, Diallo attempts to change the system from within. We should perhaps characterize her work as "womanist," for she does not attack male
domination; she simply valorizes women's experiences. According to
one critic, "Diallo's self-affirmation is not an effort to destroy the status
quo on the position of women. It is, however, a much more subtle and
tender evocation of woman and her need to express herself in her
entirety."[49]

Diallo, like other women autobiographers, presents her life often
enough in relation to the male "other,"[50] but her resistance to male
authority does not preclude love for her strict father. Indeed, she
observes that "J'aimais mon père de toutes les fibres de mon être; je
l'adorais, je l'associais à ma vie, à moi, à ma personne" (128) [I loved
my father with all the fibres of my being; I adored him, he was part of
me, of my life, of my person (129)]. Although her mother died when she
was one and a half, Diallo's autobiography depicts a happy childhood
in a large and loving family. She depicts herself as an impish child who
often disobeyed or misbehaved almost with impunity because of her
grandmother's protection. In spite of the iron rule of a conservative
grandfather and a strict father, Diallo also managed to make her own
choices about her relationships with other men. This provoked more
than one family crisis. Even though Safi's father (Nafissatou chooses to

change the obvious nickname Nafi into Safi, but otherwise offers clear signals that Safi and the author are the same person) is progressive enough to educate his daughter in French schools and allow her a certain amount of freedom, he fears that she will become an unwed mother and dishonor the family.

Nafissatou resists these ideas, even if she does so in a mild, diplomatic manner. She says her father is more conservative and jealous of his daughters' honor than her grandfather (48), and defends unwed mothers discreetly when she describes her cousin Ami's wedding.

> Les vieilles du quartier au visage ridé et à la bouche édentée l'honoraient par des phrases élogieuses. Elles adressaient des réflexions plus ou moins acerbes aux filles présentes, surtout à une fille-mère, amie de ma cousine, qui, disaient-elles, s'était vendue pour quelques "sous." La tête baissée, recroquevillée dans son coin, elle supportait l'assaut. J'avais pitié d'elle. Je maudissais ces vieilles femmes s'acharnant sur une personne qui n'était ni leur fille ni leur parente, qui n'avait pas de compte à leur rendre. Il en était ainsi dans les cérémonies de mariage et mieux valait pour les filles-mères s'abstenir de ces cérémonies (70).

> All the toothless and wrinkled old women from the neighbourhood were singing her praises. They also made some more or less acerbic observations for the benefit of the girls who were there, directed specifically at an unmarried mother, one of my cousin's friends, who, in their words, "had sold herself for a few pence." She hung her head as she endured the attack crouched in a corner. I felt sorry for her. I thought these old women were horrible for viciously attacking a girl who was neither their daughter or any relation at all and who did not have to account to them for her behavior. This always happened at every wedding and it was better for unmarried mothers to keep away from such ceremonies.[51]

Later, as a midwife, she surely had some unwed mothers as patients. Perhaps this increased her compassion for these women who faced public humiliation. Diallo clearly sees how easily such humiliation could affect almost any young girl. She describes an early infatuation and her own disappointment when she realizes that she deluded herself about the young man, as well as other inconclusive relationships and an engagement that she decided to annul after falling in love with Mambaye Diallo, whom she married in 1961. In spite of her own confusing relationships with men and the emotional crises they provoked, Diallo persistently defends women's right to choose their own partners.

Until recently, Diallo's work received little critical attention. Susan Stringer, however, insists on Diallo's importance, comparing the significance of her autobiography to Camara Laye's canonical work, *The Dark Child* (1953).[52] She believes that critics have favored other women writers over Diallo because they take a more clearly feminist stance. Indeed, some critics believe that Diallo praises patriarchy in praising her own father. Jean-Marie Volet writes that "son respect pour le père témoigne en faveur d'une vision du monde dominée par la figure du patriarche" [her respect for the father speaks in favor of a vision of the world dominated by the figure of the patriarch].[53] Other critics, however, have noted Diallo's distinctive perspective. Roger Dorsinville, editor of the collection "Vies d'Afrique," claimed that

> ce livre, placé à la charnière de deux mondes fascinait par ce qu'il supposait dans la vie de l'enfant d'intentions de démarquage, de volonté de s'extérioriser autrement que dans l'obéissance. Pour la première fois, nous avions l'histoire d'une jeune fille qui avait entrepris d'imposer à sa famille le choix de son avenir.[54]

> this book, situated on the cusp between two worlds, fascinated [readers] because it assumed the intention of setting oneself apart, and the will to express oneself other than through obedience in the life of a child. For the first time, we had the story of a young girl who had attempted to make her family accept her own choice of future.

Charlotte Bruner also situates Diallo's work within a feminist context. In an article comparing Diallo's autobiography to several other postcolonial texts about girlhood, she argues that representations of childhood are "fundamental to the understanding of women's issues."[55]

As Irène D'Alméïda has noted, however, it is Diallo's womanist attitude that allowed her to break the silence about women's lives.[56] Although she rejects any claim to literary talents, describing herself as an "ordinary" woman, her autobiography actually represents an extremely ambitious project. "Écrire? Moi? J'entends les ricanements: 'Écrire un livre pour dire qu'on a aimé Père et Grand-Mère? La belle nouvelle!' J'espère avoir fait un peu plus: avoir été au-delà des tabous de silence qui règnent sur nos émotions" (132) [Write a book? Me? I can hear you tittering: 'Write a book to say that you've loved your father and your grandmother? What's so new about that?' I hope that I have done a little more than that; perhaps I have lifted the taboos of silence that reign over our emotions (133).] Autobiographies—especially those focused on the subject's personal or domestic life—can easily be dismissed as sentimental or self-indulgent outpouring, but Diallo justifies hers by describing it as a socially useful project. In a society in which silence is considered a characteristic of nobility, writing an autobiography is a delicate task. Diallo pulls it off by revealing that the personal is political.

Diallo's work can be seen not only as a document of the family, but also, by extension, as social history.[57] As she says in her forward, her story reveals "the Senegal that was" to the new generation. Indeed, this ambitious project also aims to create a legacy that bridges the gap between the past and the present. Diallo justifies her autobiography, *De Tilène au Plateau: Une Enfance dakaroise [A Dakar Childhood]*, by placing it within the boundaries of that desire. She writes in her foreword:

> Je ne suis pas une héroïne de roman mais une femme toute simple de ce pays: une mère de famille et une professionnelle (sage-femme et puéricultrice). . . . Sur quoi écrirait une femme qui ne prétend ni à une imagination débordante ni à un talent d'écrire singulier? Sur elle-même, bien sur. Voici donc mon enfance et ma jeunesse telles que je me les rappelle. Le Sénégal a changé en une génération. Peut-être valait-il la peine de rappeler aux nouvelles pousses ce que nous fûmes.

> I am not the heroine of a novel but an ordinary woman of this country, Senegal: a mother and a working woman—a midwife and child welfare nurse. . . . What would a woman write about who has no claim to any exceptional imagination or outstanding literary talent? She could only write about herself, of course. So here are my memories of my childhood and adolescence. Senegal has changed in a generation. Perhaps it is worth reminding today's youngsters what we were like when we were their age.[58]

The preface thus presents a double vocation: that of mother and of educator. Diallo proposes to teach the new generation their country's recent history. In this context, her protestation that she is not the heroine of a novel does not mean simply that she is ordinary, but that her text presents the truth. In contrast to the many autobiographical novels written by members of her generation, this text defines itself boldly as a "true story." In addition, she immediately argues that her text has national significance. She cleverly masks her audacity with the modesty that she is supposed to display as a woman.

She also aspires to create new roles for women. Although she describes herself so humbly, Diallo clearly saw herself as a partner to members of the male political elite. Autobiography, as Carole Boyce Davies writes, signifies here an insertion of self into society, and, furthermore, marks "the process of moving from silence to voice, a 'woman-conscious' self that is ready to give the private life some public space."[59] As the first autobiography written by a Senegalese woman, *De Tilène au Plateau* toppled the silent statues of the nation erected by poets who considered Senegalese women as muses or symbols of the continent, rather than as speaking subjects in their own right. In some sense, Diallo thus aspired to take a place next to Senghor, "Father of the Nation," as midwife or even mother of the nation.

Indeed, her vision of women's role in independent Senegal comple-

ments Senghor's, for she believes that is possible for Senegalese to bor-
row and adapt French ideas to Senegalese realities, rather than accepting them wholesale, as Aïda Mbaye seems to do. As a child, Diallo
moved to a house in the elite Plateau section of Dakar—hence the title
of her autobiography, *From Tilène to Plateau*. This move represented a
rise in wealth and social status. Diallo's education paralleled this move
intellectually, for she learned Wolof and Toucouleur precepts, and
attended a Koranic school as well as a western school. She attended the
prestigious Van Vollenhoven High School, then received a degree in
midwifery. At twenty-three, she continued her education in France at
the Toulouse Institute of Obstetrics and Pediatrics. She thus presents her
education as a synthesis of Senegalese and western elements.

This synthesis fits Senghor's model for Senegalese education; however, Senghor revised the plan somewhat for women. This much
becomes clear when we turn to Senghor's address given at the Lycée des
Jeunes Filles de Dakar in 1963.

> Je l'ai souligné plus d'une fois, dans l'oeuvre de *construction nationale*,
> la femme a sa place. Elle est capable, comme l'homme, d'occuper,
> dignement, efficacement, les plus hauts postes de la société: d'être
> ingénieur, médecin, professeur, industriel, commerçante. Elle exerce,
> déjà, par vocation, certaines fonctions sociales, comme institutrice,
> assistante sociale, sage-femme, infirmière. Elle y est irremplaçable. . . .
> Cependant, la femme sénégalaise ne doit pas cesser, pour cela, d'être ce
> qu'elle a toujours été: une *épouse* et une *mère*. Vous me permettrez de
> le reconnaître, le Régime colonial a provoqué, au Sénégal, un certain
> embourgeoisement des classes moyennes: celle des fonctionnaires, des
> commerçants, des notables. L'abondance de la domesticité—une
> domesticité non éduquée, au demeurant—a détourné, souvent, la
> femme de ses devoirs d'épouse et de mère. . . . Or il n'y a pas de famille,
> il n'y a pas de *civilisation* sans ces humbles travaux domestiques. . . .
> Sans eux, on ne retiendra pas le mari, on ne fera pas l'éducation des
> enfants. Pour tout dire, on ne fera pas, de *notre* Sénégal, une nation
> moderne.[60]

> I have emphasized more than once that woman has her place in the
> work of national construction. She is capable, like man, of filling the
> highest positions in society with dignity and efficacity: to be an engi-
> neer, doctor, professor, manager or businesswoman. She already fills
> certain social functions—those of schoolteacher, social worker, mid-
> wife, or nurse—by avocation. She is irreplaceable here. . . . Neverthe-
> less the Senegalese woman should not cease to be what she has always
> been—a *wife* and a *mother*—for that reason. You will permit me to
> recognize that the colonial regime lifted the middle classes—those of
> the bureaucrats, business people, and notables—to bourgeois status in
> Senegal. The abundance of domestic labor—uneducated domestic

labor, for that matter—has often diverted the Senegalese woman from her duties as wife and mother. However, there is no family, there is no *civilization* in the absence of these humble domestic tasks. . . . Without them, one cannot retain a husband or educate children. In one word, we will not make of *our* Senegal a modern nation [without them].

Senghor outlined a rather progressive vision of women's role for his time, since he clearly promoted women professionals; however, his insistence that their most important roles are those of wife and mother not only seems calculated to placate conservative members of the audience, but also to reinforce colonial ideas of women's place (i.e., mothers were to play a role in the assimilation of their children). We might well ask why male reliance on women's domestic labor poses no danger to the nation.

Senegalese women worked and held formal political positions long before the French arrived, so Senghor's anxieties about professional women who abandon purely domestic roles seems misplaced. Indeed, colonial constructions of European sexuality seem to be the secret palimpsest of Senghor's pronouncements upon women's roles. Georges Hardy, an important spokesman for "official" cultural policy in French West Africa, claimed that the European man lost his manliness—and perhaps his Europeanness—unless he benefited from the watchful eye of a French woman.[61] As Ann Stoler has explained with regard to Dutch colonialism in Indonesia, European identities foundered under the steady influence of other cultures. In spite of extreme resistance to non-European cultures, the small number of Europeans who administrated non-settler colonies had to adapt, if ever so slightly. Anxiety about the issue demonstrates recognition of the fluid nature of European identity, rather than a belief in its stability. Europeans clearly feared that the "native" culture would mold them, rather than the reverse.[62] African influences, then, were perceived as "contamination," rather than as a "rendez-vous du donner et du recevoir."

Senghor's own cult of authenticity shows a bit of the same fear, especially with regard to change in gender roles. Although he accepts women's new professional roles, he fears that they might choose to see themselves primarily as professional women, as Amina Mbaye did. For this reason, he describes the use of hired domestics as a sort of contamination of family life. Since he views families as the building blocks of the modern nation, this "contamination" would impede national development. He explicitly states that African men will leave their wives unless the women keep a watchful eye on them. The woman's gaze, then, secures Senegalese manliness. Senghor's many poems in praise of the African woman offer further evidence for this point of view.

Diallo's autobiography presents a woman who fits the Senghorian model, for she combined a useful *feminine* profession with her domestic occupations as a wife and mother. As a midwife, she assisted other women in their fundamental role as mothers of the nation. Although her position remains within the confines of Senghor's model for national development, she also reminds the male "patrons" that if we live in a world that "vit les yeux braqués sur les grands, que [sic] les petits et les modestes sont ceux qui font, soutiennent et portent les grands" (132) [lives with its eyes fixed on great men and women, that [sic] it is the unimportant, modest folk who support and carry the weight of the great (133)]. The story of one of these "ordinary" women proves the point, for it is the first written autobiography produced by a Senegalese woman.

THE NATIONAL SCRIPT

The Haitian critic and writer Roger Dorsinville considered Diallo's autobiography highly significant, even going so far as to claim that this work marked the birth of Senegalese women's writing (an exaggeration), adding that "c'est donc avec la collection 'Vies d'Afrique' que la détermination 'nationale' trouve son ampleur et prétend à sa justification" [The category of "national literature" thus spreads its wings and has a justification in the "African Lives" collection].[63] Dorsinville's remark leads us to the closely related argument that cultural or national models of identity and generic models are linked. If we return for a moment to the arguments I made for a relational model of identity in the pre-face and in the first chapter, this seems quite reasonable. As the anthropologist Gregory Bateson argued, "'ego function' . . . is precisely *the process of discriminating communicational modes either within the self or between the self and others.*"[64] This implies that genre and subjectivity are inextricably linked in the communication process. Since these modes of communication are culturally defined (as speech genres), modes of subjectivity, too, are defined by cultural models. The cultural hybridity that French colonialism promoted thus took very specific forms in Senegal.

These forms of hybridity have clearly influenced gender politics in Senegal. As in France, woman has served the nation symbolically; poets such as Senghor replaced Marianne with the anonymous African woman celebrated in his famous poem "Femme noire." A large number of texts in the Senegalese canon of francophone literature take woman's body as the source and symbol of the nation, but few represent women as political actors. Paradoxically, critical efforts to celebrate women who defy a literary system in which they figure more often as objects than as subjects also fall prey to seductive avatars of the feminine that reflect nationalist desire, rather than a desire for sexual equality. That desire can be linked to the need to define an authentic, autonomous identity in contrast to European nationalisms founded on a social contract. The quest for national origins thus led to celebrations of the mother, "both the subject of the narrative and the symbol of that which the *act of writing* is meant to recover: Africa, the past, childhood, lost innocence."[65]

This attempt to recover the lost mother suggests a metaphorical and discursive Oedipal conflict within postcolonial francophone literature. This framework would then require the renunciation of real mothers in obedience to the Law of the White Father (whether represented by missionaries—consider the Catholic order of the White Fathers—colonial administrators, soldiers, or teachers). The Lacanian theory that the self then becomes subject to this law through the word that restructures consciousness as a language captures the dilemma of poets such as Camara Laye and L. S. Senghor, as well as those of the women their poems celebrate. The poets desperately seek to recapture the lost idyll of union with mother through writing, but simultaneously, this effort to replace the lost mother with Mother Africa excludes any real mother from consideration; this is particularly true because these poets write in French, the language of the colonizer.

Critics thus follow an imperialist literary tradition by portraying Senegalese mothers as mute. They do so most clearly when they ignore the political ramifications of writing. Writing in the narrow, colonial sense not only fixes words on a page, "memorizing" them for us, but it also signifies and reproduces power, as Vail and White, among others, so convincingly explain.[66] This political use of writing is visible in postcolonial Senegal, where official national discourse uses performance to represent an "authentic" oral sphere and simultaneously legitimate the political script written in French. Ironically, the political discourse that defines oral performance as emblematic of an authentically Senegalese identity does so to the benefit of so-called elites, who owe part of their power to their ability to read and write in French. This irony has led Ernest Gellner to dismiss African nationalisms that legitimate the postcolonial state on the basis of links to an authentic, precolonial way of life as a form of false consciousness. Elites' attempts to deploy "popular culture" to create and legitimate an elite, "high culture" inaccessible to the majority signify at best a contemptible false consciousness, at worst despotism disguised as democracy.[67] Writing in French spells out the difference between these "high" and "low" cultures.

Unlike Gellner, Miller considers the addition of French and of writing in French to the semiotic web that makes up Senegal advantageous.

"The result is not false consciousness, but hybridity, empowerment, and resistance."[68] If we consider the field of francophone literatures, it is clear that we do not determine national identity on the basis of language alone. French, Belgian, and Senegalese writers may share the French language, yet their works belong to separate national categories. As Renan argues in his famous essay "What is a Nation,"[69] a shared language may assist in nation-building, but it is not strictly necessary. In contrast, a shared literature seems to have a great deal to do with the construction of a shared national identity. Richard Bjornson, for example, stated that "a sense of national identity is obviously related to the emergence of a national literature."[70] Heated debates about the literary canon draw their energy and emotion from the sense that the canon shapes civil society and national cultural identity. In other words, we might see the canon as a sort of national script.

Written scripts, like oral performances, offer a processual, contextual means for inscribing identity. According to Barber, the scripts used in popular Yorùbá plays are collective products that do not fix performances, but offer a shape to fluid, changing improvisational forms. To the performers, the act of creating a common structure that all of them agree upon is "writing."[71] Inscribing national identity is analogous to "writing" such scripts. It follows that national literatures must include both oral and written "scripts" for the social performance of national identity. Rather than representing Senegalese political culture in light of a fixed hierarchy (high vs. low, "authentic" vs. imported), then, I would argue that hierarchies of meaning constantly shift in relation to context. In one context, a particular individual may stress her ability to communicate in French; in another, she may stress Wolof cultural literacy, or her association with another language or community. National identity does not depend on a particular written script, but on the various scripts, written and oral, that are used to collectively define and redefine what it means to be Senegalese.

The autobiographical esthetic that I have described in light of *taasu* performance thus does not exclude autobiographical texts in French, but interacts with texts in various ways. The autobiographical discourses that I have described in this chapter clearly tie motherhood to mature women's attempts to change social relations through self-expression or autobiographical self-representations. These "mothers of the nation" of the independence era clearly present themselves as partners to "fathers of the nation" such as Senghor. They accepted the goal of transforming a former French colony into a modern nation, along with the notion that modernization was in itself a good thing. These discourses of modernization and nation-building continue to influence autobiographical self-representation in various ways. A woman may mention Caterpillar tractors in a *taasu* lauding women at a naming ceremony, as one performer did, or we may reread texts by women of that generation. Whatever we may think of the goals of an earlier generation today, it is wise to recall that we, too, judge the past from a particular vantage point that shapes our perspective. This much becomes clear in Chapter Six, which focuses primarily on Ken Bugul's extraordinary autobiography, *Le baobab fou.*

CHAPTER 6

Aborted Nations

The colonial and postcolonial education and experiences of Senegalese women, inscribed in discourses that insist on their maternal role, have led many women to see themselves primarily as mothers. These discourses promote motherhood metaphorically, as well as literally; metaphorically, verbal artists are transmitters of tradition who "mother" the culture, even though they also literally mother their children. These discourses weave an intertext that neither oral nor written texts escape, as the women's autobiographical discourses we are examining demonstrate.

Yet the webs of discourse—that is, texts—catch more than we may guess. If the textual self exists only in and through language, common metaphors suggest that we can only conceive of self through the body. Indeed, scholars from a wide variety of disciplines have come to this conclusion.[1] This work has been of great interest to students of autobiography, for they are profoundly interested in the nature of selfhood and subjectivity, which is linked to the "organic roots of selfhood in the body."[2] In this sense, the text does not merely represent the body of the autobiographer, but also recreates it as a social body. This is quite clear when we think of the performer's body and the role of gesture in performance; however, it is also true of women writers, whose bodies are implicated in their writing in various ways.

Clearly, women are caught in all sorts of textual and social webs that affect their representations of self. Moreover, women are subject to various forms of state control. This control can take place in a mediated fashion, as when the colonial authorities attempted to assimilate Senegalese populations by aiming education at mothers; however, it also takes place in a literal, violent manner. The trope of the racially mixed, hybrid child of colonialism plays a special role in this history, for s/he is a living marker of the system's failure to control reproduction. Perhaps this is one reason why Senegalese women writers such as Mariama Bâ (*Un chant écarlate*) and Ken Bugul (*Le baobab fou*) continue to return to this literary topos.

Freedom of choice has long been an issue for African youth, male or female. The theme of youth rebelling against the older generation's attempts to control marriages has a venerable tradition in franco-phone fiction and theater. However, women's right to choice in the matter of motherhood has received little or no focused attention. Nevertheless, women writers have addressed the issue in a veiled manner. I will argue here that the trope of the tragic mulatto, which appears in the fiction of male Senegalese writers as a metaphor for the colonial relationship, serves women writers in another fashion. Although hybridity does play a role as a marker of cultural difference in women's fiction, particularly in Aminata Sow Fall's *L'appel des arènes,* the subject has also allowed women to discuss that taboo subject of abortion and reprouctive rights.

THE BIOPOLITICS OF COLONIALISM:
THE TROPE OF THE TRAGIC MULATTO

Hybridity is a keyword in the discussion on reproductive rights, for it presents a threat to the state: the mulatto is the site and product of uncontrolled reproduction. In his 1976 lecture, "Faire vivre et laisser mourir: La naissance du racisme" [Live and Let Die: The Birth of Racism], Foucault argues that the social contract based on the sovereign's right of life and death over his subjects has given way to what he calls "l'étatisation du biologique" [state control of biology].[3]

Theories of the social contract only recognized the individual and society; however, a third term—population—changes the state dramatically. Once the term enters the political vocabulary, procreation becomes a state affair. Foucault has described at length how states attempt to control individuals by disciplining sexual behavior;[4] however, states also attempt to regulate the population by biopolitical control of sexuality. Population control and control over individuals are then simultaneously attainable. "La sexualité est exactement au carrefour du corps et de la population" [Sexuality is situated precisely at the crossroads of the body and of population], observes Foucault.[5]

The state's efforts thus expand to include and regularize the life of the *population,* variously defined. Nineteenth- and twentieth-century states have most often and most devastatingly defined populations racially. Evolutionist ideas of the "survival of the fittest" then spur on race wars. Natural selection "est devenu, tout naturellement, en quelques années au XIXe siècle, non pas simplement une manière de transcrire en termes biologiques le discours politique . . . mais une manière de penser les rapports de la colonisation, la nécessité des guer-res, etc." [very naturally, became in a few years in the nineteenth century not simply a manner of transposing political discourse into biological terms . . . but a way of conceptualizing colonial [power] relations, the need for wars, etc.].[6]

Biopolitical control of reproduction does not do away with the state's need to control deaths; however, race wars allow the state to exercise its death rights outside of its borders. It also makes it possible for race to determine the nationality of peoples who migrated from the homeland even centuries ago—so that Russians and Rumanians of German descent have suddenly acquired German nationality and the "right of return" with the break up of the Soviet bloc. The ethnic cleansing that took place in Mauritania offers a ready example for the argument that postcolonial African states, too, have used this means to extend and maintain its control.

People of mixed race mark a slippage of the machinery, for they interrupt the logic of "either/or" with the "neither/nor" of an ambiguous racial identity. Structuralist thought proposes a list of binary pairs—black/white, man/woman, nature/culture—but the hybrid sign of the mulatto has no place in the chain. Instead, the mulatto reminds us of something the contractarian state cannot admit: "the law is based on phallic violence in an array of other names and symbols. The term mulatto/a, then, becomes a displacement for a proper name, an instance of the 'paradox of the negative' that signifies what it does not mean."[7]

In Senegalese letters, the figure of the mulatto has played a variety of political roles. During the colonial period, Senghor argued for hybridity as a means for countering colonialist efforts to control African populations. He described his utopian "Civilisation de l'Universel" not only as the product of cultural exchange, but also of intermarriage. Many of Senghor's contemporaries countered these views; perhaps the most biting critique of interracial marriage came in the form of a novel by Abdoulaye Sadji, *Nini, Mulâtresse du Sénégal* [Nini, Mulatta of Senegal] (1947).

The backdrop for Sadji's novel, Saint-Louis, was the first French trading-post in what is now Senegal. The French traders and administrators sent there contracted marriages with Wolof women for the duration of their stay. These *mariages à la mode du pays*, or customary marriages, resolved many problems for the French—not only did these wives take care of their domestic and personal needs, but they also provided useful business contacts. When a Frenchman finally returned to France, his *signare* would contract another, similar alliance. The children of these unions became extremely powerful businesswomen in their own right.[8] Although the French did not usually attempt to bring their mixed-race children to France when their contracts ended, they did offer them some privileges.

The French first introduced their own constructions of racial identity to Senegal through these domestic arrangements. The *signares* and their children became a separate caste in a sense, as did the *Naar i Kajóor* (Moors of Kajoor), the descendants of Mauritanians of Arab and Berber descent who had settled and married in Kajoor. A racial caste system gradually superimposed itself on the Wolof caste system based on hereditary professional status. This racial caste system resembled the primary caste system in that it was enforced most stringently in marriage. Although the *signares* gradually lost their power as the French moved from assimilationist policies to a policy of association,[9] the addition of race to the set of markers of social class in Senegal has persisted since the colonial era.

Sadji's psychologically flat characters mark different positions in this racial caste system. Unable to examine the system critically, they simply submit to its effects. The following passage from the novel analyzes the insidious nature of this racial caste system. "A Saint-Louis l'élément mulâtre se distingue nettement de l'élément noir. On dirait les immigrants d'une race d'aristocrates déchus vivant dans un perpétuel effort pour en imposer à leur entourage, les Nègres"[10] [The mulatto element in Saint-Louis distinguishes itself clearly from the black element. One might think them immigrants, a race of fallen aristocrats living in a perpetual effort to dominate their entourage, the Negroes]. The mocking tone of the full passage expresses a caustically critical attitude toward those who think themselves better than others simply by virtue of purportedly noble French ancestry.

Sadji ridicules these pretensions even more harshly in light of French indifference to the claims of their mixed-race children. The title character, Nini, is very proud of her status as a first-class mulatta with pale skin, blond hair, and blue eyes. She sees herself as "white," and attempts to make others accept her as a Frenchwoman; however, her African features stymie these efforts. Indeed, her primary strategy for indicating her racial status consists in treating her black compatriots rudely and making racist remarks. Ironically, this behavior merely accentuates the fact that no one accepts her as French. Nini's racist attitude toward her black compatriots signals the social performance of her "white" identity more than anything else, for she hopes that her rudeness will show solidarity with whites. The strategy backfires, showing how different she is from the novel's French characters, who always treat black Senegalese with respect.

In any case, the French characters define all people of African descent as Negroes (*nègres* in the French text)—they make no distinctions between "first" and "second-class" *métis*. Martineau, Nini's lover, expresses this clearly when he exclaims,

> Blanche . . . la blancheur importe peu en l'occurrence; une négresse c'est une négresse, on n'en saurait faire une blanche. . . . Et quand on

veut flirter on aimerait tomber sur une môme qui soit bien f. . . . N'as-
tu pas remarqué, d'autre part, que malgré une apparente vigueur le
corps de Nini donne une impression de malaise et de fragilité?
—On pourrait en dire autant de toutes les mulâtresses qui ne sont pas
fortement teintées de sang noir (32).

White . . . whiteness is of little importance in this case; a Negress is a
Negress, and one couldn't make a white woman of her. . . . And when
one wants to flirt, one would like to have the good-luck of picking a
kid who is well m. . . . Haven't you noticed, by the way, that in spite
of a superficial vigor, Nini's body gives the impression of malingering
fragility?
—One could say the same of all mulattas who are not markedly col-
ored by black blood.

Sadji's style here shows a marked discomfort with colloquial, slangy
French; Madior Diouf writes that his style reminds readers of the didactic style of the schoolteacher.[11] Stylistically, then, the passage is a failure,
for it awkwardly juxtaposes two disparate linguistic registers. As an
attempt to capture the French attitude, however, this stylistic "failure"
is a brilliant success, for it vividly contrasts the high moral tone of tracts
on the *mission civilistrice* with the vulgar language of men who see
African women as their sexual objects.

Although he criticizes the mulatto class severely, Sadji does not criticize the Frenchmen who take these women as mistresses after deceitfully
promising marriage for sexual favors. Rather, he explains that "on ne
peut pas leur faire grief d'oublier la mission civilisatrice de leur pays
lorsqu'il se trouve constamment sur leur chemin de petites mulâtresses
grassouillettes et pimpantes qui ne demandent qu'à se donner . . . à eux"
(43) [one cannot blame them for forgetting their country's civilizing mission when they constantly find plump, fresh little mulattas in their way
who ask nothing more than to give themselves . . . to them]. Ironically,
Sadji pardons the French, who instituted the racial caste system that he
criticizes. They represent racial and cultural purity, as do the African
women (mixed-race women included) who "vivent à l'indigène" (22)
[live in native style].

In contrast, Sadji considers the mulattas "easy women" who only
have themselves to blame for their disappointments. In addition, these
women do not meet his code of decorum. They drink alcohol and dress
in revealing western fashions. In addition, Nini and her friends are
depicted as childlike, stupid, and uncultivated young women. Sadji
stresses Nini's childishness by describing her at almost all times as
"small," "amusing," or as a "môme" [kid]. She makes grotesque faces,
thinks that whites' cruelty is a sign of affection, and knows so little
about French literature that she calls Montesquieu "le poète de l'amour"

(34) [the poet of love] in hopes of impressing her French colleagues. Moreover, her social class is sterile (reminding the reader that the roots of the word "mulatto" refer to racist depictions of mixed-race people as sterile mules), as these women refuse all suitors except the Frenchmen who will never marry them. Sadji insistently reminds the reader that Nini and her sisters will all occupy the dull status of their aging aunts, mothers, and grandmothers, perpetually in mourning for their wasted youth.

Sadji's "tragic mulatta" lives in a zone that falls between black and white, constantly attempting to pass for white or, if this is impossible, to improve her social status by association with whites. These efforts fail, as whites will never accept her, and the blacks who would have accepted her can only disdain her racist attitudes. In other words, assimilation inevitably leads to abortive, sterile products. The literary trope of the tragic mulatto thus surfaces as Sadji's primary argument against assimilation. In his foreword, Sadji claims that his novel is important because this is a time when "le mythe de races supérieures et de races inférieures tend à disparaître, au moins en théorie; où des unions mixtes ont lieu maintenant, chaque jour, entre individus de race différente" [the myth of superior races and of inferior races has a tendency to disappear, at least in theory; when interracial unions take place every day now between individuals of different races]. Yet he also attacks these unions, arguing that

> Nini est l'éternel portrait moral de la Mulâtresse, qu'elle soit du Séné-gal, des Antilles ou des deux Amériques. C'est le portrait de l'être physiquement et moralement hybride qui, dans l'inconscience de ses réactions les plus spontanées, cherche toujours à s'élever au-dessus de la condition qui lui est faite, c'est-à-dire au-dessus d'une humanité qu'il considère comme inférieure mais à laquelle un destin le lie inexorable-ment. On peut plaindre cette catégorie des êtres ou les blâmer. Je crois qu'il est plus charitable de ne la plaindre ni la blâmer, mais de lui offrir, comme dans un miroir, la réalité de ce qu'elle est. Ce n'est pas agir en moraliste ou en bourreau mais en philosophe.[12]

> Nini is the eternal moral portrait of the Mulatta, whether she is from Senegal, the Antilles, or the two Americas. It is the portrait of a being who is physically and morally hybrid and who always seeks, in her most unconscious and spontaneous reactions, to lift herself above the condition given her—that is to say, above a humanity she considers inferior, but to which her destiny inexorably links her. One can pity this category of beings or blame them. I believe it more charitable nei-ther to pity nor blame, but to offer them, as in a mirror, the reality of what this category is. That is not to act as a moralist or as an executioner, but as a philosopher.

Sadji's belief that the mulatto's moral character is biologically determined reveals an acceptance of essentialist definitions of cultural identity that flies in the face of all evidence. He himself praises mixed-race women who "vivent à l'indigène," demonstrating that he also sees racial identity as a cultural and social construction, rather than as a simple biological fact. In addition, his extension of this trope to universal status allows us to examine other cases that prove how culturally specific notions of racial status and of mixed-race identity have been. In Latin America, mestizo status means something quite different than the label "half-breed" does in Anglo-dominated North America. As Linda Alcoff writes, the large mestizo population in Latin America made it possible for assimilation to mean "an antixenophobic cosmopolitanism"[13] rather than pretentious rejection of one's roots. In contrast, North American evidence shows that the "one drop" rule made it impossible for mixed-race children to choose their racial identity until recently. In those cases when people were able to "pass," most of them chose to identify themselves as African Americans in spite of racial discrimination and oppression.[14]

Displacement occurs on another level as well. Sadji assigns all of the insulting characteristics that racist French discourse developed about Africans to one group—that of people of mixed race. In his fiction, the French respect the "pure" African, but see the mulatto as lascivious, childish, stupid, lazy, and untrustworthy. In other words, the novel reorganizes the racial hierarchy out of respect for racial "purity." The either/or of black and white identities modeled in Sadji's novel and in Senghor's theories depends on the neither/nor of the racially hybrid mulatto. As Hortense Spillers argues, "the mulatta mediates between dualities,"[15] for she becomes the repository for the many anomalous characteristics that fit neither white nor black identity, constructed as unified and essentialist categories. Denied personhood, the mulatta "locates in the flesh a site of cultural and political maneuver."[16] Although the mulatta is erased from the scene as the impossible, unnameable site of contamination (of a name and of a bloodline), she does so because she arouses the uneasy recollection that the races are similar, rather than different.

Stoler's discussion of the class system among whites in the colonies turns upon this pivotal point. The discursive machinery used to justify white domination depends upon the forgetfulness of the common humanity that binds colonizer to colonized, but the mulatta reminds both of that spot of discursive emptiness. In other words, the mulatto figure of Sadji's novel simply serves to emphasize the *essential* distinction between black African and white French characters. The policy of association depends on such essential differences, for if the two castes were to blend, it would be impossible to maintain Sadji's stance that the solution to colonial injustice is the establishment of "separate, but equal" spheres.

Nini's real importance, then, lies in her liminal status as the empty term making either/or distinctions possible. As a blank marker, the mulatta remains nameless. Sadji, for example, gives his mulatto characters pet-names such as Nini, Madou, Riri, and Nénée, but readers only learn Nini's real name (Virginie) when her grandmother and aunt tell her to respect her African origins. This anonymity betrays Sadji's fundamentally patriarchal attitude toward the body. The body is the basis for the distinctions essential to his social world, yet he forgets that women's bodily experiences give rise to another set of distinctions that are equally valid.

THE PROPER NAME

Nini's European patronym, Maerle, links her irrevocably to France, yet the social inscription of her body's African traits makes that identification impossible. Ironically, both the hybrid child and her mother remain nameless. Frequently enough, mixed-race children have been denied paternity and a name; indeed, women never earn the right to their own names. Feminist thinkers have argued that the contractarian state denies women subject status in this way. Proper names supposedly fix the identity of the person named; however, the "proper" refers to the patronym.[17] Women, then, are marked as the father's property. In Senegal, women usually retain their father's name after marriage; "Anta Sarr" will remain "Anta Sarr" even after she marries "Karim Diop." However, the French usage has influenced Senegalese usage as well. For instance, Anta Sarr may also be Madame Diop. One informant mentioned that calling oneself "Madame So-and-So" marks status and education, so young women now prefer more and more to take on their husband's patronym in this fashion. The problem of naming and identifying women takes on special significance within the framework of a contractarian theory of the state and civil society, for the nameless cannot enter into contracts.[18]

Names also found the "autobiographical pact"—the contractual relationship between author, text, and reader. Lejeune claims that

> autobiography is a literary genre which, by its very content, marks the confusion of author and person, confusion on which is founded the whole practice and problematic of Western literature since the end of the eighteenth century. Whence the kind of *passion for the proper name*, which exceeds simple "author's vanity," since through such passion it is the person him/herself who claims existence. The deep subject of autobiography is the proper name.[19]

Although Lejeune quite correctly restricts himself to his own area of expertise (western literature), his point is valid for Senegalese literature as well. The proper name has such importance there that the long genealogies chanted by *géwël* not only move listeners to great generosity, but also have real importance in social relations.[20] These performances highlight the proper name. Many *taasu* do so as well. Indeed, the proper name is so important that it can sometimes function as a miniaturized autobiography, as Foucault implies. "One cannot turn a proper name into a pure and simple reference. It has other than indicative functions: more than an indication, a gesture, a finger pointed at someone, it is the equivalent of a description."[21] There is little doubt, then, of the importance of the proper name in Wolof communities and in Senegalese literature of French expression.

Although French and Senegalese autobiographical discourses both insist on the proper name, discursive *deployment* of the proper name may well differ. Lejeune's own model of the autobiographical pact shows that many variations are possible. One of the admissible autobiographical uses of the proper name includes the pseudonym, for an author is not a person, but a personage who writes and publishes. The 1984 autobiography *Le baobab fou* [*The Abandoned Baobab*], written by "Ken Bugul," thus fits Lejeune's model. Or does it? In a published interview, Ken noted that the (male) publishers persuaded her to use a pseudonym for fear of scandal.[22] She herself did little to hide her "real" identity, and even participated in a televised interview. Forced to choose a pseudonym, the author, Mariétou Mbaye, chose the telling name "Kenn bëggul" [The Unloved One]. Others have translated this name as "nobody wants."[23] As she explains in a published interview, Wolof give this name to the children of women who have had several still-born babies as a sort of protection. The name protects the child from any malevolent forces which might harm it.[24] Names, then, have an effect on the persons they identify.

Feminist critics make this point explicitly, arguing that the Law of the Father imprints itself on women named by men. "Man," writes Sidonie Smith, "whether a member of the dominant culture or of an oppressed subculture maintains the authority to 'name' his woman."[25] This naming does not respect individual sentiments; whether a man has feminist sympathies or not, his daughter must be identified by the *discursive system* in place. She will thus bear his patronym.[26] By forcing Mbaye to use a pseudonym in the name of the status quo, then, the publishers (however well-meaning), reinforced that patriarchal status quo.

In her sequel to *The Abandoned Baobab*, *Cendres et braises* (1994) [*Ashes and Embers*], Bugul plays with the ambiguous significance of naming yet again. Although she retains the pseudonym, she renames her central character Marie. The name of the character does not coincide with that of the "author," but it *does* coincide with that of the person who uses the pseudonym. Marie is simply the French version of Mariétou. Forced to create two personae—a social persona named "Mariétou Mbaye" and a literary persona named "Ken Bugul"—the author of *Cendres et braises* then fuses the two in a work that resists standard definitions of either the novel or the autobiography. Her new publisher (L'Harmattan), however, categorizes the work as a novel and even redesignates the previous work as a novel. This implies that women's texts, too, may bear the name of the father. Nevertheless, the text clearly continues Ken's story within the framework of a narrative told after her return to Senegal. Ken had already started work on the text in the 1980s, when she described the sequel to Magnier as *autobiography.*[27]

Since proper names also serve to fix bodies in social space, one strand of feminist thought links renaming oneself to liberation.[28] Indeed, the pseudonym Ken Bugul allows the autobiographer to transform compliance with the publishers' demand into an act of liberation. The name denotes that she is the unwanted, unloved child, but it also bears the connotation that she is the precious one who must be saved at all costs.[29] Names mean little unless they are made public through an official baptism and recognized by the social order. Ken first inserts her new name into discourse by adding her own childhood experiences to the mythical history of her village entitled "Ken's Prehistory." The autobiography thus presents this "newly born woman" to the world, but Ken also wishes social recognition in the genealogical discourse of the village. Fusing her story with that of the village allows her to overcome whatever resistance that project might meet.

In his study of autobiographical self-invention, Eakin writes that the realization that "I was I" represents a second baptism.[30] This is indeed how Ken presents the experience, for her description of her actual baptism flows seamlessly into her description of this coming to consciousness. Consciousness of self presupposes a consciousness of embodiment for Ken, whose ambivalent understanding of the body pervades the autobiography. Her new name, for example, refers explicitly to the body in pain, for it presumes that the child who bears it faces a physical threat. In fact, Bugul's coming to embodied consciousness occurs through a painful experience.

> Soudain un cri! Un cri perçant. Un cri qui venait briser l'harmonie, sous ce baobab dénudé, dans ce village désert. L'enfant s'enfonçait de plus en plus profondément, la perle d'ambre dans l'oreille.[31]

> Suddenly a scream! A piercing scream. A cry from underneath the denuded baobab tree came to shatter the harmony of the deserted village. The child was pushing the amber bead into its ear, deeper and deeper.[32]

The child's new self-awareness does not find speech until much later. For this reason, Mortimer sees the incident as a sign that "language also fails, for silence follows the initial cry."[33] Only later can the child verbalize her feelings in autobiography.

Although Mortimer's logic is impeccable, this answer seems a bit facile, since later crises re-enact this first, painful event. The reader never learns how the bead was dislodged from the child's ear; indeed, Ken's recurrent references to the bead suggest that the bead—a symbol for some painful reality—continues to trouble her. According to Scarry, physical pain resists language and cannot be shared without transformation (i.e., analogies and the like).[34] This resistance seems related to the enigma of the body, seen as the "ground of experience." Although our perceptions and sensations must traverse the body, we can only share them through the resistant medium of language. Thomas Csórdas proposes a methodological distinction similar to the sex/gender distinction as a solution. He sees "'body' as a biological, material entity and 'embodiment' as an indeterminate methodological field defined by perceptual experience and mode of presence and engagement in the world."[35] This describes current scholarly usage in a helpful way, but also reproduces the mind/body split it is meant to analyze.

Since we can only define the body on the basis of perceptions and experiences filtered through that body, attempts to avoid "thinking through the body," as Jane Gallop puts it, are in fact illusory. They also seem to lead to a naive universalism that assumes that everyone's perceptions/sensations will match. Gallop, on the other hand, defines the body without separating it from the subject:

> Not just the physical envelope, but other puzzling and irreducible givens, arising from the "body" if that word means all that in the organism which exceeds and antedates consciousness or reason or interpretation. . . . But the theorizing is precisely endless, an eternal reading of the "body" as authorless text, full of tempting, persuasive significance, but lacking a final guarantee of intended meaning.[36]

This is the perspective of a woman who seeks to understand the meaning(s) of her own body, as well as those of other bodies. Ken Bugul shares that perspective, for her deep fascination for others' bodies cannot rival her passionate interest in her own.

Although she calls it "hers," both texts deny her any right of possession over the body. She cannot master the discourses that racialize and sexualize it; indeed, she can hardly recognize the body mirrored in the other's gaze. When she arrives in Belgium as a scholarship student, she first remarks that no one pays attention to her (or to anyone else, for that matter). "Etait-ce la fin du monde ou quoi? Vous ne m'avez pas

vue? Vous ne m'avez pas reconnue? Mais c'est moi" (47) [Was it the end
of the world, or what? Didn't you see me? Didn't you recognize me?
This is *me*] (35). Soon she cannot recognize the body mirrored in shop
windows as her own. "La façade en miroir d'une vitrine me renvoya le
reflet de mon visage. Je n'en crus pas mes yeux. Je me dis rapidement
que ce visage ne m'appartenait pas: j'avais les yeux hors de moi, la peau
brillante et noire, le visage terrifiant" (*Le baobab fou*, 50) [The front of
a shop window of mirrored glass reflected my face. I couldn't believe my
eyes. That face couldn't belong to me, I quickly told myself: my eyes
were bulging, my skin was shiny and black, the face terrifying] (37). Ken
literally becomes the slave of these mirrors, for "it is in this context that
Ken is cast and agrees to assume the role, à la Jean Genêt, of primitive
sexual enchantress, heir to Fatou Gaye [of *Le roman d'un spahi*] and the
Hottentot Venus."[37]

Role-play and reality melt into one as Ken loses the illusion that
she can control her body. She becomes addicted to drugs, prostitutes
herself, and accepts the physical abuse of her partners. Although men
control her with these images of the black temptress, she prefers to
believe that she can change the game by reinterpreting it. Ken takes
slight consolation in the illusory hope that the object can influence the
desiring subject. This hope is predicated on the belief that men will
allow her to negotiate her sexuality as at an auction. The metaphor
returns us to the world of the social contract based on the free consent
of individuals who own property *in themselves*. Ken, however, cannot
be said to own that primary piece of property.[38] Her ability to shatter
the story that the "decadent West" was telling itself about her is thus
nullified.

As many feminist thinkers have noted, this story effectively disguises
the violence used to enforce this system. In *Cendres et braises*, the dis-
guise slips. In this work, Marie/Ken leaves Senegal again as the mistress
of a Frenchmen; she identifies her new "master" only as Y. Although he
parades her as his pet beauty and dresses her in the finest fashions, he
begins to beat her after his wife divorces him. Later he rejects her completely and even has her arrested as a thief in the home they have shared
for months. Male violence metonymically represents racist and colonial
violence for Ken, as it has for other African writers.[39]

Although she indicts an auction system that means that "as soon as
women are alone together they seem so much like tarts" who "have the
same destiny" (43), Bugul blames assimilation for her victimization.

> L'école française, nos ancêtres les Gaulois, la coopération, les
> échanges, l'amitié entre les peuples, avaient créé une nouvelle dimen-
> sion: l'étranger. Ne pouvant plus reconnaître chez les siens, les liens
> vrais qui façonnaient et pouvaient guider les destins. (129)

> The French school, our ancestors the Gauls, cooperation, foreign exchanges, friendship between peoples had all created a new dimension: the foreigner, no longer able to recognize among one's own people the true bonds that used to shape and could guide destinies. (111)

She identifies herself as that foreigner, a cultural mulatta as ill at ease in Africa as in the West. At the same time, she sees the "foreigner" who fails to recognize the "true bonds" as a guilty party to colonialism, rather than as its victim. The baobab of the title becomes the symbol of those bonds.

This identification highlights the ambiguous nature of Ken's search for the proper name. According to Lévi-Strauss, proper names function as signs of the totem in the West.[40] These allusions to totems are far from innocent, for they bear the weight of the word's long colonial history in the west. Lévi-Strauss's acute observation encapsulates the "fetishism" of the name, if we define fetishism (actually the invention of western discourses on "the primitive") as "the collapse of representation, the primitive inability to tell sign from being."[41] Proper names are supposed to identify attached bodies in all "possible worlds," yet Ken makes of her name a floating signifier, subverting the colonial order embedded in the term "fétichiste."

Although Ken later learns to accept her totem as the sign of her "authentic" being, the totem itself refuses her. "J'avais pris rendez-vous avec le baobab, je n'étais pas venue et je ne pouvais pas l'avertir, je n'osais pas. Le rendez-vous manqué lui avait causé une profonde tristresse. Il devint fou et mourut quelque temps après" (181) [I had made a date with the baobab tree, I hadn't shown up and couldn't let it know, I didn't dare. The missed date had caused it deep sorrow. It went mad and died shortly thereafter (158)]. Other critics have noted the polysemy of the baobab symbol; it stands for continuity and rebirth, as well as for Ken herself.[42] In addition, the baobab is one of Senegal's national symbols. It even gives her birthplace its name, for Gouye [guy] is the Wolof word for baobab. We need hardly ask why Ken "chooses" the baobab as a totem. In his discussion of the figure of the totem in *L'Enfant noir*, Miller writes that the totem's significance is not "a matter of 'choice' but of inheritance and genealogy."[43] Although this is true, both of these autobiographies controvert that point. French education interrupted Laye's Malinke training, so he does not know what his totem is. In Ken Bugul's case, the totem dies when she does not recognize its call. Laye remains "suspended" between the past and the colonial present, as Miller argues,[44] but Ken has killed her past with the poison of assimilation.

The Abandoned Baobab thus becomes an epitaph to the precolonial past. It also marks Ken's rejection of her role as the "exotic" African who lacks the capacity to distinguish between sign and being, and of a discourse that defines her in terms of lack. In a rather ironic twist, she associates the totem with her neurosis, just as Freud associated the two in his *Totem and Taboo*. At the trunk of the dead tree, she gives up her neurotic preoccupation with her parents' divorce. "Sans paroles, je prononçais l'oraison funèbre de ce baobab témoin et complice du départ de la mère, le premier matin d'une aube sans crépuscule. Longtemps, je restai là devant ce tronc mort, sans pensée" (182) [Wordlessly, I pronounced the eulogy of the baobab tree that had been witness to and accomplice in the mother's departure, the first morning of a dawn without dusk. I stayed there in front of the dead trunk for a long time, without a thought (159)].

Proper names in Wolof are usually marked for gender.[45] The name Ken Bugul, however, does not mark gender. This in itself shows that Ken could not insert herself into the genealogy represented by the totemic baobab. The genealogy, of course, is the product of a certain sexual regime. Seen from a different angle, a genealogy provides the history of the nation's population. Unlike Nafissatou Diallo, however, Ken does not accept the state's appropriation of her sexuality as a tool for regulating the population. The tree's death, then, marks the end of a certain sexual regime. Ken mourns its passing primarily because she suffers from the violent and chaotic transition to some other, as yet unknown, discourse of sexual identity.

ALIEN BODIES

This new discourse of sexuality can be related to the incident of the bead that Ken discovers underneath the baobab as a child. In addition, it represents yet another possible future that she rejects. The bead, manufactured in France, replaces the fecund baobab seed, according to Mortimer.[46] As the analogy suggests, the incident marks Ken's painful awakening to an embodied consciousness that includes an awareness of the social meaning of her female body.

> A deux ans je ne marchais pas encore. Je pouvais ramper dehors. Une fois, c'est ce que je fis. Je jouais dans le sable, sous un immense baobab, face à la maison familiale. J'avais trouvé une perle d'ambre. Un enfant qui joue avec le sable ne fait que chercher quelque chose. . . . Dans mon village, les femmes portaient des perles enfilées des épingles de nourrice aux oreilles. J'avais associé la perle d'ambre trouvée dans le sable à cette image de la femme de mon village pour m'enfoncer la perle dans l'oreille. (30)

> At two years old, I still wasn't walking. I could crawl around outside. One time that is what I did. I was playing in the sand, underneath an

immense baobab tree, across from the family house. I found an amber bead. A child who plays with sand is bound to find things. . . . In my village, the women used to wear beads on diaper pins in their ears. I made a connection between the amber bead found in the sand and that image of the women in my village, and so I pushed the bead in my ear. (22)

The recurrent images of the painful bead and its connection to the village women's earrings suggest that the bead reminds her of her own painful "social body," overdetermined by sexuality. The earrings, intended to highlight the woman's (sexual) beauty, also indicate motherhood, for they are made of diaper pins. In addition, the bead itself refers to motherhood, for it represents a seed or ovum. For Ken, who affirms her sexuality almost with desperation, it is a painful alien body lodged in her own.

Motherhood and the quest for identity as Ken understands it are incompatible. Pregnancy makes it impossible for us to see the body as a physical envelope separating us from others, for the mother and child are one "split subjectivity." Drawing on Kristeva's remarks on this subject,[47] Iris Young writes that "pregnancy challenges the integration of my body experience by rendering fluid the boundary between what is within, myself, and what is outside, separate. I experience my insides as the space of another, yet my own body."[48] Ken, however, experiences split subjectivity as a pain she associates with a failed colonial assimilation.

Ken would like to be able to choose a simpler model of identity based on either/or distinctions, possibly because this is the model those around her use to judge her. She thus uses her first romance in Belgium "à m'expliquer, à m'intégrer, à montrer que j'étais comme eux: qu'il n'y avait aucune différence entre nous, que eux et moi, nous avions les mêmes ancêtres" (54) [to explain myself, to integrate me, to show that I was like them, that there was no difference whatsoever between us, that they and I had the same ancestors" (42)]; however, her lover proves to be "l'instrument inutile" (54) [a useless tool (42)], for she remains "rien que moi: ma réalité" (54) [nothing other than myself: my reality (42)]. Although Louis cannot make his society accept her, he begs her several times to marry him and return to Africa (where he thinks a mixed couple will be accepted). Ken does not love him (42), she says, and refuses to marry him.

This decision probably reflects her painful realization that most whites will never accept her as she is. Even Louis seems to have made her his symbol of "exotic Africa." When the doctor who examines her and verifies her pregnancy asks if the father is white or black, then suggests that she had better abort a child he views as a product of miscegenation, Ken has no power to express her outrage at his racism. As a result, she feels a sudden hatred for Louis, even after living with him "comme une jeune mariée" (55) [like a young bride (43)], as he put her into this doctor's office. Louis suddenly becomes the representative of her oppression in the doctor's office. Her ambiguous response thus represents a complex knot of feelings about racism, colonialism, sexism, and the news of her pregnancy.

Pregnancy and colonialism both split subjectivity, creating ambiguous identities. Since she already suffers from the split consciousness of the colonized, Ken wishes above all to create a unified, autonomous identity. As a result, she can only perceive her pregnancy as an unwanted burden. The doctor's "scientific" claims that mixed-race children are degenerate (60/47) only reinforce these feelings. Although Louis proposes to her again, she cannot see that as a solution either. "Pour moi, il n'en était pas question. J'avais quitté l'Afrique depuis à peine trois mois. Comment pourrais-je y retourner avec une grossesse et un mari blanc" (63) [I wouldn't hear of it. I had left Africa just barely three months earlier. How could I go back there, pregnant and with a white husband" (50)]?

Caught in the toils of the "either/or" model, Ken imagines such a child only as the sign of a sterile, "neither/nor" compromise. She thus sees the embryo as an alien body that she must dislodge. Since abortion was then illegal in Belgium, Ken accepts the doctor's offer to perform one on her kitchen table. Mariama Bâ's novel *Un chant écarlate* (1981) [*Scarlet Song*] presents an analogous situation. In that work, the mother of a biracial child murders her son, rather than going through an abortion; however, she, too, believes that her son is irredeemably foreign to the communities of both of his parents. This infanticide marks a desire to erase past choices that led to the child's birth. Given Bâ's strong interest in social issues, this anomalous murder may "stand in" for abortion, allowing her to address the issue in ways that would otherwise be impossible, given the strong emotions that abortion inspires. Ken's somewhat exhibitionist autobiography spurns such maneuvers.

The trope of the tragic mulatto, then, knits itself into that of the "ambiguous (colonial) adventure." Ken herself relates the abortion directly to her first experience of embodied consciousness. "Là-bas, si j'y étais restée, comme avant la perle d'ambre dans l'oreille, je n'aurais jamais eu à subir un avortement. Un système de valeurs pré-établies, une approche plus saine de la sexualité empêchent cette situation" (65) [Had I stayed down there, remained as I was before the amber bead in my ear, I never would have had to submit to an abortion. A system of preestablished values, a healthier approach to sexuality prohibit such a situation

(51)]. This complaint does not explain her refusal to accept that sexual regime; she not only rejects her village suitor, but also rebels against it. In complete disregard of the social and religious norms that she praises elsewhere, she states "je m'étais fait 'dévierger' par mon professeur d'histoire" (163) [let my history teacher deflower me (142)]. As Eileen Julien has noted, she herself undermines these attempts to present life in Senegal as an uncomplicated idyll.[49] Her remark thus expresses nostalgia for an uncomplicated, unified identity that she can only imagine.

This concept of identity resembles the contractarian definition of the individual as the sole and autonomous owner of his body. The irony lies in the fact that Ken seeks salvation in the very system that has denied this right of ownership to women and Africans. This has very specific implications for motherhood as a social institution. Indeed, the question of identity has haunted legal and ethical discussions of reproductive rights, as the debates on abortion and surrogate motherhood show. In her historical review tracing the links between nineteenth-century and contemporary conceptualizations of women's reproductive rights, Reva Siegel shows that the regulation of reproductive rights also functions as gender-caste regulation intended to control women.[50] In other words, regulation of reproduction also influences women's roles, and thus their social identities.

These definitions not only reduced women to the reproductive role, but also directed women's reproduction in specific ways. Nineteenth-century discourse aimed at banning contraceptive and abortion rights, for instance, defined the woman as the receptacle of the fetus. The fetus was redefined as an autonomous form of life that "seemed to have scant relation to the woman bearing it."[51] This supposed autonomy then pits the mother against her child, for their rights and best interests are presumed to conflict under a regime that can order women to bear children.

This conception of pregnancy thus makes it impossible for women to attain the status of owners of their own bodies. As a result, many pro-choice feminists have attempted to redefine pregnancy in ways that might allow women to be seen as proprietors of their bodies. Their arguments in defense of women's right to choose are also based on contractarian definitions of identity. Drucilla Cornell, for instance, argues that "denying a right to abortion is not a wrong to the 'self,' but a wrong that prevents the achievement of the minimum conditions of individuation necessary for any meaningful concept of selfhood."[52] Cornell posits bodily integrity as the universal condition for selfhood,[53] thus setting aside the enigma of the body. She argues that the fetus is a part of the mother's body; however, she also chooses to see the body as the dividing line between self and other. Cornell thus takes the right to bodily integrity as the basis for the right to abortion.

Pregnant women's perceptions of their condition, however, seem to resist this logic. Certainly, Ken's experience suggests that the fetus is part of the mother. After the abortion, she feels that "I'd been done in. It was not the medical procedure, it was the abortion itself that had killed me" (51). The equation between woman and fetus here does not reflect some "symbol," but Ken's embodied experience. That split, however, also negates the concept of bodily integrity as a universal factor in determining individuation. Paradoxically, Cornell herself recognizes the imaginary, enigmatic status of bodily integrity, but defends it as a basis for legal rights because "there is no self without this imaginary projection."[54] Furthermore, she understands the person as a work in progress—an aspiration, rather than a destination, "implicated in an endless process of working through personae."[55] This describes Ken's autobiographical quest for identity quite precisely. According to Cornell, women may masquerade as sexual personae, but they may also strive to unmask these personae to become "that which shines through" the mask—a person.[56]

This quest for the "real" person provides the impetus for Ken Bugul's autobiographical quest for identity. She vacillates between an unworkable concept of African authenticity (*Baobab*, 74) and an equally unfeasible concept of assimilation. In *Cendres et braises*, she tries on another mask—her Muslim identity. Ken's search for a unified identity circles around a lack that she defines as the lack of a mother. In accordance with Muslim law, her mother did indeed leave her with her father after their divorce.[57] This traumatic separation becomes the sign of the split in consciousness and consequently, of Ken's alienation in *The Abandoned Baobab*. As the passage above shows, Ken seeks some "transcendental signifier" to fill that lack. The Marabout becomes her "therapist," then marries her. Nevertheless, the lack remains; Ken attempts unsuccessfully to shift the blame for this inner lack onto her brother after renewing her ties to her mother in *Cendres et braises*. Although we cannot completely identify the author with the character, nor the person behind the text with the author, it is interesting to note that she later ended her marriage to the marabout.

These failed attempts to find a "transcendental signifier" in order to create a unified subjectivity illustrate the problem that Cornell seeks to resolve. Even though Cornell (and Ken, too) realizes that such a unified subject will always be a legal fiction, she believes that women must pursue the imaginary persons behind the personae in order to acquire equal rights.[58] Bodies anchor that legal fiction, for they represent the "real" in this discourse. As Judith Butler argues, however,

> as resistance to symbolization, the "real" functions in an exterior relation to language, as the inverse of mimetic representationalism, that is,

as the site where all efforts to represent must founder. . . . To freeze the real as the impossible "outside" to discourse is to institute a permanently unsatisfiable desire for an ever elusive referent: the sublime object of ideology.[59]

Given the indeterminacy of the body, Butler concludes that the term "woman" marks "a permanent site of contest."[60] Yet surely, it is the very relationship between the "real" (represented here by women's bodies) and discourse that is contested. As a referential art, autobiography plays a major role in that contest. The autobiographical text constantly teases the reader by presenting and simultaneously withdrawing the "real" person. Indeed, the autobiographical exchange seems to parallel Freud's "Fort-Da" game in some sense. Both players agree to pretend that the object that has disappeared will reappear in time. The true focus of the game, however, is the exchange, rather than the object itself.

Debates on women's reproductive rights can be recast in this light. Cornell's defense of women's reproductive rights, for instance, should be read within the wider context of her goal of democratizing the contest so that women will be able to participate as equals. Unfortunately, her reinterpretation of contractarian identity limits individuality and embodied experiences in ways that may impede women from "entering differently." This reinterpretation freezes the exchange by taking one culture's definition of the body as the basis for universal human rights.

Other readings of cases involving women's human rights make this point sharply. Françoise Lionnet writes that excision offers an "ideal test case, as it apparently illustrates absolute and total cultural conflict between the rights of the individual to bodily integrity and the individual's need to be satisfactorily integrated into a community." Since male circumcision, tonsilectomy and appendectomy, for instance, do not disturb western sensibilities, bodily integrity is not an absolute value, even in the West.[61] In other words, no definition of bodily integrity is likely to be universal. Cornell's own definition of bodily integrity as the "real" that anchors the "imaginary domain" frees an abstract, universal "woman" while simultaneously trapping women in an ethnocentric framework.

Lionnet's test case highlights this problem. She examines the 1991 sentencing of three Malian immigrants to France who continued to practice excision and were thus trapped between two legal systems. Lionnet argues that they were punished for their inability to choose one legal identity over the other, for in her view, excision, or the removal of part or all of the clitoris, can be compared to other procedures—such as abortion—that can arguably be defended by their proponents as cultural steps taken to avoid biological determinism.[62] Abortion is legal in France; excision is not. If this was a contest between two systems, rather than a matter of individual identity, it was pointless "to claim that the issue opposes communitarian values to universal ones; the actual conflict hinges on the opposing claims of two different communities, one of which would like to believe that its culture is a 'universal' one."[63]

For the purposes of my argument, the crucial point is that the individual becomes the locus for a competition staged between two ideological regimes. Reproductive rights in particular serve as a scorecard in the contest, for population control indicates the ascendancy of the state, according to Foucault. Reproduction, then, is tied to other social concerns. Siegel, for example, highlights the nineteenth-century concern that women "preserve the ethnic character of the nation."[64] Twentieth-century European states' attempts to promote the reproduction of the white population have the same goal.[65] They also seem to promote what Foucault called "race war" within the state, for the white population is pitted against an immigrant population from former colonies that is perceived as an alien body.

The multicultural population in many West European countries today reflects a plurality of loyalties and identities that blocks the rebirth of a totalitarian state based on racial identity. That plurality, much like the double vision ascribed to members of minorities, the colonized, and the oppressed, poses a danger to the state's goal of population control. The many attempts to create homogeneous populations—from early antimiscegenation laws in the United States to the recent ethnic cleansing in the former Yugoslavia or in Mauritania—offer evidence enough to make the point. Homogeneous populations, of course, are easier to control than heterogeneous ones. This is particularly true because those who are afflicted—or blessed—with double vision perceive their subject position in the order of things with a clarity denied to the unified subject.[66]

As they bear the brunt of the assaults in this new "race war," however, immigrants and their children suffer a great deal. Mame Seck Mbacke's collection of interviews and fictionalized life histories, Le froid et le piment: Nous, travailleurs immigrés (1983), as well as novels such as Marie NDiaye's En famille (1990) represent only a few of the available texts on this conflict. In this context, Ken's abortion represents rejection of a possible future, rather than a successful resolution of her identity conflict. Since Ken compares her feelings to those of her mother on the day that she learned of her son's death, we can assume that she mourns the death of her hopes of building a hybrid cultural identity along with the death of a future métissage.

ETHICAL ESTHETICS

In *Cendres et braises*, Ken Bugul offers some insight into the ethical problems involved in the construction of identity when she writes that the individual can only assume responsibility within a social framework (133–34). As I argue in the introduction, individuality exists only within community. The interactions between individual agent and community simultaneous shape both of them. This does not preclude individuality or agency; indeed, we can only perceive human agency in these interactions. Ken's flight from responsibility to herself and to others thus represents passivity. Babacar Thioune characterizes the autobiographical figure in *The Abandoned Baobab* as "un personnage passif, sans initiative ni responsabilité, se limitant à réagir à des contraintes sociales contradictoires" [a passive character without initiative or responsability, limited to reacting to contradictory social constraints].[67] This statement could also represent the conflict between African immigrants and the French state as it appears in Lionnet's account.

Although the fictional self here appears to be a passive gauge of this conflict, Ken's autobiographical work marks various attempts to resolve the problem. First she accepts assimilation, then she rejects it completely—just as she rejects the possibility of a postcolonial *métissage* when she decides to go through with the abortion. Nevertheless, she cannot accept mere "association" for long, for she sees and mocks essentialism even when it seduces her. Ironically, Ken ends her second work in the place that some have denounced as the site of a colonialism worse than French domination. She decides that "la femme devait se battre pour conquérir son indépendance matérielle, économique, si elle voulait être libre. Mais la liberté économique n'était pas la liberté de la femme. L'homme demeurait le problème fondamental" (189) [Woman had to fight to conquer her material and economic independence, if she wanted to be free. But economic liberty was not woman's liberty. Man remained the fundamental problem]. This contradictory statement marks the collision between different needs: the need for a fulfilling sexual relationship with a man; the need for material independence so that no man can "master" her, as Y. did; the need for affection, and the need for communication as a basic form of exchange necessary to social identity.

These needs link Ken to social reality, but her personal desire makes the fiction of an autobiographical self possible. Desire is singular, individualistic, while needs are collective; however, the two meet in the autobiographical exchange. Readers' differing relationships to autobiographical texts make this much clear. Many readers choose to see autobiographies almost as self-help manuals, for they focus on the collective needs represented in the experiences of the individual autobiographer. However, the autobiographical *art* consists at least in part in the imaginary fusion of collective needs and singular desires.

The Franco-Senegalese critic Cathérine N'Diaye proposes a "radical esthetic" as the solution to the cultural alienation that makes this fusion seem unattainable to Ken Bugul. "En quête d'identité, nos écrivains croyaient souffrir d'un manque. Ils ont cru qu'ils avaient le devoir de répondre à un besoin—de boucher un creux. En fait, ils voulaient inconsciemment, naïvement, oblitérer la littérature" [Searching for an identity, our writers believed that they suffer from a lack. They believed that they had a duty to respond to a need—to stop up a hole. In fact, they unconsciously, naively, wanted to obliterate literature].[68] In contrast, N'Diaye sees the esthetic project as the conversion of a need into a desire; indeed, she claims that "il faut convertir le manque d'être jusqu'à le rendre méconnaissable" [it is imperative to transform the lack of being until it is unrecognizable].[69]

Although the protagonist of *Cendres et braises* continues to sense a lack that she now traces to her relationship with her brother, she ends the text by claiming to have found an answer to the problem of the desiring subject who must meet social needs. Even though she has not yet succeeded in adapting to the point of being able to farm her own field, she writes that "ma Mère vient d'apprendre par la Mauresque et sa voisine que le Marabout m'avait épousée. Mille Gloires Au Créateur des Harmonies Eternelles" [My Mother just learned from the Moorish woman and her neighbor that the Marabout had married me. A Thousand Glories to the Creator of Eternal Harmonies] (190). It is striking that, for the first time, she claims the mother as her own, rather than distancing her by calling her "La Mère," which specifies her function but does not indicate any relationship to the speaker. Does this mean that Ken Bugul, too, has attempted to "boucher le creux" [fill the emptiness]? In N'Diaye's terms, this would mean an esthetic failure, rather than a successful fusion between the collective and the personal. Although *Cendres et braises* lacks the sheer power of *Le baobab fou*, it reflects an effort to redefine the terms—identity, need, lack—that move the protagonist of the first text to rage and desperation when she must return to Senegal.

Ken Bugul's autobiographical practice, then, reflects an ambivalent attitude. It also fits d'Alméïda's notion of autobiography as dé/couverte,

the process of discovering [the self] as covering/uncovering/recovering. In that sense, my initial belief that autobiography provides for women a "safe" entry into writing becomes untenable. It is, on the contrary, a daring undertaking that cannot even cover itself under the guise of the novelistic form, which is rightly or wrongly seen as the "real" fictional mode.[70]

Le baobab fou uncovers many of the masks that deface Ken by making her unrecognizable even to herself, but Ken learns that this dé/couverte destroys that which she sought—the baobab that represents her "true" self. In other words, she transforms the terms so that "either/or" becomes "neither/nor." Ken's obsessive questioning of the various systems used to construct social identities—whether they are based on cultural origins, race, religion, or sex—thus leads her to recreate *herself* as an ironically tragic mulatto (neither/nor). The characteristics assigned to the tragic mulatto, then, shift from characters like Nini, the *métisse* who has never left Senegal, to Ken, who writes of her experiences in both Europe and Senegal.

Although the first text resists the trope of the tragic mulatto in more ways than one, the second finally dismisses the trope by retreating to a new either/or model based on religious belief. This marks a retreat from what N'Diaye calls radical esthetics, for desire has been redefined as a "lack to be filled" in this text. As Norman Rush writes in a review of the English translation of *The Abandoned Baobab*, the reader "comes away with a salutary reminder of how difficult it is truly to cast a cold eye on what we are and on the obstacles we face in the attempt to make ourselves into something we would prefer to have been."[71] In spite of itself, this textual retreat indicates a new way of combining ethics and esthetics.[72] The trope of the tragic mulatto only functions in the discourse of either/or; as Hortense Spillers notes, it is not a figure of self-referentiality.[73] Since Ken Bugul puts herself into the position of the tragic mulatto, this discursive displacement explodes both "either/or" and "neither/nor" as models for identity.

The trope then disappears into the larger political project that Lionnet proposes as a definition for *métissage*.

> We have to articulate new visions of ourselves, new concepts that allow us to think *otherwise*, to bypass the ancient symmetries and dichotomies that have governed the ground and the very condition of thought, of "clarity," in all of Western philosophy. *Métissage* is such a concept and a practice; it is the site of undecidability and indeterminacy, where solidarity becomes the fundamental principle of political action against hegemonic languages.[74]

As a site of radical indeterminacy, *métissage* foils the totalitarian state based on rigid population control that Foucault fearfully envisioned. New and hybrid "nations" have grown up within Europe's modern nation-states through *métissage*, yet this practice will only liberate those who freely choose it. As long as we seek to anchor ourselves in a contractarian world of unified, proprietary subjects, however, this choice will remain forever in abeyance, and the state will continue to regulate ownership and identity.

CHAPTER 7

Terms of Exchange

Critical enthusiasm for *métissage* and related notions like hybridity sometimes succeeds in erasing all doubts about the difficulties involved in embracing hybrid identities. Yet Ken Bugul's struggle to bypass identities that others ascribe to her reminds us not only how difficult it is to cast a cold eye on ourselves and our past, as Rush suggests, but also how many external obstacles African women face in their efforts to increase their options. *Métissage* as an historical process and as an historical reality also reminds us in sobering fashion that creole, hybrid societies often exist because of slavery, colonialism, and other injustices. Although we may celebrate the new identities and cultures that survivors have created, this history means that we cannot forget that individuals are never completely free to choose their identities. An understanding of *métissage* that ignores or dismisses the consequences of racism and sexism, or pretends to signal our arrival at some postethnic utopia would be unethical, as well as erroneous, in this context.

At the same time, *métissage* allows us to conceptualize identity in such a manner that the "neither/nor" of the aborted child may be transformed into the joyous naming ceremony of a new child, whose painful birth leads to a life of new choices. Very probably, these new alternatives will hold some risks, as every new life presents as many new dangers as hopes and promises. On one hand, the dilution of identity may be an inherent danger of *métissage*. On the other hand, the concept offers the theoretical possibility of circles of exchanges based on shared identities that reflect more than our ethnic, national, racial, and sexual identities. This is the problem that Kwame A. Appiah addresses in arguing that identities are now "too tightly scripted," thus criticizing the almost obsessive focus on ethnicity and race that leads some people to "forget that their individual identities are complex and multifarious—that they have enthusiasms that do not flow from their race or ethnicity, interests, and tastes that cross ethnoracial boundaries."[1]

Similarly, the generic *métissage* that I have constructed by comparing *taasu* to autobiography presents problems as well as some promise. First, partners in exchange must agree upon the terms used in that exchange, or the exchange will fail. Second, the blurring of genres that makes the expansion of our hermeneutic horizons and new exchanges possible may blur necessary distinctions, thus endangering the exchange itself. Finally, cross-cultural exchanges often fail because the terms of the exchange collapse as the partners transform them. Although different individuals and groups vary in their definition of what a "necessary distinction" might be, most of them agree to call them "truths." This chapter addresses the problem of the necessary distinction in relation to autobiographical discourse.

TRUTHFUL LIES

Autobiographical discourse marks the cross-roads where many different genres of truth meet, just as the individual represents the meeting-place of various competing discourses. Readers generally define autobiography according to some notion of truth or referentiality. As Eakin argues, acknowledgment of the fictional qualities of autobiography does not do away with the referentiality of the genre. Indeed, the double vision of the autobiographer and her reader enriches the contact. Similarly, audiences of *taasu* accept the fictional and purely formulaic aspects of the performance, but also recognize the performer's *referential* powers, which make the *taasu* into a form of social action. Autobiography, I hold, is never simply mimetic. Moreover, genre distinctions are crucial to our ability to evaluate the truth-value of all narratives.

For these and other reasons, many scholars of autobiography have linked the genre to confession, thus presuming that the autobiographer at least intends to tell the truth. Here I find it useful to turn to Bakhtin, who considers confession in light of the relationship forged between speaker and listener. This relationship is predicated upon a *self*-objectification from which the other is excluded; "the only principal that organizes the utterance here is the pure relationship of the *I* to itself.[2] That other may function as a judge at times, but s/he then merely supplements the confessor's conscience. Confession essentially represents the divided self judging *itself* before a witness.

However, autobiography also allows the self to create a double, fictitious self in relation to others. "The other is not I myself as produced through the agency of the other, but the valued other himself in me, another human being in me."[3] This concept succinctly explains the quintessence of autobiography: through this genre, the autobiographer initiates a gift exchange that allows her to give of her *self*. Furthermore, this gift of the self is a self-ish gift in another sense, for the autobiographer receives something from her audience in return. She may receive another's confidences, material gifts, or a more meaningful relationship, as the Wolof *taasukat* does; however, she may receive more intangible benefits as well, as Bakhtin suggests.

The truth value of such exchanges may appear dubious at times; Wolof women, for example, never forget self-interest as they exchange secrets in public through the transparent veil of allusions typical of *taasu*. Bakhtin addresses this problem briefly, linking autobiographical intersubjectivity to facticity and truth. This link remains implicit, yet Bakhtin clearly subscribes to the idea that dissonance leads to a rough form of objectivity or truth. That is, the hybrid form of consciousness that Bakhtin proposes is based on an interior form of competition that makes it possible to confront and analyze ideas and ideologies, then move toward a synthesis we may call a truth. Bakhtin's model stands in sharp contrast to the introspective and limited truths that the confessional mode offers. This model also suggests that genre distinctions have a clear role to play, not only in histories of subjectivity, but also in judgments about truth value.

Indeed, we understand intuitively that genre offers us a useful tool for evaluating truth-value, which depends upon context. We understand irony, for instance, because of contextual clues; in other words, the truth-value of an ironic statement is of a certain kind that we recognize because we can recognize the rhetorical category of "ironic statement." This may even explain why theorists of genre, and of autobiography in particular, have long focused on questions of truth and truth criteria. As Richard Bauman notes, "the truth value of narrative—one dimension of the relationship of stories to the events they recount—has been a basic typological criterion in the classification of narrative. . . . Folklorists, for their part, have relied rather heavily on the truth factor in classifying oral narrative forms."[4] Clearly, scholars of autobiography, too, have relied extremely heavily on this distinction when defining the genre.[5] Narrative poems can and have been judged in the same way; the best example is perhaps the epic, which has been used as a source of historical data more often than most other poetic forms.

However, the concerns of these theorists have often been dismissed, as most discussions of genre and truth remain tautological: the truth-value of a text or statement serves in many of these discussions to define the genre, while in fact, that truth-value could only be determined based on the genre of the statement or text. This theoretical failing has promoted a disingenuous disavowal of the importance of truth, a disavowal often accompanied by a skewed version of the borrowed notion of indeterminacy. Indeterminacy as I understand it does not remove the possibility of truth so much as it expands the possibilities, forcing us to consider the issue of perspective in truth production. This is a narrative issue, and truth is a matter related to storytelling.

Although distrust of the "truthful lie"[6] is long-standing in many cultures, in others, the ambivalent nature of fictional truth is accepted. Indeed, the words "lie" and "story" are almost interchangeable in some communities. According to Karim Traoré, the concluding formula of many Mande popular tales is "'I brought the lie back to the place where I found it,' signaling to the audience that everyone should come back to reality."[7] This ambiguity makes many scholars uneasy; some resolve this as Linda Dégh and Andrew Vázsonyi do, by arguing that "objective truth and the presence, quality, and quantity of subjective belief are irrelevant. . . . [What is important is that legend] takes a stand and calls for the expression of opinion on the question of truth and belief."[8] This stance begs the question by removing truth-value from the discussion. Cultural relativism and the notion of indeterminacy do not necessarily erase truth-value as a valid issue, but indicate that the standard western distinction between objectivity and subjectivity is inoperative here.[9]

Concepts of truth are not "objective," in other words, but depend on culturally defined criteria of veracity and saliency.[10] This culturalist conception of truth does not deny the existence of truths, but seeks to investigate the conditions under which "truth" is produced. As the cultural anthropologist Renato Rosaldo points out,[11] it is possible to disagree with one standpoint without accepting a predictably contrary perspective. If we accept the premise that truth is culturally determined, we can re-examine questions of truth, rather than blandly arguing that truth does not matter as long as some stand is taken. Indeed, a new area of research springs into view, for we must investigate different cultural conceptions of truth. Questions of truth or reference to "reality," vital to the social sciences, are no less vital to literary theories of genre, as Bauman argues. "Considerations of truth and belief will vary and be subject to negotiation within communities and story-telling situations,"[12] or indeed, in any communicative event. Truth-value thus depends on cultural and historical negotiations that crystallize for a moment in a particular genre of discourse. Of course, such negotiations are reciprocal, as genres are culturally defined categories of discourse.

In the following, I attempt to outline the basic paradox that we encounter when discussing some Wolof notions of truth. Since I had not planned on doing research on truth criteria in Wolof society, the following observations are the unexpected fruit of an intense period of participatory fieldwork. Among many Wolof, a certain ambivalence toward truth and fiction can be detected. On one hand, the definition of truth is so rigorous that even an unintentional error can be considered a lie. A well-known story about the seventeenth-century Wolof sage Kócc Barma offers an example. The ruler, or Damel, jealous of Kócc's reputation for wisdom, decides to play a trick on the sage. Preparing for his departure, one foot in the stirrup of his horse, the other on the ground, the ruler orders Kócc to precede him and announce his arrival to the villagers he wishes to visit. As soon as Kócc leaves, the ruler changes his plans and decides to stay at home. Prudently, Kócc tells the villagers that "au moment où je quittais le roi, il avait l'intention de venir vous rendre visite, il avait déjà posé un pied sur l'étrier tandis que l'autre était resté à terre. Je ne sais pas lequel des deux pieds a rejoint l'autre après mon départ" [When I left the king, he had the intention of visiting you; he had already placed one foot in the stirrup, while the other remained on the ground. I don't know which foot joined the other after my departure].[13] The narrative offers proof that Wolof definitions of truth are extremely rigorous. Indeed, before I had heard the story, Wolof friends advised me to avoid discussing future plans unless I was sure that I was telling "the truth," meaning that I should say nothing until these plans were realized. Clearly, the story still has relevance in contemporary Senegal.

On the other hand, truth is often a matter of negotiation, rather than one of proof or evidence, among many Wolof. The divergence between my own attitudes toward truth and those of informants and friends in Louga struck me most clearly because of a slight misunderstanding. On a hot summer day, I offered everyone a *radi*, or locally made popsicle (sold in plastic baggies) after lunch. One of the children had already left the courtyard in order to play with the neighbor's children; when he returned, I simply gave him 20 CFA and asked him to buy another *radi*. I assumed that the other children had told him that he should ask for his treat. Souleymane, on the other hand, assumed that I wanted him to run an errand for me. Since Wolof children are expected to run errands for their elders, this was a logical conclusion. In many cases, one gives the child a small treat in return, but it is not obligatory to do so. Souleymane ran off to accomplish the errand, and soon returned with a red circle around his mouth and a *radi* worth only 10F CFA. The child's action did not surprise me so much as the adults' reactions. Souleymane's aunt began to laugh and to praise him, exclaiming "Dafa-y muus" [He's clever]! Given my own upbringing, however, I was startled and thought to myself that this was a form of dishonesty. This idea startled Souleymane's aunt, who repeated that Souleymane had shown how shrewd or clever he is, for he not only accomplished the task, but also made sure that he received a reward for it. In other words, he was both honest and dishonest at the same time. Since moral standards are usually formed at a very young age, the contrast in educational styles is significant.

Wolof are proud of their reputation for shrewdness, as this anecdote illustrates; indeed, "muus" is a quality that serves to define Wolof identity, to some extent. Members of other ethnic groups sometimes complain that Wolof "se croient plus malins que les autres" [Wolof think they are cleverer than other people] (Diola informant, Dakar 2/93). Wolof informants, when questioned, agreed with this statement, and added that they believe that Wolof are in general cleverer than members of other groups. Shrewdness is carefully distinguished from intelligence in Wolof. An intelligent person "amna xel" [literally, "has intelligence"], while a shrewd or clever person "dafa-y muus" [is clever].

The Canton (Texas) dog-traders studied by Bauman show the same ambivalence toward truth-telling and lying. Indeed, Bauman's depiction of dog-trading in Canton suggests that truth can only be seen as a contingent, socially negotiated matter.

> The narratives that are the instruments of these negotiations do not fall into clear-cut categories of factual and fictional, truthful and lying, believable and incredible, but rather interweave in a complex contextual web that leaves these issues constantly in doubt, ever susceptible to strategic manipulation.[14]

Many Wolof narratives reflect the same ambivalent attitude toward truth-telling. Indeed, indirect, allusive speech indicates that an individual has attained the highest level of linguistic competency in Wolof. Two of the tales in Emil Magel's collection of Wolof folktales from the Gambia, "The Marriage of Two Masters of the Wolof Language I and II," explicitly praise such speech.[15] *Taasukat* as well must master the art of expressing themselves indirectly. Given the admiration for indirect speech, one might even expect directly self-referential speech to attract criticism or disapproval. Indeed, veiled references to oneself are more common than directly self-referential *taasu*; however, those exceptional poems in which the performer openly discusses herself and her experiences immediately win great fame for the performer. In addition, audience members often cite these as the most memorable *taasu*.

Before attempting to explain this paradox, I wish to discuss yet another self-referential *taasu*. The following example of a virtuoso performance, collected in the village of Jillilu Sylla on 4/6/93, provides insight not only into the performance of truth, but into the performance of autobiography.

4/6/93, Jillilu Sylla. Performer: Anta Bouna Dieng

Man duma dellooti Gànnaar	[As for] myself, I will never return to Mauritania
Chorus	
Man duma dellooti Gànnaar	I will never return to Mauritania
Ma ne Gànnaar, duma fa dox di dee	I say Mauritania, I will not go there to die

Chorus

Ma ne Gànnaar, duma fa dox di dee
I say, Mauritania, I will not go there to die

Ma ne Gànnaar duma fa dox di dee
I say, Mauritania, I will not go there to die

Foo dëju dee
Wherever you rest, death

Foo taxaw dee
Wherever you stand, death

Foo gëstu dee
Wherever you look, death

Duma dellooti Gànnaar
I will not return to Mauritania

Yaayi Njabate Faal di maami Naxe
Mothers of Njabate Fall and mothers of Naxe[16]—

Duma dellooti Gànnaar
[I swear to you that] I will never return to Mauritania

Chorus
Duma dellooti Gànnaar
I will never return to Mauritania

Ma ne Baba Njeme
I say Father Njeme

Njàmbaar ga ca Waalo
Hero of Waalo[17]

Mayaasin Demba
Mayaasin Demba[18]

Duma dellooti Gànnaar
[I swear to you that] I will never return to Mauritania

Chorus
Lutax doo dellooti Gànnaar?
Why won't you ever return to Mauritania?

Faatimata wat ma nag
Fatimaata shaved my head and

Ma dem ak saam nel
I went about with my bald pate

Xam nga ne bilaay
You know, I swear by God

duma dellooti Gànnaar
I will never return to Mauritania

Chorus
Dinga dellooti Gànnaar
You will never return to Mauritania

Wool ma Omar
Call Omar to me

Wool ma Baay Lambi
Call Father Lambi

Mu rëddal ma kër
So he'll mark the foundations of my house

Chorus
Mu rëddal ma kër
He'll mark the foundations of my house

Ma ne Baba Ñemme
I say Father Ñemme

Njàmbaar ga ca Waalo
Hero of Waalo

Mayaasin Demba daal
Mayaasin Demba too

Ne Jillilu daa neexa neexa neex
Say, Jillilu is better than good, the best

Waay Baba Ñemme
But Father Ñemme

Màkkaay sa kër baay	Màkka is the house of your fathers
Wool ma Omar	Call Omar to me
Wool ma Baay Lambi	Call Father Lambi
Mu rëddal ma kër	So he'll mark the foundations of my house
Wool ma Omar	Call Omar
Wool ma Baay Lambi	Call Father Lambi
Mu rëddal ma kër	So he'll mark the foundations of my house

The performer, an older *géwël* woman, perhaps in her late sixties, but full of energy, comes from the nearby village of Màkka-Barage, one of a group of three villages called Màkka that were founded by former inhabitants of Jillilu Sylla (*Boróom kër* or headman, of Màkka Barage, 6/93). She and other villagers from Màkka had come to attend a naming ceremony at Jillil u Sylla. The following *taasu* was so famous in the surrounding region that people had forgotten the woman's name, and called her Mother Mauritania. When I visited her in Màkka, no one knew who Anta Bouna Dieng was, but as soon as I mentioned Mother Mauritania I was shown the way to her house.

The day that she performed in Jillil u Sylla, she encountered resistance from the *géwël* of that village, who found her to be stiff competition. Her performance commanded the attention of the audience. She declaimed extraordinarily well, provoking infectious laughter because she had attached wooden representations of male and female genitals to her hips. As she performed, she manipulated these carvings in lewd and hilarious fashion. Jealous, other performers made her abbreviate the performance. She was well aware of their reaction, for she began to praise the village in order to appease them—"Ne Jillilu daa neexa neexa neex" [Say, Jillilu is better than good, the best]—contrasting the pleasure of being in Jillilu Sylla with the horrors of her experiences in Mauritania.

On another occasion, I was able to record a more complete version of the poem, which Anta had first performed at a naming ceremony in her home village of Màkka after she was forced to leave Mauritania. Anta was not present that day, but her daughter chose to perform the well-known *taasu*. As we will see, however, she redirected the poem so that it explains her own experiences as well. Follow-up interviews with Anta proved that Bassine remembered the original version better than her mother.

6/9/93, Màkka. Performance by Bassine Guèye, daughter of Anta Bouna Dieng

| Wool ma Omar | Call Omar to me |
| Wool ma Baay Lambi | Call Father Lambi |

Ñu rëddal ma kër

That they trace the foundations
of my house

Chorus
Wool ma Omar
Wool ma Baay Lambi
Ñu rëddal ma kër

Call Omar to me
Call Father Lambi
That they trace the foundations
of my house

Waay Gànnaar duma fa dox di
dee

Oh, Mauritania, I will not go
there to die

Chorus
Waay Gànnaar duma fa dox di
dee
Ni siggi dee
Taxaw dee
Gëstu dee foo yëngu mu dig dee

Oh, Mauritania, I will not go
there to die
If you raise your head, you die
Stand, you die
Look, you die
Wherever you move, death
promises to come

Dee gaanga Gànnaar
Gànnaar duma fa dox di dee

Death is in Mauritania
Mauritania! I will not go there to
die

Chorus
Gànnaar duma fa dox di dee

Mauritania! I will not go there to
die

Naar xartaane ca yees

Haratine Moors[19] are the worst
[in Mauritania]

Ñoo jàpp xuur aki dambal

They grab your balls and uproot
them

niko nàmmit boroom nelew

In a flash, the owner sleeps
forever[20]

Xarafaat baa nga wall wa

A second circumcision from
which your blood springs

Chorus
Naar xartaane ca yees

Haratine Moors are the worst [in
Mauritania]

Maay ñàkk sama ndeye
Tég ca sama baay ba yalnaa dee

I lost my mother
Add to that my father, who
almost died

Ni duma dellooti Gànnaar

Say, I will never return to
Mauritania

Mane maami naxati

I say, the ancestors have cheated
again

yaayi Njamata

Mothers of Njamata

Man duma dellooti Gànnaar	Me, I will never return to Mauritania
Naar xartaane ca yees	Haratine Moors are the worst there
Chorus:	
Naar xartaane ca yees	Haratine Moors are the worst there

Bassine redirects the poem slightly to introduce her own feelings in the sixth stanza of her poem (the sixth if we exclude the refrains), when she explains that she had been separated from her mother. When she returned alone to her village, her "father" [probably an uncle, in this case] almost died when he learned that she had lost her mother. Indeed, Bassine felt extremely guilty for having brought her mother to Mauritania in the first place. She had done so because her own father, Anta's first husband, had died. The village chief had given Anta in marriage to a wealthy man from another village, but this marriage was extremely unhappy. Anta described her first marriage as a perfect union. She stressed that she was the only wife that her first husband took; however, in her second marriage, she had two co-wives. In order to escape her marital problems, Anta joined Bassine in Mauritania in order to help her run a small restaurant. When the continuing friction between Senegal and Mauritania evolved into open conflict, they became refugees.

Although these performers are Senegalese and can depend on family and village ties, they faced great difficulties. According to Diop and Diouf,

> Le conflit sénégalo-mauritanien constitue un révélateur de la crise sociale sénégalaise. . . . L'intégration au sein de la société de milliers de Sénégalais rapatriés et de Mauritaniens noirs déportés aggrave la crise sociale et économique du pays.

> The Senegalo-Mauritanian conflict constitutes an indicator of the Senegalese social crisis. . . . The social integration of thousands of repatriated Senegalese and deported black Mauritanians aggravates the country's social and economic crisis.[21]

The refugees' chances for economic re-integration in Senegal are slim.[22] Anta and Bassine returned to their village almost naked. Anta's poem was a plea for help directed at her family's hereditary patron, the village chief. He indeed responded, and offered her a modest home. She still lives there, rather than with the husband she left when she went to Mauritania.

The emotional power of self-referential *taasu* performances appears quite strongly in the context of this performance. Obviously, Anta and her daughter were not the only refugees from Mauritania in the area; indeed, I met several others quite by chance. Perhaps the experience has even given rise to a new social identity based on this common experience of genocidal terror. Indeed, Dieng links her own pain to that of male victims of torture, showing an empathy that allows her to cross even those boundaries of gender that we so often presume to be fixed and immutable. Anta Dieng's decision to describe her experience in a *taasu* also reflects the urgency of her need in a society that prefers indirect, allusive speech in most circumstances. As we noted in reference to Ngoné Mbaay's famous *taasu* "Loo làkkale," directly self-referential *taasu* are among the most famous examples of the genre.

NEGOTIATING TRUTHS

In the context of a very real case of human rights abuses and victimization, it may seem callous to examine the truth-value of the victim's representation of her experience. However, we must do so on a regular basis. This is the dilemma that the Rwandan tribunals and the South African Truth and Reconciliation Commission face as I write. The dilemma itself suggests that we must always ask what *kind* of truth the speech act offers, for truth is never a given, but always a matter for negotiation. If this were not true, it would be impossible to judge or sentence anyone, in any court of law, for the claims of the victim and those of the plaintiff must by definition be opposed. Furthermore, it would be naive to believe that language could transmit a transparent version of the facts; indeed, language is by definition a form of mediation between ourselves and the referent.

The extremely ambivalent attitude of most Wolof toward direct, referential speech also suggests that naïve notions of truth-value fall short of the mark when applied to the self-referential *taasu*. Indeed, the *taasu* underscores this point as it exists because of intersubjective exchanges. As we have seen, Mbaay's poem may offer a direct and honest presentation of an event—the fire that destroyed her home. However, it is also possible that Mbaay's poem, like most praise poems, is a highly allusive, indirect description of her marital problems. Anta and Bassine, as well as their audiences, confirmed the facts: they did indeed face death in Mauritania, and barely escaped. Nevertheless, their performances also signal attempts to negotiate truth. They presented their experiences in a manner calculated to gain assistance. Indeed, the poems exist *only* because of the possibility of gaining that assistance.

Juxtaposing Mbaay's text and the seemingly straightforward texts that Anta and Bassine performed thus forces us to re-examine the problem of the intentional fallacy.[23] As William Wimsatt and Monroe Beardsley argue in reference to written texts, the text itself cannot explicate the intentions of the author. Although the author may include comments about his/her intentions within a text, the very notion of the text as a work of art makes it impossible to accept such statements at face value. First, authors do not always succeed in fulfilling their intentions. Second, authors cannot completely control the meaning of their texts. Since the reader interacts with the text, rather than the author, the author can perhaps limit the number and variety of plausible interpretations, but s/he cannot direct possible readers' interpretations. Third, authors are not always aware of all of the intentions that they may have had when writing. In other words, interviewing the author about his/her intentions cannot resolve the problem of the intentional fallacy.

Many students of oral literature have relied on the performer's statements of intention in order to decipher the "true" meaning of the text; however, we cannot do so unless we ignore the aesthetic and playful aspects of oral performance. Although the notion of the intentional fallacy has hitherto been applied almost exclusively to written texts, the principle is applicable to any enunciation at all. In addition, performers may at times joke, lie, or obscure the "truth" in other ways. As Americo Paredes has argued, it is naive and ethnocentric simply to accept informants' statements at face value.[24] The notions of "truth" that provide the underpinnings for the failings of ethnography described in Paredes' work are indeed specific to a particular group of western cultures.

The problem of the intentional fallacy, then, affects social scientists as well as literary critics. Whether the research concerns social texts or literary texts, the problems of interpretation remain; however, the methods for dealing with these problems differ. The split between the social sciences and literature that Peter Zima deplores[25] stems at least in part from the divergent methods that social scientists and literary critics have used to deal with the problem. Social scientists consistently refer to facts external to the text—to the context—in order to interpret specific social texts.[26] Literary scholars, however, rely far more heavily on textual data to support their interpretations.

Scholars of oral literature and performance genres too choose to anchor their interpretations contextually. This approach is not unproblematic; as members of the Prague School such as Roman Jakobson realized early on, "context" is a loaded word. References to context cannot anchor an analysis if context itself remains an unexamined or blank category. Jakobson, for example, criticized scholars in the social sciences for refusing to revise the philosophical basis for their work, arguing that "c'est là seulement que s'est poursuivie, voire même intensifiée, encore au début de notre siècle, l'extension du réalisme naïf" [Here alone, even at the beginning of our century, has the extension of naïve realism been pursued and indeed, even intensified.][27] The criticism stands to the present, for in spite of structuralist and poststructuralist attempts, the battle over "truth" continues to rage.

The question of subjectivity takes a central place in this debate, for experience seems to offer the last available foothold for naive realism. Poststructuralist and new-historical criticisms of the western belief in an immanent, present subject and the coherent reality within which that subject moves not only present the truth-value of oral and written texts as doubtful, but also question the very possibility of locating the "truth." Perhaps the intense interest in autobiography and life-history within the social sciences as well as the humanities in the past fifteen years is a reaction to these criticisms, for autobiography appears to offer incontrovertible evidence of selfhood and a truth validated by experience.[28] As a genre purporting to communicate "true" experiences, autobiography apparently participates in this untenable western myth of metaphysical presence. In a sense, of course, autobiography has been an important vehicle for this "myth."[29] In another sense, the genre demolishes the myth even when it serves it, for by definition, it offers a record of self-invention that controverts the myth of immanent self.

Some theorists of autobiography have argued quite explicitly that reality is constructed, thus autobiography cannot represent empirical fact. The belief that autobiography

> remains in essence the record of a self with its own autonomous existence . . . must seem a naive sort of empiricism, assuming as it does a realm of 'fact' that is independent of description. . . . Facts are never "bare": they are the trajectory of the questions with which one began and the needs which initiated the inquiry. It is not simply a matter of impurities. Observation would be impossible without some initial guide for recognizing similarities and significance. Lacking an informing interest or intention, experience is chaotic and data are meaningless. Categories are the prior condition of perception and knowledge, not the natural outgrowth of experience.[30]

Bruss' "constructionist" position is that of most anthropologists, who assume that wider cultural patterns shape the trajectory of an individual life. The focus on a typical life-cycle as the pattern of individual experience so common to ethnographic writing depicts other societies convincingly only if we accept this assumption. Clearly, most individuals are socialized so that they may not even realize that they conceive their experience in terms of well-established cultural models. Consequently, some of the recent scholarly discussion of the dramaturgical theory of self-presentation has taken sincerity to be the crucial problem, following Victor Turner and Erving Goffman, who distinguish a performed self from a "real" self. This is simply another version of the same problem of metaphysics.

In contrast to humanist theories of autobiography, however, the dramaturgical theory assumes that sincerity is practically impossible, for even individuals who believe in norms do so naively. Less skeptical than Goffman, Abu-Lughod believes that social agents have real choice in these matters. In her view, a purely dramaturgical view not only misinterprets the importance of moral values, but also misinterprets the meaning of social conformity. She claims that individuals in the Egyptian community of the Awlad 'Ali "perceive the moral standards less as norms than as values; therefore, it is a matter of self-respect and pride that the individual achieve the standards, not an obligation."[31] In other words, we also choose to believe certain truths rather than others.

The distinction matters in the context of *taasu* performances because performers often criticize specific behavior. Since the audience is full of witnesses, the performance will not be effective as a tool for negotiation if no one believes the performer's claims. In addition, the performer's claim on the patron depends on her ability to stir his/her sympathy, as well as on long-established ties. Furthermore, the *taasu* often serves as a form of verbal self-defense, as Ngoné Mbaay's *taasu*, "Loo làkkale," demonstrates. These are traits that the *taasu* shares with written autobiographies, for as Eakin notes, "autobiography not only records an imaginative coming-to-terms with history, it functions itself as the instrument of this negotiation."[32] At bottom, conceptualizing truth as a matter for negotiation means recognizing the limitations of language as a tool for telling the truth.

The problems central to anthropological theories of self-representation thus parallel those familiar to students of autobiography. The problematic relationship between reference and sincerity recurs in studies of autobiography, but with a difference. Many of the most influential theories of the genre have been embedded in theories of reader response or reception theory. Rather than referring to an abstract social code or charter that stands outside of the text in order to anchor a textual interpretation, reader-response critics often view the text itself as a variable, fluid artefact that shifts slightly depending on the factors that affect each reading experience. Interpretation, then, involves the negotiation of meaning. Whether we are interpreting a social text or a literary text, we must be prepared to bargain for a kind of truth.[33]

CONTINGENCY AND CONVERGENCE

Negotiating truth also means recognizing another's pain in a meaningful way. In Senegal, this is now particularly necessary in light of the political conflicts opposing Mauritania and Senegal or the rebels in the Casamance and the government in Dakar. The Moors who dispossessed Anta Bouna Dieng and other refugees justified their actions by claiming historical primacy in the region. Similarly, the ongoing conflict in the Casamance has claimed many victims partly because none of the parties involved can agree on the historical status of that region, even though external authorities, supposed to be neutral, have already pronounced decisions based upon French colonial documents. An acceptable concept of historical truth thus appears to be the condition for furthering human rights in the region.

Unfortunately, scholarly debate thus far seems unlikely to offer many clear answers to the questions this situation presents. Given the blurring of genres and of truths that has followed in the wake of a popularized version of indeterminacy, the very concept of truth-value seems likely to disappear into the vagueness of literature (an undefined concept) and ideology. In fact, many scholars claim that truth is always already ideological. Feminist thinkers such as Michèle Barrett and Leigh Gilmore make a particularly strong case for an ideological notion of truth-value.[34] While it is true that all truths are political, it is necessary to distinguish politics from ideology in this discussion. In her work on theories of double-consciousness, Sandra Adell draws upon Hannah Arendt's theories to explain that some feminist scholars may ignore gender itself at times because of the ideologies that led many of them to the field of feminist studies in the first place. This happens when "everything is interpreted, explained, and comprehended from one single premise."[35] Arendt's work has demonstrated that this characteristic defines totalitarian ideologies. Ideology may thus reduce the awareness of competing perspectives or truths. Politics, on the other hand, always includes negotiation of power with others. It assumes that truths exist in competition.

Theories of postcolonialism, cultural studies, feminist theory, and, indeed, most of the scholarly work on so-called "marginal" communities are predicated on political truths, for scholars in these fields endeavor to recuperate and present the truths that the hegemonic majority (male, white, western, heterosexual, etc.) either fails to see or refuses to see. These truths can cross the borders of ideologically constructed subject positions, for we can *share* experiences. The power of the texts (autobiographical or not) created in order to express "subaltern truths"[36] depends upon this possibility for border-crossing.

This has obvious implications for cross-cultural scholarship. The kind of interdisciplinary work that has been the hallmark of African studies since its inception also demands a willingness to negotiate and rethink current boundaries and paradigms. As Appiah claims, such negotiations require an understanding of the contingency of values.[37] If we recognize the contingency of values, equal respect for all cultures should follow; however, recognition of the contingency of values alone cannot lead to true respect for unfamiliar discourses, according to Charles Taylor.

> For a culture sufficiently different from our own, we may have only the foggiest idea *ex ante* of what its valuable contribution might consist. Because, for a sufficiently different culture, the very understanding of what it is to be of worth will be strange and unfamiliar to us. To approach, say, a raga with the presumptions of value implicit in the well-tempered clavier would be forever to miss the point. What has to happen is what Gadamer has called a "fusion of horizons." We learn to move in a broader horizon, within which what we have formerly taken for granted as the background to valuation can be situated as one possibility along the different background of the formerly unfamiliar culture. The "fusion of horizons" operates through our developing new vocabularies of comparison, by means of which we can articulate these contrasts. So that if and when we ultimately find substantive support for our initial presumption, it is on the basis of an understanding of what constitutes worth that we couldn't possibly have had at the beginning. We have reached the judgment partly through transforming our standards.[38]

Such a fusion of horizons provides the necessary space for meaningful dialogue. Creating such spaces is the true goal of cross-cultural, cross-disciplinary scholarship. Merging horizons of value implies merging differing standards of truth-value in scholarship as well. Since different disciplines define the "truth" that scholarly research is supposed to purvey according to different standards, interdisciplinary work that seeks to combine different disciplines may find it necessary to engage in the kind of intellectual exchange that leads to a fusion of disciplinary horizons as well as a fusion of interpretive horizons.

In attempting to reach a "fusion of critical horizons," I have characterized a cross-section of performances of the *taasu* as autobiographical discourse. The term *taasu* cannot be translated as autobiography, and covers texts that belong to several different genres, from a western perspective. My use of a western generic term to interpret and analyze this cross-section does not mark an attempt to subsume a wholly different system of generic classification or the particular genre of *taasu* under a familiar rubric. It is my hope that this usage marks the site of an interdisciplinary exchange that will transform how audiences and critics view both *taasu* and autobiography.

The convergences I have outlined in this study seem all the more important to me in light of the issues raised in the first part of this chapter. Cross-cultural exchanges hold the power to transform the disciplinary and generic boundaries that make judgments of truth-value possible. As Clifford Geertz has suggested,[39] blurring genres across disciplines and across cultures might actually sharpen our vision. The resulting convergences might then allow us to see our Others as thinkers whose perspectives deserve the same critical regard that we too often reserve for those critics who work within a western theoretical framework. Negotiating truth-values cross-culturally is a necessary part of the process of this form of exchange, but does not require us to sacrifice the notion of truth itself. Indeed, exchange requires more, not less critical thinking. No single subject position offers a view of the final "truth." Indeed, we may hesitate before seeking the final truth, since its most memorable twentieth-century formulation was Hitler's "final solution."

POST-FACE

Selfish Gifts

This very literary study attempts to address key issues of representation, gendered subjectivity, and identity. In my desire to *know*, I have been forced to seek in many places. Some critics might equate this desire with actual resistance. Rebellion represents the "authentic" critical encounter to Jane Gallop, for we then "experience not only the object's force but equally our own powerful drive to understand, to possess, that which moves us so intensely."[1] Conversely, "knowledge that has lost the truth of its roots in desire and aggression is in its very objectivity a lie."[2] This open acceptance of critical desire and need offers a much-needed antidote to a false objectivism.

Nevertheless, it seems reductionist to me to see critical reactions only as so many rebellions against resisting texts. Senegalese women's autobiographical discourses neither move me to seek mastery over "the mute object," nor do they move me to aggressive rebellion. Although I agree with Gallop that critical practice risks becoming a mere conceit unless it is predicated on a genuine desire for understanding, autobiographical discourses offer a theoretical alternative to critical assault. As I have argued throughout this study, the autobiographical act is an invitation to exchange. Exchanges take place in a very concrete way in the *taasu* performance; however, they also take place in the world of writing.

> In the specular reciprocity of the world of autobiography the author as reader is matched by the reader as author, for the reader's involvement in authorial consciousness, which seems to be intrinsic to the functioning of the autobiographical text, is ultimately self-referential; readers, perhaps especially critics, are potentially autobiographers themselves.[3]

The desire for understanding does not always imply a need to master the text; it may signify a need for reciprocal exchange across disciplines, cultures, languages and media. This study is the fruit of such boundary-crossings. I have chosen to draw upon several disciplines in order to formulate new questions and solutions to problems central to literary studies.

CHANGING COLORS

The need for a model of criticism and theory based on exchange and translation is particularly pressing in the field of postcolonial studies.

147

Given the broad range of cultures and literary traditions that scholars from many different subject positions have begun to address and compare as the Eurocentric canon of knowledge has been cracked open to receive other knowledges and esthetics, Gallop's model of aggressive criticism no longer seems empowering (as she clearly intends it to be), but dangerous to both the peoples of the postcolonial world and to the critics who seek to make honest and ethical contributions.

As I observed in the pre-face, my identity as a white westerner has had a real significance during the long process from research proposal to published text. As Frantz Fanon has shown us with great eloquence, the inverted image of the Other that we see in another's gaze is really our own. My experience does not escape this rule. This is why the obstacle that led to so many misunderstandings—my identity as a white, western researcher—also led to the perspectives on autobiography as exchange presented in this book. Yet identities are rarely stable, as the individual depends upon the community, and vice versa. As Chinua Achebe teaches us, the individual and the community exist in dialogue, a form of exchange. The dialectic that founds the relationships between individual and community varies across cultures, yet human society is "inconceivable" without it.[4]

This intersubjective model of identity informs my project, which involved the work of establishing a dialogue with another community, and thus the reconfiguration of my notions of individuality and individual identity. In this sense, an intersubjective approach goes beyond the banality of remarking that fieldwork teaches us more about the researcher's culture than it does about other cultures. Fieldwork is so difficult because it requires change on the most personal of levels. In other words, we can only learn about the Other by becoming strangers to ourselves, as the title of Julia Kristeva's book suggests.[5]

Of course, this approach has limitations. Theories of multiculturalism and Afrocentricity that question the role of the white researcher who undertakes research in Africa or the African Diaspora effectively highlight these limitations. In a recent article, Mineke Schipper (a white, European scholar of African literatures) addresses this issue with reference to the widely known proverb, "However long the tree trunk lies in the water, it never becomes a crocodile." Schipper interprets the proverb as a way of stifling diversity by dividing the world into us and them.[6]

Certainly, this proverb can be interpreted in this way, as proverbs depend on context for meaning; however, the proverb also tells us an undeniable truth. White researchers working on African or Diaspora literatures do not have the same kind of relationships, nor the same kind of access, to the relevant communities that our African or African-American counterparts enjoy as part of their birthright. In short, researchers cannot change their colors. Yet recognition of the importance of the researcher's social identity need not negate the value of her research; rather, it may lead to a renewed sense of the importance of multiplying the perspectives available on, say, Wolof verbal arts. Such a view contrasts sharply with an earlier paradigm, when some anthropologists took a proprietary view toward "their" cultures because they happened to be the only westerner to have conducted fieldwork there. In rejecting this paradigm, we might open the way to new forms of cultural exchange.

The process of translation offers a felicitous metaphor for forms of cultural exchange that are not based on possession, but on sharing. Translations inevitably transform the original text, yet they also enlarge the horizons of the text's host culture and language. Such translations are necessary if we are to overcome the parochialism and ethnocentrism that Henry Louis Gates decries. He writes that

> the central questions asked in Western critical discourse have been asked, and answered, in other textual traditions as well. The Eurocentric bias presupposed in the ways terms such as *canon, literary theory,* or *comparative literature* have been utilized is a culturally hegemonic bias, a bias that the study of literature could best do without. Europeans and Americans neither invented literature and its theory nor have a monopoly on its development.[7]

Rather than attempting to assimilate and erase difference, the kind of intellectual exchange that Gates proposes in *The Signifying Monkey* offers a model for efforts toward creating a larger intellectual community.[8] This study, too, represents an attempt to translate the literary terms of one culture into those of another. I hope that this "translation" will give African discourses greater influence on western notions of autobiography. As Gates argues, we cannot understand literary theory solely as a product of western cultures, for it is a vital function of verbal performance itself.

Such a notion of expanded literary borders may be the only solution to the trap Paulin Hountondji describes when he warns that the western researcher, consciously or unconsciously, plays an imperialist role simply because of the social structures and global inequalities that currently define knowledge production. "Fieldwork" can imply a search for raw materials to be refined in order to produce the end product of another western theory based on African raw materials.[9] Clearly, knowledge production according to this model repeats (neo)colonial use of African raw materials in industrial production. It is my hope that we will be able to contruct another model, one based on exchange and translation. In this context, the military metaphor of changing colors to indicate changed loyalties might shift toward the Senegalese esthetic of *njaxas*, or patchwork cloth, far more colorful and variegated than the stark contrast of military colors.

SELFISH GIFTS

I have discussed fieldwork problems at length because they resemble those of the autobiographer. She, too, must create and perform a new persona or personae as an adult. This process actively involves others, for in constructing a textual self or selves, the autobiographer must also imagine an audience or the responses of the audience before her. The implied audience of autobiographical discourse thus draws the outlines of autobiographical selves. Authorial function then collapses into an overpowering but chimerical autobiographical figure that is created through exchanges that take place between autobiographer and audience.

Possessive individualism cannot serve here as an explanation for the individual's identity, as autobiography presents us with the knowledge that we cannot own what seems most our own—our lives. The autobiographer generously offers us the gift of her life. However, the gift demands reciprocation, for gifts signify exchange, rather than gratuity. The title of this study, *Selfish Gifts*, attempts to encapsulate this notion. An autobiographer will not offer her most precious gift—that is, her life—without good reason. Frequently, she does so because of significant life crises. Moreover, the gift of the self is always a selfish gift, for it demands reciprocity. The pact that links autobiographer and audience, then, clearly roots itself in concrete experiences of giving and receiving gifts.

Knowledge production also depends upon exchange. For this reason, and to honor the Senegalese who made this study possible, I must share what I have learned, translating their words and my experience into this text. Sharing their words thus means sharing a part of myself, for I can only reflect upon what I have learned through the mirrors of memory and personal experience. In a very real way, this, and perhaps all literary analyses, are not only translations, but also autobiographical acts. I accept these human limitations on scholarship, for they offer unexpected gifts of insight. True gifts are selfish gifts—gifts of the self that seek a response.

As reader and researcher, I have given much of myself in order to respond to Senegalese women's invitations to join the autobiographical exchange. These gifts of the self have been selfish, for the exchange has satisfied some, if not all, of my critical desire to know more about these discourses. Paradoxically, self-ish gifts may be more genuine than those offered out of a gratuitous altruism that does not distinguish one person from another. Derrida and others argue that the need to reciprocate negates the gift; however, I see the self-ish gift as an invitation to further exchange and interaction. It is my hope that this particular self-ish gift will invite readers to share my passionate interest in Senegalese women's autobiographical acts.

NOTES

PRE-FACE

1. Michael Jackson, *Paths toward a Clearing: Radical Empiricism and Ethnographical Inquiry* (Bloomington: Indiana UP, 1989).

2. Or the observer may become an object under observation, with interesting repercussions; for a thorough discussion of the issue, see Michel Serres, *Hermès IV: La distribution* (Paris: Minuit, 1977): 271ff.

3. Sylvia Ardyn Boone, *Radiance from the Waters: Ideals of Feminine Beauty in Mende Art* (New Haven: Yale UP, 1986).

4. Such definitions neatly make it almost impossible to value art in market terms, founding an ideology that cheapens or even devalues certain forms, in practical terms, by offering them at little cost to consumers who often evaluate products according to cost.

5. Veit Erlmann writes that it took some time before he realized that musicians expected to receive *gifts*, rather than payment. "Dieses Beschenken ermöglichte aber dann auch erst, daß die Musikproduzenten ihrerseits ihre rollenspezifischen Verhaltensmuster demonstrieren konnten." [This giving, however, also made it possible for the first time for music producers to demonstrate the behavior pattern specific to their role.] Veit Erlmann, *Die Macht des Wortes: Preisgesang und Berufsmusiker bei den Fulße des Diamaré (Nordkamerun)* (Hohenschäftlarn: Klaus Renner Vlg., 1980): 5. My translation.

6. Boone is African-American. In addition, her problem was unrelated to her status as an outsider to the community; the problem of secrecy described in her book affects Mende researchers as well.

7. Maivân Clech Lâm, "Feeling Foreign in Feminism," *Signs* 19.4 (1994): 876. Lâm notes two possibilities: an inability to accept gifts, for they imply subordination, and some colonialists' inability to reciprocate, for they saw gifts as tribute.

8. Johannes Fabian, "Ethnographic Misunderstanding and the Perils of Context," *American Anthropologist* 97.1 (1995): 41–50.

9. Catherine N'Diaye, *Gens de sable* (Paris: P.O.L., 1984): 34–35. For another interesting discussion of the topic, see Abena Busia, "Performance, Transcription and the Languages of the Self: Interrogating Identity as a "Post-Colonial" Poet," *Theorizing Black Feminisms: The Visionary Pragmatism of Black Women*, eds. Stanlie M. James and Abena P. A. Busia (London: Routledge, 1993): 203–13.

10. Deborah Heath, *The Politics of Signifying Practice in Kaolack, Senegal: Hegemony and the Dialectic of Autonomy and Domination* (Diss. Johns Hopkins U, 1988): 129.

11. The *boubou* is a voluminous, caftan-like garment worn by both men and women in West Africa.

12. Judith Butler, *Gender Trouble: Feminism and the Subversion of Identity* (New York: Routledge, 1990): 25.

13. See especially Pat Caplan, "Spirits and Sex: A Swahili Informant and His Diary,"*Anthropology and Autobiography*, eds. Judith Okely and Helen Callaway (London: Routledge, 1992): 64–82.

14. Butler, *Gender Trouble*, 51.

15. Judith Okely, "Anthropology and Autobiography: Participatory Experience and Embodied Knowledge," *Anthropology and Autobiography*, eds. Judith Okely and Helen Callaway (London: Routledge, 1992): 16.

16. Lila Abu-Lughod,*Veiled Sentiments: Honor and Poetry in a Bedouin Society* (Berkeley: U of California P): 18.

17. As I have noted, Senegalese are highly aware of racial politics, thus my racial category clearly marked my efforts to fit in as performances.

18. Paris: Harmattan, 1991. Mouralis wrote the foreword. Feminists criticized this ethnocentrism earlier in the context of their critique of male-centered studies of autobiography. See Estelle C. Jelinek, *The Tradition of Women's Autobiography: From Antiquity to the Present* (Boston: Twayne, 1986) for a brief discussion of Egyptian funerary epitaphs as autobiography. She also mentions Asian autobiographical works.

19. Amadou Koné, "Tradition orale et écriture du roman autobiographique: L'exemple de Camara Laye," *Autobiographical Genres in Africa/Genres autobiographiques en Afrique: Actes du 6e Symposium international Janheinz Jahn*, eds. János Riesz and Ulla Schild (Berlin: Dietrich Reiner, 1996): 53–64.

20. Edward Saïd, Introduction, *Culture and Imperialism* (New York: Vintage Books, 1994): xx.

21. Leroy Vail and Landeg White, *Power and the Praise Poem: Southern African Voices in History* (Charlottesville: U of Virginia P, 1992).

22. There is nothing artless about oral performance, as Charles Briggs argues in the following passage from *Competence in Performance: The Creativity of Tradition in Mexicano Verbal Art* (Philadelphia: U of Pennsylvania P, 1988): "Performers do not simply 'reflect' the natural and cultural world around them, unconsciously replicating structures of which they have no understanding. . . . The performer draws on these resources as needed, selecting those elements that prove relevant to the purpose at hand" (18).

23. Samba Diop, for example, briefly notes that some scholars redefine writing as inscription, yet he seems to define writing in the traditionally narrow sense of the word for the most part. Samba Diop, *The Oral History and Literature of the Wolof People of Waalo, Northern Senegal. The Master of the Word (Griot) in the Wolof Tradition* (African Studies vol. 6. Lewiston: Edwin Mellen Press, 1995): 277–90.

24. Harold Scheub, "Review of African Oral Traditions and Literature," *African Studies Review* 28 (1985): 1.

25. Alain Ricard, "Histoire d'âmes et autobiographie au Zaïre," *Littératures autobiographiques de la francophonie*, ed. Martine Mathieu (Paris: L'Harmattan, 1996): 139.

CHAPTER 1. AUTOBIOGRAPHICAL SUBJECTS

1. The full text is presented in chapter 7. Parts of this chapter were published in an article entitled "Autobiographical Subjects," *Research in African Literatures* 28.2 (1997): 83–101.

2. I particularly wish to stress that Anta Dieng created this poem. Much of the early literature on oral performance genres ignores the individual creator or even describes all oral works as collective products. Although this *taasu* performance clearly depended on group participation in a chorus, Anta Dieng was the individual agent behind the performance.

3. Fredric Jameson, "Third-World Literature in the Era of Multinational Capitalism," *Social Text* 15 (1986): 69.

4. Lila Abu-Lughod, *Writing Women's Worlds: Bedouin Stories* (Berkeley: U of California P, 1993): 7.

5. Jacqueline Rabain, *L'enfant du lignage: Du sévrage à la classe d'âge chez les Wolof du Sénégal* (Paris: Payot, 1979): 36.

6. Paul John Eakin, *Fictions in Autobiography: Studies in the Art of Self-Invention* (Princeton: Princeton UP, 1985).

7. James Olney, "Autobiography and the Cultural Moment: A Thematic, Historical and Bibliographical Introduction," *Autobiography: Essays Theoretical and Critical*, ed. James Olney (Princeton: Princeton UP, 1980): 8–9.

8. Georges Gusdorf, "Conditions and Limits of Autobiography," *Autobiography: Essays Theoretical and Critical*, ed. James Olney (Princeton: Princeton UP, 1980): 29.

9. James Olney, *Tell Me Africa: An Approach to African Literature* (Princeton: Princeton UP, 1973).

10. Olney, *Tell Me*, 39–40.

11. Olney, *Tell Me*, 53–54.

12. Olney, *Tell Me*, 58–59.

13. Honorat Aguessy, "Visions et perceptions traditionnelles," *Introduction à la culture africaine* (Paris: Unesco, 1977): 158–59.

14. János Riesz, "Autobiographische Gattungen in Afrika und Europa: Historische Einbindung und Vision eines anderen Lebens," *Koloniale Mythen— Afrikanische Antworten,* Europäisch-afrikanische Literaturbeziehungen I. (Frankfurt a.M.: Vlg. für interkulturelle Kommunikation, 1993): 265–66.

15. Jean-Jacques Rousseau, *Du contrat social* (Paris: Garnier-Flammarion, 1966).

16. Philippe Lejeune, *On Autobiography,* ed. Paul John Eakin and trans. Katherine Leary (Minneapolis: U of Minnesota P, 1989): 11.

17. In particular, see Jacques Derrida, *De la grammatologie* (Paris: Minuit, 1967) for a rereading of Rousseau's theory of the social contract.

18. Social norms create biologically differentiated groups, according to many anthropologists and feminists. Sex and race are not natural categories, but socially constructed ones, according to these thinkers. The problem of another "natural" group—the family—provokes similar paradoxical situations. Critiques of social contract theory, from Engels to Pateman, have often focused on this paradox.

19. See Michel Foucault's essay "What Is an Author?" *Foucault Reader*, ed. Paul Rabinow (New York: Pantheon Books, 1984): 101–20.

20. bell hooks, *Black Looks: Blacks and Representation* (Boston: South End Press, 1992) and Henry Louis Gates, "The Master's Pieces: On Canon Formation and the African-American Tradition," *Loose Canons: Notes on the Culture Wars* (Oxford: Oxford UP, 1992): 34–38.

21. *The Alchemy of Race and Rights* (Cambridge, Mass.: Harvard UP, 1991).

22. Peter Ekeh, "Colonialism and the Two Publics in Africa: A Theoretical Statement," *Comparative Studies in Society and History* 17.1 (1975): 91–112.

23. Michael Sprinker, "The End of Autobiography," *Autobiography: Essays Theoretical and Critical*, ed. James Olney (Princeton: Princeton UP, 1980): 142.

24. Paul John Eakin, *Touching the World: Reference in Autobiography* (Princeton: Princeton UP, 1992).

25. Elizabeth Fox-Genovese, *Feminism without Illusions: A Critique of Individualism* (Chapel Hill: U of North Carolina P, 1991): 198.

26. Kéba Mbaye, "L'Afrique et les droits de l'homme," *Revue juridique et politique* 48.1 (Jan.-Apr. 1994): 10.

27. Kéba Mbaye, "L'Afrique et les droits de l'homme," 3.

28. Marilyn Strathern, *The Gender of the Gift: Problems with Women and Problems with Society in Melanesia* (Berkeley: U of California P, 1988): 272.

CHAPTER 2. THE GIFT OF PRAISE

1. Leslie Kurke, *The Traffic in Praise* (Ithaca: Cornell UP, 1991).

2. *Teraanga* is extremely difficult to translate, for it means hospitality, honors, gifts, and the gift-exchanges that are obligatory during events such as name-giving ceremonies.

3. Arame Fal, Rosine Santos, and Jean Léonce Doneux, *Dictionnaire wolof-français* (Paris: Karthala, 1990): 27.

4. Lilyan Kesteloot and Bassirou Dieng have provided a short taxonomy of Wolof oral genres; they briefly define the *taasu* as "Chants d'éloges ou satiriques chantés par des griots en maintes circonstances" [Praise songs or satires sung by griots in many circumstances]. Lilyan Kesteloot and Bassirou Dieng, *Du Tieddo au Talibé: Contes et mythes wolof II* (Paris: Présence Africaine, ACCT and IFAN, 1989): 14. In his otherwise highly useful "Folklore wolof du Sénégal," *Bulletin de l'I.F.A.N.* 37, Série B #4 (1975), Amar Samb does not mention the *taasu*.

5. Chérif Mamadou Thiam, "Introduction à l'étude d'un genre satirico-laudatif: Le taasu wolof" (M.A. thesis, Dakar: UCAD, 1979): 208.

6. Lila Abu-Lughod, *Writing Women's Worlds: Bedouin Stories* (Berkeley: U of California P, 1993): 7.

7. Thiam, Introduction, 144.

8. Mariama Ndoye Mbengue, "Introduction à la littérature orale léboue: Analyse ethno-sociologique et expression littéraire," Thèse de doctorat de

troisième cycle, Université Cheikh Anta Diop de Dakar (UCAD), 1982, and Abdoulaye Kéïta, "Approche ethnolinguistique de la tradition orale wolof (contes et taasu)," Mémoire de maîtrise, UCAD, 1986.

9. Ruth Stone, *Let the Inside Be Sweet: The Interpretation of Music Event among the Kpelle of Liberia* (Bloomington: Indiana UP, 1982): 72.

10. Deborah Heath, "The Politics of Signifying Practice in Kaolack, Senegal: Hegemony and the Dialectic of Autonomy and Domination" (Diss. Johns Hopkins U, 1988): 93.

11. Ndoye, 39.

12. Margaret Thompson Drewal, "The State of Research on Performance in Africa" (Paper prepared for the Joint Committee on African Studies of the American Council of Learned Societies and the Social Science Research Council, 1990): 24.

13. Fall, Pape, "Lekku Ndey: Les dessous d'un commerce lucratif," *Le Soleil* (19 August 1993): 8–9 and Anonymous, "Vers une évolution du mariage sénégalais," *Bulletin de l'"Institut Français de l'Afrique noire* 13 (1951): 542–46.

14. Archives Nationales du Sénégal. Document 11D1.1268. The French gave between 2,000 and 5,000 F for griots at public ceremonies organized in the 1930s, judging from the limited documentation.

15. Marcel Mauss, *The Gift: Forms and Functions of Exchange in Archaic Societies*, trans. Ian Cunnison (New York: Norton, 1967).

16. Emmanuel S. Ndione, *Le don et le recours: Ressorts de l'économie urbaine* (Dakar: ENDA, 1992): 16.

17. Ndione, *Le don*, 17.

18. David W. Ames, "The Rural Wolof of the Gambia," *Markets in Africa*, eds. Paul Bohannon and George Dalton (Evanston: Northwestern UP, 1962): 54.

19. Ndione, *Le don*, 21.

20. Ndione, *Le don*, 63.

21. Arjun Appadurai, "Disjuncture and Difference in the Global Cultural Economy," *Public Culture* 2.2 (1990): 16.

22. Abdoulaye Bara Diop 1981, 185. See also Pathé Diagne, *Pouvoir politique traditionnel en Afrique occidentale* (Paris: Présence Africaine 1967).

23. See Judith T. Irvine, "When Talk Isn't Cheap: Language and Political Economy," *American Ethnologist* 16.2 (1989): 248–60.

24. See Lila Abu-Lughod's *Veiled Sentiments: Honor and Poetry in a Bedouin Society* (Berkeley: U of California P, 1986) for a fascinating study of the way poetry allows Egyptian Bedouins the possibility of expressing sentiments that would otherwise be unacceptable in light of the reigning social values.

25. Wolof *géwël* (griot) families were once tied to specific noble families, thus nobles may speak of their *géwël u júddoo*. These are *géwël* whose family specialized in praising a particular noble family. In some ways, these *géwël* become almost a subclan of the noble family. As A.B. Diop has noted in *La société wolof*, intercaste marriages most often take place between *géwël* and nobles because of this.

26. *Kel* is a very hard, rigid wood.

27. The Baay Fall are Mourides, followers of Cheikh Amadou Bamba. However, they adhere to the code set by Bamba's fervent disciple Cheikh Ibra

Fall, whose extremism led Bamba to give him certain dispensations (notably, from the duties to pray five times daily, abstain from alcohol and pork, and to fast during Ramadan). In exchange, the Baay Fall make work their prayer. However, many now beg or perform religious songs. See Neil J. Savishinsky, "The Baye Faal of Senegambia: Muslim Rastas in the Promised Land?" *Africa* 64.2 (1994): 211–19.

28. According to Qu'uranic law. Wolof society now only shows vestiges of the matrilineal side of the former system of double-descent (Wright, 44), thus men are normally responsible for the needs of the family.

29. Diop, 1985, 181.

30. For further information on the role of the *njëkke*, see Abdoulaye Baara Diop. *La famille wolof: Tradition et changement* (Paris: Karthala, 1985): 39, 72–73.

31. This probably refers to the family delegation who visited her family to ask for her hand in marriage.

32. This formula is much more optimistic than the widely used proverb, "Bant bu dëng, kenn mëna ko jubal" [Nobody can straighten the crooked branch]. I have heard this proverb used in order to compare a crooked or vicious person to a crooked branch—you cannot straighten it without breaking it. In other words, the truly "crooked" can never take the straight and narrow. This idea is in keeping with the concept that one's character is innate and related to one's caste status.

33. This is an onomotopeia signifying the sound of laughter.

34. Usually, *gaaruwaale* are indirect, veiled attacks. The intensity of the conflict in Fatou's household can be inferred from the directness of the criticisms.

35. Karl Polanyi, *The Great Transformation* (New York: Farrar & Rinehart, 1944): 75. According to Polanyi, this is a constant in *all* types of economies.

36. Bonnie Wright, "The Power of Articulation," *Creativity of Power: Cosmology and Action in African Societies,* eds. W. Arens and Ivan Karp (Washington, D.C.: Smithsonian Institution Press, 1989): 39.

CHAPTER 3. PANEGYRICS

1. The *géwël* caste is one of the most complex, as the many specialized forms of entertainers are ranked and named differently. The *mbàndkat* were once buffoons, clowns, and acrobats; however, after the French did away with the kingdoms of Waalo, Jolof, Kajoor-Baol, and Siin-Saalum, the distinctions between specialist *géwël* seem to have lost some of their importance. One of the current male stars who performs *taasu*, Abdou Ndiaye, is *mbàndkatt*. Although he is a comic performer, one cannot, however, typecast him as a *mbàndkatt*.

2. Judith Irvine, "Caste and Communication in a Wolof Village" (Diss., U. of Pennsylvania, 1974), and Abdoulaye Bara Diop, *La société wolof.*

3. Irvine, "Caste," 146–47.

4. The *géwël u juddu* is the "hereditary griot." That is to say, her family has been attached to that of her noble patron for generations. See Abdoulaye Bara Diop (1980) for a detailed discussion of this concept.

5. For a brief analysis of the origins and current social roles of the Laobé, see Cheikh Anta Diop, *L'Afrique noire pré-coloniale* (Paris: Présence Africaine, 1960): 164–65. Diop insists on Laobé ethnic particularism, but notes that some observers have considered them to be simply another caste. This backs my point that markers of caste and ethnicity change over time.

6. In response to the popular attitude of disdain, the Laobé have formed an effective political pressure group, the Union Nationale Coopérative des Laobés du Sénégal.

7. Interviews: Njañ, 5/23/93; Fatou Dioum. St. Louis, 7/10/93, Degen Dioum; Louga, 5/26/93, Fatou Sow.

8. Ndoye, 28.

9. Mame Rokhaya Diouf, 4/20/93.

10. St. Louis (Pikine), 11/18/93.

11. bell hooks, *Black Looks: Race and Representation*. South Hadley, MA: 1990.

12. The interpretation of Wolof social structure that Diop and Irvine present as most prevalent is marked by a belief that "personality is inheritable; personality differences will, therefore, follow the lines of caste endogamy." Judith Irvine, "Caste," 126.

13. Irvine, "Caste," 131.

14. For a different analysis of power relationships in Senegal that also relies on Bakhtin, see Deborah Heath (1988, 1994). Although Heath also draws upon Voloshinov and Bakhtin to interpret the Wolof, she neglects the aspects of Bakhtin's theory that I have chosen to emphasize.

15. Mikhail Bakhtin, "Discourse in the Novel," *The Dialogic Imagination*, trans. Caryl Emerson and Michael Holquist (Austin: U of Texas P, 1981): 342.

16. For further information, see Stéphane Robert, *Approche énonciative du système verbal: Le cas du Wolof* (Paris: Editions du CNRS, 1991): 117–48.

17. This transcription is obviously problematic, since it is not consistent. In addition, the accepted standards of transcription have changed since Thiam wrote his thesis, thus many of the diacritical marks do not follow the form of the other transcriptions that I give. Given the great expense of hiring transcribers for the texts I collected myself, I made the purely practical decision to use this transcription.

18. Wrappers of *dënk* and *Njor* are made of expensive, locally produced woven cotton fabrics of high quality.

19. *Kaar* is a formula that Wolof use to avert bad luck or *cat*, malicious gossip. Since Mbaay here details her former wealth, she fears that she will bear the brunt of jealous gossip or ill fortune because of her pride.

20. This detail is used to prove that Mbaay is an excellent housewife who works extra hard to please her husband.

21. See Abdoulaye Baara Diop. *La famille wolof: Tradition et changement* (Paris: Karthala, 1985): 185. "Les Wolof sont plus facilement polygames que les autres ethnies" [The Wolof are more likely to be polygamous than other ethnic groups]. Some 66.7 percent of married women have co-wives.

22. Diop 1985, 197, "*Sagoy jigéen mooy wujj wu dee ci ngóópté .*"

23. For a critique of such homologies, see Fredric Jameson, *The Political Unconscious: Narrative as a Socially Symbolic Act* (Ithaca: Cornell UP, 1981): 44ff.

24. Ruth Finnegan, *Oral Literature in Africa* (Oxford: Clarendon Press, 1970): 116.

25. Isidore Okpewho, *African Oral Literature: Backgrounds, Character, and Continuity* (Bloomington: Indiana UP, 1992): 143–44.

26. E. Casalis quoted in M. Demane and P. B. Sanders, *Lithoko: Sotho Praise Poems* (Oxford: Clarendon Press, 1974): 18.

27. Demane and Sanders 18.

28. Demane and Sanders 18.

29. G. P. Lestrade, "Traditional Literature," *The Bantu-Speaking Tribes of South Africa*, ed. I. Schapera (London: Routledge, 1937): 291–308.

30. I. Schapera, *Praise-Poems of Tswana Chiefs* (Oxford: Clarendon Press, 1965): 2.

31. Elizabeth Gunner, "Songs of Innocence and Experience: Women as Composers and Performers of *Izibongo*, Zulu Praise Poetry," *Women and Writing in South Africa: A Critical Anthology*, ed. Cherry Clayton (London: Heinemann, [1979] 1989): 12–39.

32. Joseph Nsengimana, "*Ukwivuga* (Parler de soi-même), genre autobiographique rwandais," *Genres autobiographiques en Afrique/Autobiographical Genres in Africa*, eds. János Riesz and Ulla Schild (Berlin: Dietrich Reimer, 1996): 39–52.

33. Y. I. Rubanza, *Fasihi Simulizi: Majigambo (Ebyebugo)* (Dar-es-Salaam: Dar-es-Salaam UP, 1994): 12. My translation. For a good example, see Rubanza, 12–13.

34. Karin Barber, *I Could Speak until Tomorrow: Oriki, Women and the Past in a Yoruba* Town (Washington D.C.: Smithsonian Institute, 1991): 110–11.

CHAPTER 4. GENRE AND GENDER IN THE AUTOBIOGRAPHICAL EXCHANGE

1. *Teraanga* also means hospitality.

2. Fatou Sow, "Femmes, socialité et valeurs africaines," *Notes africaines* 168 (1980): 108.

3. Usually, men perform *taasu* for comic effect; for example, the male members of the popular group Lemzo Diamono, dressed as women, performed *taasu* in a 1997 music video. This is the traditional role of men like the professional buffoons, or *mbàndkatt*, who perform *taasu*. Popular musicians (Youssou NDour, Baaba Maal) have also exploited the popularity of rap, incorporating *taasu* in some of their songs.

4. See Sidonie Smith, *A Poetics of Women's Autobiography: Marginality and the Fictions of Self-Representation* (Bloomington: Indiana UP, 1987).

5. Germaine Brée, "Autogynography," *Studies in Autobiography*, ed. James Olney (New York: Oxford UP, 1988): 171–179.

6. Celeste Schenck, "All of a Piece: Women's Poetry and Autobiography," *Life/Lines: Theorizing Women's Autobiography*, eds. Bella Brodzki and Celeste Schenck (Ithaca: Cornell UP, 1988): 291.

7. Many studies of American women's autobiographical poetry have appeared recently. See Carol Muske, *Women and Poetry: Truth, Autobiography, and the Shape of the Self* (Ann Arbor: U of Michigan P, 1997), Carmen Birkle, *Women's Stories of the Looking Glass: Autobiographical Reflections and Self-Representations in the Poetry of Sylvia Plath, Adrienne Rich, and Audre Lorde*, American Studies Monograph Series vol. 72 (Munich: Wilhelm Fink, 1996) and chapter 2 of Jeanne Perreault, *Writing Selves: Contemporary Feminist Autography* (Minneapolis: U of Minnesota P, 1995).

8. James Olney, *Metaphors of the Self: The Meaning of Autobiography* (Princeton: Princeton UP, 1972): 45.

9. James Olney, "Some Versions of Memory/Some Versions of *Bios*: The Ontology of Autobiography," *Autobiography: Essays Theoretical and Critical*, ed. James Olney (Princeton: Princeton UP, 1980): 239.

10. Olney, 1980, 242.

11. If we consider the nuclear structure of most western families, it is clear that women are separated, rather than united in a women's sphere. The image of the suburban housewife comes to mind: she cooks, cleans, and cares for children in isolation. This isolation was one of the primary motivations for Betty Friedan's work.

12. Schenck, 292.

13. Two recent studies offer nuanced views on the importance of motherhood in African literatures—*The Politics of (M) Othering: Womanhood, Identity and Resistance in African Literature*, ed. Obioma Nnaemeka (New York: Routledge, 1997) and Juliana Makuchi Nfah-Abbenyi, *Gender in African Women's Writing: Identity, Sexuality, and Difference* (Bloomington: Indiana UP, 1997). As Nnaemeka and Nfah-Abbenyi argue, motherhood cannot be seen in a hegemonic manner, given the shifting and ambiguous realities of African women's lives.

14. Dorothy Davis Wills, "Economic Violence in Postcolonial Senegal: Noisy Silence in Novels By Mariama Bâ and Aminata Sow Fall," *Violence, Silence and Anger: Women's Writing as Transgression*, ed. Deirdre Lashgari (Charlottesville: U of Virginia P, 1995): 161.

15. In the 1960s, sociological findings indicated that employment opportunities were the primary concern of women in Senegal. Pierre Fougeyrollas, *Où va le Sénégal?* (Paris: Ed. Anthropos, 1970): 117–214, for instance, focuses on this issue in a chapter entitled "Les Sénégalaises." This continues to be the case, according to my informants.

16. Victoria Bernal, "Gender, Culture, and Capitalism: Women and the Remaking of Islamic 'Tradition' in a Sudanese Village," *Comparative Studies in Society and History* 36.1 (1994): 44–45.

17. Barbara Callaway and Lucy Creevey, *The Heritage of Islam: Women, Religion, and Politics in West Africa* (Boulder, Colo.: Lynne Rienner Publishers, 1994): 82.

18. Riss, 96.

19. Bernal, 45.

20. Diop, 1985, 213. Diop found that urban divorce rates were higher than rural rates, and that unrelated couples divorce more frequently than those who have followed cultural prescriptions and married their cross-cousins. Earlier studies, however, show that Wolof communities have long sustained extreme marital mobility. See V. Martin, *Etude socio-démographique de la ville de Dakar* (Paris: Ministère du Plan, 1962), L. Thoré, "Mariage et divorce dans la banlieue de Dakar," *Cahiers d'Etudes Africaines* 16 (1964) and D. W. Ames, *Plural Marriage among the Wolof in the Gambia* (Evanston, Ill.: Northwestern UP, 1953).

21. Marie-Denise Riss, *Femmes africaines en milieu rural: Les Sénégalaises du Sine Saloum* (Paris: L'Harmattan, 1989): 96.

22. Rabain, 226.

23. Kate Modic, "Negotiating Power: A Study of the *Ben Ka Di* Women's Association in Bamako, Mali," *Africa Today* 41.2 (1994): 25–37.

24. Sow, 1980, 108.

25. Heath, 1988 confirms this.

26. Pape Fall, "Lekku Ndey," 7.

27. Heath, 1988, 133.

28. Y. Wane, "Sur une forme de solidarité: Le baptême toucouleur," *Notes Africaines* 97 (1963): 42–46.

29. Wane, 46.

30. "African expressionism sidesteps the necessity of mimesis without having to exclude or deny the reality of the world of things and people and feelings. A Dogon mask is an artifact in wood; the mask, too, is a face or a body, or a bird, with features that clearly bear more than a potential correspondence to some very specific and recognizable forms of reality. It is neither a representation nor a mere impression. It is a statement, not an imitation." Michael Echeruo, "Redefining the Ludic: Mimesis, Expression, and the Festival Mode," *The Play of the Self*, eds. Ronald Bogue and Mihai I. Spariosu (Albany: State U of New York P, 1994): 139.

31. Echeruo, "Redefining the Ludic," 140.

32. Wolof informants treated me as a guest; however, I defined my presence at these events in terms of research. Near the end of my stay, I finally had time to go to events that I did not plan on recording.

33. Used to get rid of a cat, much as "shoo" is used in English to make chickens move.

34. This playful use of the verb "to heap up" also suggests the jal-jali, or waist-beads worn by women who are sexually active and by nubile girls.

35. "Diggu Manding" is a field that has been fertilized by burning undergrowth.

36. Abdu refers to President Abdou Diouf; Elisabeth is his wife. Habib Thiam was the prime minister at the time.

37. The Bamba referred to is Cheikh Amadou Bamba, the founder of Mouridism. Metaphorically, Fatou Sarr Dieng *is* Bamba for the poet, who specifically suggests that she is as just and generous as Bamba.

38. Dakar, 1/12/93.

39. "Baleese" is derived from the French "blesser"—to hurt or wound. Here, it refers to the competition between women giving gifts to gain prestige.

40. *Mbokk* actually refers to the relatives who make up the extended family, but here I believe that "friend" makes more sense in the English translation.

41. See Paul Riesmann's posthumously published *First Find Your Child a Good Mother: The Construction of Self in Two African Communities* (New Brunswick, N.J.: Rutgers UP, 1992).

42. Nnaemeka, *The Politics of (M)Othering*, 5.

43. Sometimes bold women will use similar styles, but men are more likely to make hand gestures indicating the groin area, and often provoke laughter by moving their hips in a movement suggestive of penetration.

44. Strathern, 287. This definition is problematic in light of Strathern's own example of Vanuatuan women who take on male roles in exchange, for it appears to exclude the possibility of creativity in performance.

45. I owe this insightful question to Adolphe Sanon.

46. Johannes Fabian, *Power and Performance: Ethnographic Explorations through Proverbial Wisdom and Theater in Shaba, Zaire* (Madison: U of Wisconsin P, 1990): 13.

47. Margaret Thompson Drewal, *Yoruba Ritual: Performers, Play, Agency* (Bloomington: Indiana UP, 1992): 16.

48. Chérif Thiam, personal communication (Dakar, July 1993).

49. See Gayle Rubin, "The Traffic in Women: Notes on the 'Political Economy' of Sex,"*Toward an Anthropology of Women*, ed. R. Rayner (New York: Monthly Review Press, 1975): 157–210 and Michelle Zimbalist Rosaldo, "Woman, Culture, and Society: A Theoretical Overview,"*Woman, Culture and Society* (Stanford, Calif.: Stanford UP, 1974): 17–42.

50. Jacques Derrida, *Given Time: I. Counterfeit Money*, trans. Peggy Kamuf (Chicago: U of Chicago P, 1992). For another critique, see Paul de Man's essay on Bakhtin, "Dialogue and Dialogism," *The Resistance to Theory* (Minneapolis: U of Minnesota P, 1986): 106–14. In de Man's essay, I see a very pertinent, if different, conceptualization of the same problem. Drawing on a critique of Husserlian phenomenology, de Man perceives the competition that Bakhtin names heteroglossia as a form of imperialistic warfare that makes true dialogism (exchange) impossible. Derrida's Heideggerian argument strikes me as more convincing, for when de Man accuses Bakhtin of "uncritically assimilating the structure of language to the structure of a secure perception," he seems to assume that Bakhtin believed in an ultimate truth-value. Since Bakhtin argued that all truth is ideological, this seems rather unlikely. Nonetheless, I think we might fruitfully interrogate de Man's idea that "we are within a reflective system of *mise en abyme* that is anything but dialogical" with reference to gift exchange *and* to hermeneutics. Although Derrida does not quote de Man on this point, his essay seems to take up the same problem from a Heideggerian vantage that is far more pertinent to performance issues, in my view.

51. Derrida, 1992, 25.

52. *The Hélène Cixous Reader*, ed. Susan Sellers (New York: Routledge, 1994). See chapter 6 for a more detailed discussion of this subject.

53. Barber, *I Could Speak until Tomorrow*, 249.

54. Eakin, *Touching the World*, 99.

55. See Bronislaw Malinowski, *Argonauts of the Western Pacific* (London: Routledge, 1922).

56. I prefer to recall Derrida's notion of the supplement, rather than Lévi-Straussian notions of bricolage. Both are useful, yet Derrida's notion has a liberating power that Lévi-Strauss's additive model lacks. Perhaps my reliance on these concepts will seem suspicious to those who now seek to "go beyond poststructuralism." Ironically, some critics choose to see postcolonial studies as the substitute for a now stale poststructuralism. Given the immense debt postcolonial studies owes to poststructuralism, it seems more likely that this field is a successor to poststructuralism. In my opinion, any attempts to go beyond poststructuralism must inevitably build on the achievements of that once-dominant school of theory.

CHAPTER 5. THE POLITICS OF PRAISE

Parts of this chapter appeared in an article on Nafissatou Diallo in *Post-Colonial African Writers: A Bio-Bibliographical Source Book*. Eds. Pushpa Pareth and Fatou S. Jagne (Westport, Conn.: Greenwood Press, 1998): 123–28.

1. Carole Boyce Davies, "Private Selves and Public Spaces: Autobiography and the African Woman Writer," *Neohelicon* 17.2 (1990): 187.

2. Molara Ogundipe-Leslie and Carole Boyce-Davies, "Women as Oral Artists: Introduction," *Research in African Literatures* 25.3 (1994): 2. This statement must be qualified, for several distinguished researchers have either worked or are working on women's oral performances. Apart from the works cited in this study, we might look to Thomas Hale's research on griottes in Niger, or Beverly Mack's work on Hausa women in Nigeria. Many other scholars have been working in this area as well. Perhaps it would be more accurate to claim that studies of oral performances have yet to receive the attention they deserve. Few universities in North America support folklore institutes, and few literary scholars greet new monographs in that field with the same serious attention that they would the latest work in critical theory.

3. Sharon B. Stichter and Jane L. Parpart, "Introduction: Towards a Materialist Perspective on African Women," *Patriarchy and Class: African Women in the Home and the Workforce* (Boulder: Westview Press, 1988): 23.

4. Ekeh, "Colonialism and the Two Publics in Africa," 91–112.

5. Nfah-Abbenyi gives a good overview of African women's responses to western feminism in chapter 1 of her *Gender in African Women's Writing*. In addition, she promotes greater critical awareness of local discourses on sexuality and women's rights. For a more text-based introduction to the problems facing feminist critique in Africa, see Odile Cazenavè, *Femmes rebelles: Naissance d'un nouveau roman africain au féminin* (Paris: L'Harmattan, 1996).

6. Julien, *African Novels* 47.

7. Charles L. Briggs and Richard Bauman, "Genre, Intertextuality, and Social Power," *Journal of Linguistic Anthropology* 2.2 (1992): 161.

8. Diop and Diouf, *Le Sénégal sous Abdou Diouf*, 251–52. See also pages 16–17 of Linda Beck's article, "Senegal's 'Patrimonial Democrats': Incremental Reform and the Obstacles to the Consolidation of Democracy," *Canadian Journal of African Studies* 31.1 (1997): 1–31, for a discussion of Abdou Diouf's use of ties to marabouts.

9. Quoted in Jean-François Bayart, *The State in Africa: The Politics of the Belly* (London: Longman, 1993): 212.

10. For political scientists' analyses of these elections, see Leonardo Villalón, "Democratizing a (Quasi) Democracy: The Senegalese Elections of 1993," *African Affairs* 93 (1994): 163–93, and Linda Beck, "Senegal's 'Patrimonial Democrats': Incremental Reform and the Obstacles to the Consolidation of Democracy."

11. Africanists have long examined popular performance genres for insight. One of the first classic studies on popular arts and their political importance is J. C. Mitchell, *The Kalela Dance: Aspects of Social Relationships among Urban Africans in Northern Rhodesia* (The Rhodes-Livingstone Papers, no. 27. Manchester, 1956).

12. Ould Taya, a military leader, was the Mauritanian head of state during the events in 1989 which almost led to war between Mauritania and Senegal.

13. Momar Coumba Diop and Mamadou Diouf, *Le Sénégal sous Abdou Diouf: État et société* (Paris: Karthala, 1990). For further information, see *Book of Facts, Conflict with Senegal* (Nouakchott: Islamic Republic of Mauritania, 1989); Durman Daxxel, *Mauritania in Black on White* (Oslo: D. Daxxel, 1989); *Mauritania 1986–1989: Background to a Crisis, Three Years of Political Imprisonment, Torture and Unfair Trials* (New York: Amnesty International, 1989); Ron Parker, "The Senegal-Mauritania Conflict of 1989: A Fragile Equilibrium," *Journal of Modern African Studies* 29.1 (1991): 155–72.

14. Diop and Diouf, 1990, 396.

15. Robert Fatton considers it an example of a successful "passive revolution" because of the transition from a one-party to a multiparty system that took place in 1981. See his "Clientalism and Patronage in Senegal," *African Studies Review* 29 (1986): 61–78.

16. Miller, *Theories*, 260.

17. Gayatri Chakravorty Spivak, "Imperialism and Sexual Difference," *The Oxford Literary Review* 8 (1986): 229.

18. Walter J. Ong, *Orality and Literacy: The Technologizing of the Word* (London: Methuen, 1982): 12–13.

19. Miller, *Theories*, 255.

20. Jack Goody, *The Interface between the Written and the Oral* (Cambridge: Cambridge UP, 1987).

21. John Miles Foley, *The Singer of Tales in Performance* (Bloomington: Indiana UP, 1995): 79.

22. This translation is adequate, for the Wolof also use the image of "holding one's tongue"; however, I want to stress that in Wolof this means knowing how to control one's speech, rather than remaining silent.

23. Literally, "Your leg is short."

24. This word is the key to my argument that the performer has inscribed literacy in French in her performance. In Wolof, "fuy" means "to disrespect" someone; "fou" means "crazy" in French. The performer has used this near-homonymy to indicate that disrespectful behavior is crazy.

25. Gilmore, *Autobiographics*.

26. Julien, *African Novels*, 154.

27. See chapter 6, "Senegalese Women Writers, Silence, and Letters: Before the Canon's Roar" in Christopher Miller, *Theories of Africans*, and Irène Assiba d'Alméïda, *Francophone African Women Writers*. Although these critics discuss oral performance, they are primarily interested in the works of African women writing in European languages.

28. For a sophisticated analysis of gender assumptions behind the "vernacular" model linking literacy to liberation, see Katherine Clay Bassard, "Gender and Genre: Black Women's Autobiography and the Ideology of Literacy," *African American Review* 26.1 (1992): 119–28.

29. Eileen Julien, *African Novels*, 46.

30. Michel Foucault, *The History of Sexuality*, vol. I, trans. Robert Hurley (New York: Vintage, 1990): 139.

31. Lüsebrink, *Schrift*, 236.

32. Lüsebrink, *Schrift*, 50–54.

33. Arlette Chemain-Degrange, *Emancipation féminine et roman africain* (Dakar: Les Nouvelles Editions Africaines, 1980): 112.

34. Christopher Miller, *Blank Darkness: Africanist Discourse in French* (Chicago: U of Chicago P, 1985): 122.

35. The *évolués*, or "evolved" Africans, were supposed to be able to gain French citizenship and its privileges by proving that they had assimilated French culture. Very few requests for citizenship were granted on this basis.

36. For a few examples, see Ousmane Socé, "L'éducation des femmes," *Paris-Dakar* (10 November 1937): 2; Ouezzin Coulibaly, "La colonisation française vue par un indigène évolué. La magnifique aventure des noirs français," *Dakar-Jeunes* 22 (4 June 1942): 3.

37. Denise Bouche, *L'enseignement*, 405.

38. For example, see Governor General Carde's 1924 Circular, in which he writes that it is important to educate women because "par la femme, nous touchons au coeur même du foyer indigène, où pénètre notre influence. 'Quand on s'adresse à l'homme, a dit Saint-Simon, c'est l'individu qu'on instruit. Quand on s'adresse à la femme, c'est une école qu'on fond.'" Reprinted in Denis Turcotte and Hélène Aubé, *Lois, règlements et textes administratifs sur l'usage des langues en Afrique Occidental Française (1826–1959): Répertoire chronologique annoté* (Laval: Presse universitaires de Laval, 1983): 83.

39. Although the first school for girls in Senegal opened in 1819, enrollment declined precipitously after 1880, and never reached the level of boys' enrollment. Bouche, *L'enseignement*, 400.

40. She was born in 1941; Amina Mbaye was born in 1937.

41. Diane Barthel, "Women's Educational Experience Under Colonialism: Toward a Diachronic Model," *Signs* 11.1 (1985): 144, 147.

42. "These men now wished to ensure their class advantage for both sons and daughters, although the education they envisioned for the two sexes was not identical. Their sons, like themselves, would be educated as leaders; their daughters would be educated as wives of leaders, skilled in Western forms of sociability and feminine accomplishments." Barthel, "Women's Educational Experience," 147. Barthel sees this as a "first stage" in women's education.

43. See Ann Laura Stoler, *Race and the Education of Desire: Foucault's History of Sexuality and the Colonial Order of Things* (Durham: Duke UP, 1995).

44. Chemain-Degrange, *Emancipation féminine*, 348.

45. Barthel, "Women's Educational Experience," 139.

46. Barthel, "Women's Educational Experience," 154.

47. Beverley Ormerod and Jean-Marie Volet, "Écrits autobiographiques et engagement: Le Cas des Africaines d'expression française," *French Review* 69.3 (1996): 426–44.

48. Amina Sow Mbaye, *Mademoiselle* (Dakar: Nouvelles Éditions Africaines/EDICEF, 1984): 157.

49. Régine Lambrech, "Three Black Women, Three Autobiographers," *Présence Africaine* 123 (1982): 142.

50. Mary G. Mason, "The Other Voice: Autobiographies of Women Writers," *Autobiography: Essays Theoretical and Critical*, ed. James Olney (Princeton: Princeton UP, 1980): 235.

51. Nafissatou Diallo, *A Dakar Childhood*, trans. Dorothy S. Blair (Harlow: Longman, 1982): 66.

52. Susan Stringer, "Nafissatou Diallo—A Pioneer in Black African Writing." *Continental, Latin-American, and Francophone Women Writers*, Selected Papers From the Wichita State University Conference on Foreign Literature II, 1986–1987, eds. Ginette Adamson and Eunice Myers (Lanham, Md.: UP of America, 1987), *The Senegalese Novel By Women: Through Their Own Eyes* (New York: Peter Lang, 1996).

53. Jean-Marie Volet, *La parole aux Africaines: L'idée du pouvoir chez les romancières d'expression française de l'Afrique sub-Saharienne* (Amsterdam: Rodopi, 1993): 196.

54. Roger Dorsinville, "Vies d'Afrique: Une collection vérité," *Notre Librairie* 81 (1985): 148.

55. Charlotte Bruner, "First Novels of Girlhood," *College Language Association Journal* 31 (1988): 324.

56. Irène Assiba D'Alméïda, *Francophone African Women Writers: Destroying the Emptiness of Silence* (Gainesville: U Presses of Florida, 1994).

57. Carole Boyce Davies, "Private Selves and Public Spaces: Autobiography and the African Woman Writer," *Neohelicon* 17.2 (1990): 188.

58. Trans. Dorothy Blair, ix.

59. Boyce Davies, "Private Selves," 207.

60. Léopold Sédar Senghor, "La jeune fille et le latin," Allocution-Réponse à un Discours de Distribution des Prix, Lycée des Jeunes Filles de Dakar, 26 June 1963, *Liberté I: Négritude et humanisme* (Paris: Seuil, 1964): 438.

61. Stoler, *Education of Desire*, 129.

62. Stoler, *Education of Desire*, 105.

63. Dorsinville, "Vies d'Afrique," 148.

64. Gregory Bateson, *Steps toward an Ecology of Mind* (New York: Chandler Publishing, 1972): 205.

65. Eileen Julien, "Avatars of the Feminine in Laye, Senghor and Diop," *From Dante to García Márquez: Studies in Romance Literatures and Linguistics*, eds. Gene H. Bell-Villada, Antonio Giménez, and George Pistorius (Williamstown, Mass.: Williams College, 1987): 336–48.

66. Vail and White, 1992.

67. Ernest Gellner, *Nations and Nationalism* (Ithaca: Cornell UP, 1983).

68. Christopher Miller, "Nationalism as Resistance and Resistance to Nationalism in the Literature of Francophone Africa," *Yale French Studies* 82 (1993): 90.

69. Ernest Renan, "What is a Nation?" trans. Martin Thom, *Nation and Narration*, ed. Homi Bhabha (London: Routledge, 1990): 16.

70. Richard Bjornson, *The African Quest for Freedom and Identity: Cameroonian Writing and the National Experience* (Bloomington: Indiana UP, 1991): 14.

71. Karin Barber, "Literacy, Improvisation and the Public in Yorùbá Popular Theater," *The Pressures of the Text: Orality, Texts and the Telling of Tales*, ed. Stewart Brown (Birmingham: Centre of West African Studies, University of Birmingham, 1995): 6–27.

CHAPTER 6. ABORTED NATIONS

1. A host of feminist studies springs to mind, as does the work of anthropologist Michael Jackson.

2. Eakin, *Touching the World*, 186, 189.

3. Michel Foucault, "Faire vivre et laisser mourir: La naissance du racisme," *Les temps modernes* 46.535 (1991): 38.

4. See Michel Foucault, *The History of Sexuality*.

5. Foucault, "Faire vivre et laisser mourir," 50.

6. Foucault, "Faire vivre et laisser mourir," 55.

7. Hortense Spillers, "Notes on an Alternative Model—Neither/Nor," *The Difference Within: Feminism and Critical Theory*, eds. Elizabeth Meese and Alice Parker (Amsterdam: John Benjamins, 1989): 168–69.

8. See George Brooks, "The *Signares* of Saint-Louis and Gorée: Women Entrepreneurs in Eighteenth-Century Senegal," *Women in Africa: Studies in Social and Economic Change*, eds. Nancy J. Hafkin and Edna G. Bay (Stanford: Stanford UP, 1976): 19–44.

9. Although French and British colonial systems are frequently depicted as diametrical opposites, the French did not follow a strictly assimilationist policy. Rather, they wavered back and forth between assimilation and association (which implied more cultural freedom but no chance of gaining the rights of French citizens, as Senghor understood). For a clear historical and political contrast of the two, see François Manchuelle, "Assimilés ou patriotes africains?

Naissance du nationalisme culturel en Afrique française (1853–1931)," *Cahiers d'études africaines* 138/139 (1995): 333–68.

10. Abdoulaye Sadji, *Nini, mulâtresse du Sénégal* (Paris: Présence Africaine, 1965): 38–39.

11. Madior Diouf, *Nini mulâtresse du Sénégal: Étude critique*, Collection C.A.E.C./Université 1 (Dakar: Editions Khoudia, 1990): 67.

12. I quote from unpaginated prefatory material.

13. Linda Alcoff, "Mestizo Identity," *American Mixed Race: The Culture of Microdiversity*, ed. Naomi Zack (Lanham, Md.: Rowman & Littlefield, 1995): 264.

14. Paul R. Spickard, *Mixed Blood: Intermarriage and Ethnic Identity in Twentieth-Century America* (Madison: U of Wisconsin P, 1989): 329–39.

15. Spillers, "Notes," 181.

16. Spillers, "Notes," 173.

17. Judith Butler, *Bodies That Matter: On the Discursive Limits of "Sex"* (London: Routledge, 1993): 217.

18. It is easy to speculate that this factor justified male control over women's labor contracts, property, and so on until the twentieth-century in most western nations. Leigh Gilmore reinscribes the patronym in the binary system as a "play on authority, staged through the recoding of the mother's maiden name as 'secret' in order to enforce the 'public' authority of the name of the father." Leigh Gilmore, *Autobiographics*, 88. Of course, there is a double bind: even the woman doesn't know her "maiden name," as that refers to her father's name.

19. Philippe Lejeune, *On Autobiography*, trans. Katherine Leary (Minneapolis: U of Minnesota P, 1989): 20.

20. For a fictional account that highlights the importance of genealogy, see Aminata Sow Fall, *Le jujubier du patriarche* (Dakar: Editions Khoudia, 1993).

21. Foucault, "What Is an Author?" 105.

22. Bernard Magnier, "Ken Bugul ou l'écriture thérapeutique," *Notre Librairie* 81 (1985): 151–55.

23. This literal translation locks us into non-transferable syntactic categories. Wolof, like many West African languages, uses verbal elements for a wider range of functions than English does. Rather than attempting to force English into another language's straitjacket, I have chosen to make the name a noun.

24. Magnier, "Ken Bugul," 153.

25. Sidonie Smith, *A Poetics of Women's Autobiography: Marginality and the Fictions of Self-Representation* (Bloomington: Indiana UP, 1987): 51.

26. Some experiments have taken place in this regard; for example, one Oregon family numbered the children, rather than naming them. However, these experiments appear to be dead ends.

27. Magnier, "Ken Bugul," 155.

28. See Audre Lorde, *Zami: A New Spelling of My Name* (Trumansburg, N.Y.: Crossing, 1983).

29. Irène d'Alméïda, *Francophone African Women*, 45.

30. Eakin, *Fictions in Autobiography*, 217.

31. Ken Bugul, *Le baobab fou* (Dakar: Les Nouvelles Editions Africaines, 1983): 25.

32. Ken Bugul, *The Abandoned Baobab: The Autobiography of a Senegalese Woman*, trans. Marjolijn de Jager (Brooklyn: Lawrence Hill Books, 1991): 17.

33. Mildred Mortimer, *Journeys Through the French African Novel* (Portsmouth, N.H.: Heinemann, 1990): 169.

34. Elaine Scarry, *The Body in Pain*, 5.

35. Thomas J. Csórdas, "Introduction: The Body as Representation and Being-in-the-World," *Embodiment and Experience: The Existential Ground of Culture and Self*, ed. Thomas J. Csórdas (Cambridge: Cambridge UP, 1994): 12.

36. Jane Gallop, *Thinking through the Body* (New York: Columbia UP, 1988): 13.

37. Eileen Julien, "The Horror! The Horror! Going Native in Ken Bugul's Brussels," Unpublished paper (New York: MLA Conference, 1992): 8.

38. For an important analysis of this problem, see Patricia Williams, *The Alchemy of Race and Rights* (Cambridge, Mass.: Harvard UP, 1991).

39. See Eileen Julien's analysis of Yambo Ouologuem's *Le devoir de violence* (1968) and Sony Labou Tansi's *La vie et demie* (1979) in "Rape, Repression and Narrative Form in *Le devoir de violence* and *La vie et demie*," *Rape and Representation*, eds. Lynn A. Higgins and Brenda R. Silver (New York: Columbia UP, 1991): 160–81.

40. In a discussion of the proper name as sign, Lévi-Strauss comes to the following conclusion: "Everything takes place as if in our [western] civilization every individual's own personality were his totem: it is the signifier of his signified being." Claude Lévi-Strauss, *The Savage Mind*, trans. George Weidenfeld and Nicolson, Ltd. (Chicago: U of Chicago P, 1966): 214. See also Claude Lévi-Strauss, *Totemism*, trans. Rodney Needham (Boston: Beacon, 1963).

41. Miller, *Theories of Africans*, 153.

42. D'Alméïda, *Francophone African Women*, 53.

43. Miller, *Theories of Africans*, 143.

44. Miller, *Theories of Africans*, 177.

45. Lest the reader think names are always marked for gender, I wish to note that names in certain African languages such as KiKongo do not serve as gender markers.

46. "The amber bead, an instrument of pain, replaces the baobab seed, a portent of happiness," Mortimer, *Journeys*, 169.

47. Julia Kristeva, "Women's Time," trans. Jardine and Blake, *Signs* 7 (1981): 31.

48. Iris Marion Young, *Throwing Like a Girl and Other Essays in Feminist Philosophy and Social Theory* (Bloomington: Indiana UP, 1990): 163.

49. Julien, "The Horror," 3.

50. Reva B. Siegel, "Abortion as a Sex Equality Right: Its Basis in Feminist Theory," *Mothers in Law: Feminist Theory and the Legal Regulation of Motherhood*, eds. Martha Albertson Fineman and Isabel Karpin (New York: Columbia UP, 1995): 45.

51. Siegel, "Abortion as a Sex Equality Right," 46–47.

52. Drucilla Cornell, *The Imaginary Domain: Abortion, Pornography and Sexual Harassment* (New York: Routledge, 1995): 33.

53. Cornell, *The Imaginary Domain*, 33–35.

54. Cornell, *The Imaginary Domain*, 46.

55. Cornell, *The Imaginary Domain*, 5.

56. Cornell, *The Imaginary Domain*, 4.

57. Children under seven stay with the mother, but once they are considered old enough (usually seven years old), they return to the father's family.

58. Cornell, *The Imaginary Domain*, 236.

59. Butler, *Bodies*, 207.

60. Butler, *Bodies*, 221.

61. Françoise Lionnet, *Postcolonial Representations: Women, Literature, Identity* (Ithaca: Cornell UP, 1995): 159.

62. Lionnet, *Postcolonial Representations*, 161. The analogy is problematic, yet Lionnet's work does serve to highlight the ethnocentrism behind much of the debate.

63. Lionnet, *Postcolonial Representations*, 166.

64. Siegel, "Abortion as a Sex Equality Right," 45.

65. In 1988, for example, a French advertisement campaign promoted maternity. All of the babies depicted were white. In addition, the government subsidizes children by giving parents a fixed amount of money per child. Germany does so as well. Since the subsidy cannot be denied to legal residents and immigrants, there is some social tension about the topic.

66. Since the unified subject is a legal fiction, I assume that any speaking subject experiences this duality. Indeed, psychoanalysis teaches that a split between sensation and consciousness generates subjectivity. Within the social order, however, dominant subject positions not only allow those who hold them to forget this, but induce them to do so.

67. Babacar Thioune, "L'Exploration de l'écriture féminine au Sénégal: La Tentation autobiographique" (Diss. U of Paris IV, 1987): 117.

68. N'Diaye, *Gens de sable*, 159.

69. N'Diaye, *Gens de sable*, 160.

70. D'Alméïda, *Francophone African Women*, 70.

71. Norman Rush, "The Woman in the Broken Mirror," *The New York Times Book Review* (Dec. 15, 1991): 28.

72. See also Paul Gilroy, *Small Acts: Thoughts on the Politics of Black Cultures* (London: Serpent's Tail, 1993): 136.

73. Spillers, "Notes," 167.

74. Lionnet, *Autobiographical Voices*, 6.

CHAPTER 7. TERMS OF EXCHANGE

1. Kwame Anthony Appiah, "Race, Culture, Identity: Misunderstood Connections," *Color Conscious: The Political Morality of Race* (Princeton: Princeton UP, 1996): 103.

2. Mikhail Bakhtin, "Author and Hero in Aesthetic Activity," *Art and Answerability: Early Philosophical Essays by M. M. Bakhtin*, eds. Michael Holquist and Vadim Liapunov, trans. Vadim Liapunov (Austin: U of Texas P, 1990): 141.

3. Bakhtin, "Author and Hero," 153.

4. Richard Bauman, *Story, Performance, and Event: Contextual Studies of Oral Narrative* (Cambridge: Cambridge UP, 1986): 11.

5. Roy Pascal, *Design and Truth in Autobiography* (Cambridge, Mass.: Harvard UP, 1960) offers the most obvious example; however, Philippe Lejeune as well has relied on the notion of "sincerity" in his definition of the genre.

6. See Biodun Jeyifo's 1987 study of African theater, *The Truthful Lie: Essays in a Sociology of African Drama* (London: New Beacon Books, 1985). In contrast, the western philosophical tradition shows little of this tolerance for the verbal arts as an ambiguous form of truth-telling; Plato, for instance, banished poets from his utopian republic. In the *Cratylus* as well, language (particularly poetic language) is described as duplicitous.

7. Karim Traoré, "Kourouma's *Monnè* and the Aesthetics of Lying," Unpublished paper presented at the African Studies Association conference 1992, Boston. See also Zora Neale Hurston, *Dust Tracks on a Road* (Urbana: U of Illinois P, 1984): 197–98.

8. Quoted in Bauman, 1986, 11.

9. Michel Serres, *Hermès IV: La distribution* (Paris: Éditions de Minuit, 1977). Serres' work on the importance of noise to meaning has particular significance here:

> Ou je suis plongé dans les échanges de signaux, ou j'observe l'ensemble global des échanges. Mais désormais je comprends et j'explique ce qui se passe lorsque l'observateur change de site, quand le sujet devient objet. . . . Le champ du subjectif, celui de l'objectif, ne répugnent plus. L'observateur comme l'objet, le sujet comme l'observé, sont travaillés par un partage plus stable et plus puissant que leur antique séparation: ils sont, ensemble, de l'ordre *et* du désordre. 270–71.

> Either I am plunged into the exchanges of signals, or I observe the global ensemble of these exchanges. But from now on I understand and I explain what happens when the observer changes place, when the subject becomes object. . . . The field of the subjective, that of the objective, no longer repels. The observer as object, the subject as the observed, are affected by an exchange that is more stable and more powerful than their classical separation: together, they are of order *and* of disorder. (my translation)

Although this translation closes rather clumsily, I do not wish to resolve the problem because doing so would erase Serres' insight that the subjective and the objective orders of discourse are both constituted *by* order and chaos, and constitutive *of* order and chaos.

10. Pascal Boyer, *Tradition as Truth and Communication: A Cognitive Description of Traditional Discourse* (Cambridge: Cambridge UP, 1990).

11. Renato Rosaldo, *Culture and Truth: The Remaking of Social Analysis* (Boston: Beacon Press, 1989): 224.

12. Bauman, *Story, Performance, and Event*, 11.

13. Assane Sylla, *La philosophie morale des Wolof* (Dakar: Sankoré, 1978), 114.

14. Bauman, *Story, Performance, and Event*, 32.

15. *Folktales from the Gambia: Wolof Fictional Narratives*, trans. Emil A. Magel (Washington, D.C.: Three Continents Press, 1984): 163–71.

16. These are the performer's female ancestors, the matrilineage called the *meen* in Wolof.

17. Waalo was a precolonial kingdom in the northern part of modern Senegal. See Boubacar Barry, *Le Royaume du Waalo: Le Sénégal avant la conquête* (Paris: Karthala, 1985).

18. Here the performer refers to her *gëño*, or patrilineage.

19. Haratines are the former slaves of Arab-descended Moors. They define themselves culturally as Moors, rather than identifying with other black communities in Mauritania, such as the Wolof, Fulani, or Soninke.

20. dies.

21. Diop and Diouf, *Le Sénégal sous Abdou Diouf*, 401.

22. Indeed, the Senegalese and Mauritanian governments continue to negotiate the future of the refugees to the present. See "Refugiés mauritaniens au Sénégal: Les Petits pas du dossier," *Sud-Weekend* 590 (March 11, 1995): 12.

23. For the classic essay on the problem, see William Wimsatt and Monroe C. Beardsley, "The Intentional Fallacy," *The Verbal Icon: Studies in the Meaning of Poetry* (Lexington: U of Kentucky P, 1954): 3–18.

24. Américo Paredes, "On Ethnographic Work among Minority Groups: A Folklorist's Perspective," *New Directions in Chicano Scholarship*, eds. Ricardo Romo and Raymund Paredes (La Jolla, Calif.: Chicano Studies Monograph Series, 1978): 1–32.

25. Peter Zima, *Die Komparatistik: Einführung in die Vergleichende Literaturwissenschaft* (Tübingen: Francke, 1992): 9–12.

26. Although structuralism led social scientists to analyze texts, social and literary, solely on the basis of internal structural relationships, few would link the two schools of interpretation.

27. Roman Jakobson, "Le folklore, forme spécifique de création," *Questions de poétique*, trans. Jean-Claude Duport (Paris: Le Seuil, 1986): 59.

28. For a brilliant discussion of the problems of textual unity (analogous to the problem of unity of memory necessary to individual selfhood) that relates praise poetry and critical theory, see Karin Barber, "Yoruba *oriki* and Deconstructive Crticism," *Research in African Literatures* 15.4 (1984): 496–518.

29. See Paul de Man's "Autobiography as De-Facement," *Modern Language Notes* 94 (1979): 919–30, Michael Ryan, "Self-Evidence," *Diacritics* 10 (1980): 2–16, and Michael Sprinker, "Fictions of the Self: The End of Autobiography?" *Autobiography: Essays Theoretical and Critical*, ed. James Olney (Princeton: Princeton UP, 1980): 321–42.

30. Elizabeth W. Bruss, *Autobiographical Acts: The Changing Situation of a Literary Genre* (Baltimore: The Johns Hopkins UP, 1976): 128.

31. Lila Abu-Lughod, *Veiled Sentiments*, 237.

32. Eakin, *Touching the World*, 144.

33. This bargain entails hard work for the reader and the rereader, as Matei Calinescu's section on secrecy in *Rereading* (New Haven: Yale UP, 1993), makes quite clear.

34. See Michèle Barrett, *The Politics of Truth: From Marx to Foucault* (London: Polity Press, 1991).

35. Sandra Adell, *Double-Consciousness/Double Bind: Theoretical Issues in Twentieth-Century Black Literature* (Urbana: U of Illinois P, 1994): 105.

36. I use the adjective subaltern here with reference to the Subaltern Studies Group and to the postcolonial theorists such as Gayatri Chakravorty Spivak who use the term with a *differance*, a slippage of meaning that resembles *signifying*.

37. See Barbara Herrnstein Smith, *Contingencies of Values: Alternative Perspectives for Critical Theory* (Cambridge, Mass.: Harvard UP, 1988).

38. Charles Taylor, *Multiculturalism and "The Politics of Recognition,"* (Princeton: Princeton UP, 1992): 67.

39. Clifford Geertz, "Blurred Genres: The Refiguration of Social Thought," *Local Knowledge: Further Essays in Interpretive Anthropology* (New York: Basic Books, 1983): 19–35.

POST-FACE

1. Gallop, *Thinking through the Body*, 141.

2. Gallop, *Thinking through the Body*, 144.

3. Eakin, *Touching the World*, 36.

4. Chinua Achebe, "The Writer and His Community,"*Hopes and Impediments* (New York: Anchor Books, 1988): 56.

5. Julia Kristeva. *Strangers to Ourselves*, trans. Leon Roudiez (New York: Columbia UP, 1991).

6. Mineke Schipper, "Knowledge Is Like an Ocean: Insiders, Outsiders, and the Academy," *Research in African Literatures* 28.4 (1997): 122.

7. Henry Louis Gates, *The Signifying Monkey: A Theory of African-American Literary Criticism* (Oxford: Oxford UP, 1988): xiv.

8. It is important to note that African and Diaspora scholars have always adapted to the norms of the white scholarly community, and have had no real choice in the matter until recently. However, if exchange and dialogue are to occur, white scholars must adapt to the new exigencies of a "postcolonial" world. Postcoloniality, I think, refers more to this change in the West (at least in western intellectual discourse) than it does to the former colonies, where persistent neocolonialism makes it difficult to accept the "post" in postcolonialism.

9. Paulin Hountondji, "Scientific Dependence in Africa Today," *Research in African Literatures* 21.3 (1990): 5–15.

SOUND RECORDINGS

FIELD RECORDINGS

Deposited in the Archives of Traditional Music, Indiana University
94–004–F. Senegal. Lisa McNee, 1993.

4648. Wedding and performances of erotic *taasu*. Dakar: February 20, 1993.
4650. Nogay Sène. *Taasu* performance and interview. Louga: March 3, 1993.
4652. Political rallies for the legislative elections. Louga: April 25–26, 1993.
4653. Naming ceremony. Louga: May 21, 1993.
4655. *Taasu* performances. Jillil u Sylla: May 24, 1993.
4658. *Taasu* performance. Màkka: June 9, 1993.
4659. *Taasu* performance. Màkka: June 9, 1993.
4666. Laobé naming ceremony. St. Louis: July 10, 1993.
4669. *Taasu* performances. St. Louis: November 17, 1993.

Field recordings in the researcher's personal collection

Ceet. Usine (Dakar): March 29, 1993.
Guèye, Aminata. *Taasu* performance and interview. Dakar: Dec. 1, 1993.
Maal, Baba. Interview. Dakar: December 11, 1993.

ARCHIVAL SOUND RECORDINGS

Archives Culturelles du Sénégal
Wolof songs and interviews conducted at Batal (Kajóor). April 22, 1969.
Taasu and songs performed at Colom Fall and Sagata (Kajóor). April 24, 1969.
Songs, *taasu* and "divertissement" performed at Colom Fall. April 25, 1969.

RADIO-TÉLÉVISION SÉNÉGAL

Dieng, Daba. *Taasu*. October 11, 1992.
Guèye, Ami Collé. *Taasu*. Sept. 9, 1975.
———. *Taasu*. June 10, 1990.
Mbaye Mbassou, Soda. *Taasu*. May 20, 1980.
Ngoné Mbaye. *Taasu*. 1968.
———. *Taasu*. 1976.
Fatou Tacko Thioune. *Taasu*. Sept. 2, 1980.

COMMERCIAL RECORDINGS

Diop, Aby Ngana. *Thiossanou-Ngewel: Liital*. Dakar: Midi Musique, 1994.

Guewell, Fatou. *Kara*. Dakar: Wings, 1992.

Lô, Ismaël. *Xumbeul*. Ilopro, 1992.

Maal, Baba. *Tono*. Dakar: Studio 2000, 1992.

N'Dour, Youssou. *Xippi*. Saprom, 1992. (Also available on CD as *Eyes Open*).

Sow, Alassane Doudou. *Leumbeul en live*. Dakar: Wings, 1992.

Thiam, Assane. *Mame*. Saprom, 1993.

WORKS CITED

Abu-Lughod, Lila. *Veiled Sentiments: Honor and Poetry in a Bedouin Society.* Berkeley: U of California P, 1986.

———. *Writing Women's Worlds: Bedouin Stories.* Berkeley: U of California P, 1993.

Achebe, Chinua. *Hopes and Impediments.* New York: Anchor Books, 1988.

Adell, Sandra. *Double-Consciousness/Double Bind: Theoretical Issues in Twentieth-Century Black Literature.* Urbana: U of Illinois P, 1994.

Aguessy, Honorat. "Visions et perceptions traditionnelles." *Introduction à la culture africaine.* Paris: UNESCO, 1977.

Alcoff, Linda. "The Problem of Speaking for Others." *Cultural Critique* (1991): 5–31.

———. "Mestizo Identity." *American Mixed Race: The Culture of Microdiversity.* Ed. Naomi Zack. Lanham, Md.: Rowman and Littlefield, 1995. 257–78.

Ames, David W. "The Rural Wolof of the Gambia." *Markets in Africa.* Eds. Paul Bohannon and George Dalton. Evanston: Northwestern UP, 1962. 29–60.

Appadurai, Arjun. "Disjuncture and Difference in the Global Cultural Economy." *Public Culture* 2.2 (1990): 1–24.

Appiah, Kwame Anthony. *In My Father's House: Africa in the Philosophy of Culture.* New York: Oxford UP, 1992.

———. "Race, Culture, Identity: Misunderstood Connections." *Color Consciousness: The Political Morality of Race.* Princeton: Princeton UP, 1996. 30–105.

Autobiographie et récits de vie en Afrique. Paris: L'Harmattan, 1991.

Bakhtin, Mikhail. *Art and Answerability: Early Philosophical Essays by M. M. Bakhtin.* Eds. Michael Holquist and Vadim Liapunov. Trans. Vadim Liapunov. Austin: U of Texas P, 1990.

———. *The Dialogic Imagination: Four Essays.* Ed. M. Holquist. Trans. C. Emerson and M. Holquist. Austin: U of Texas P, 1981.

Barber, Karin. *I Could Speak Until Tomorrow: Oriki, Women and the Past in a Yoruba Town.* Washington, D.C.: Smithsonian Institute, 1991.

———. "Literacy, Improvisation and the Public in Yorùbá Popular Theater." *The Pressures of the Text: Orality, Texts and the Telling of Tales.* Birmingham University African Studies Series, no. 4. Ed. Stewart Brown. Birmingham: Centre of West African Studies, University of Birmingham, 1995. 6–27.

———. "Oriki, Women and the Proliferation and Merging of Orisa." *Africa* 60 (1990): 313–37.

———. "Popular Arts in Africa." *African Studies Review* 30.3 (1987): 1–78.

———. "Yoruba Oriki and Deconstructive Criticism." *Research in African Literatures* 15 (1984): 497–518.

Barrett, Michèle. *The Politics of Truth: From Marx to Foucault.* London: Polity Press, 1991.

Barry, Boubacar. *Le Royaume du Waalo: Le Sénégal avant la conquête.* Paris: Karthala, 1985.

Barthel, Diane L. "The Rise of Female Professional Elite: The Case of Senegal." *African Studies Review* 13.3 (1975): 1–17.

———. "Women's Educational Experience under Colonialism: Toward a Diachronic Model." *Signs* 7.1 (1985): 137–54.

Bateson, Gregory. *Steps toward an Ecology of Mind.* New York: Chandler Publishing, 1972.

Bauman, Richard. "Contextualization, Tradition, and the Dialogue of Genres: Icelandic Legends of the Kraftaskáld." *Rethinking Context: Language as an Interactive Phenomenon.* Eds. Alessandro Duranti and Charles Goodwin. Cambridge: Cambridge UP, 1992. 77–99.

———. *Story, Performance, and Event: Contextual Studies of Oral Narrative.* Cambridge: Cambridge UP, 1986.

———. *Verbal Art as Performance.* Prospect Heights, Ill.: Waveland Press, 1977.

Bayart, Jean-François. *The State in Africa: The Politics of the Belly.* Trans. Mary Harper, Christopher and Elizabeth Harrison. London: Longman, 1993.

Ben-Amos, Dan. "Introduction." *Folklore Genres.* Ed. Dan Ben-Amos. Austin: U of Texas P, 1976. ix–xiv.

Benga, Marie-Louise. "Journée internationale de la femme: Mobilisation pour l'égalité des droits." *Le Soleil* (8 March 1993): 7.

———. "L'exemple des femmes de Nder." *Le Soleil* (8 March 1993): 7.

Bennett, Pramila R. "A Senegalese Childhood." Review of *A Dakar Childhood. Africa* 147 (1983): 71.

Benstock, Shari, ed. *The Private Self: Theory and Practice of Women's Autobiographical Writings.* Chapel Hill: U of North Carolina P, 1988.

Bernal, Victoria. "Gender, Culture, and Capitalism: Women and the Remaking of Islamic 'Tradition' in a Sudanese Village." *Comparative Studies in Society and History* 36.1 (1994): 44–45.

Bhabha, Homi K. *The Location of Culture.* London: Routledge, 1994.

———. "Introduction: Narrating the Nation." *Nation and Narration.* Ed. Homi K. Bhabha. London: Routledge, 1990. 1–7.

Blair, Dorothy. *Senegalese Literature: A Critical History.* Boston: Twayne Publishers, 1984.

Boone, Sylvia Ardyn. *Radiance from the Waters: Ideals of Feminine Beauty in Mende Art.* New Haven: Yale UP, 1986.

Bop, Codou. "La séduction, mode d'emploi." *Africa* 171 (April 1985): 33–37.

Borgomano, Madeleine. *Voix et visages de femmes dans les livres écrits par des femmes en Afrique francophone.* Abidjan: CEDA, 1989.

Bouche, Denise. *L'enseignement dans les territoires français de l'Afrique occidentale de 1817 à 1920: Mission civilisatrice ou formation d'une élite?* Diss. U of Paris I. Lille: U of Lille P, 1974.

Bovin, Mette. "Provocation Anthropology: Bartering Performance in Africa." *Drama Review* 32 (1988): 21–41.

Boyd-Buggs, Debra. "Mouridism in Senegalese Fiction." *Faces of Islam in African Literature.* Ed. Kenneth W. Harrow. Portsmouth, N.H.: Heinemann, 1991. 201–14.

Boyer, Pascal. *Tradition as Truth and Communication: A Cognitive Description of Traditional Discourse.* Cambridge: Cambridge UP, 1990.

Briggs, Charles. *Competence in Performance: The Creativity of Tradition in Mexicano Verbal Art.* Philadelphia: U of Pennsylvania P, 1988.

Briggs, Charles and Richard Bauman. "Genre, Intertextuality, and Social Power." *Journal of Linguistic Anthropology* 2.2 (1992): 131–72.

Brodzki, Bella and Celeste Schenck, eds. *Life/Lines: Theorizing Women's Autobiography.* Ithaca: Cornell UP, 1988.

Brodzki, Bella. "'Changing Masters': Gender, Genre, and the Discourses of Slavery." *Borderwork: Feminist Engagements with Comparative Literature.* Ed. Margaret Higonnet. Ithaca: Cornell UP, 1994. 43–60.

Brooks, George. "The *Signares* of Saint-Louis and Gorée: Women Entrepreneurs in Eighteenth-Century Senegal." *Women in Africa: Studies in Social and Economic Change.* Eds. Nancy J. Hafkin and Edna G. Bay. Stanford: Stanford UP, 1976. 19–44.

Bruner, Charlotte. "First Novels of Girlhood." *College Language Association Journal* 31 (1988): 324–38.

———. Review of *A Dakar Childhood.World Literature Today* 57 (1983): 339.

Bruss, Elizabeth W. *Autobiographical Acts: The Changing Situation of a Literary Genre.* Baltimore: Johns Hopkins UP, 1976.

Butler, Judith. *Bodies That Matter: On the Discursive Limits of 'Sex.'* New York: Routledge, 1993.

———. *Gender Trouble: Feminism and the Subversion of Identity.* London: Routledge, 1990.

Callaway, Barbara and Lucy Creevey. *The Heritage of Islam: Women, Religion and Politics in West Africa.* Boulder, Colo.: Lynne Rienner, 1994.

Cazenave, Odile. *Femmes rebelles: Naissance d'un nouveau roman africain au féminin.* Paris: L'Harmattan, 1996.

Cham, Mbye Baboucar. "Islam in Senegalese Literature and Film." *Faces of Islam in African Literature.* Ed. Kenneth W. Harrow. Portsmouth, N.H.: Heinemann, 1991. 163–86.

Chemain-Degrange, Arlette. *Emancipation féminine et roman africain.* Dakar: Les Nouvelles Éditions Africaines, 1980.

Chodorow, Nancy J. *The Reproduction of Mothering: Psychoanalysis and the Sociology of Gender.* Berkeley: U of California P, 1978.

Cixous, Hélène. "Castration or Decapitation?" Trans. Annette Kuhn. *Signs* 7 (1981): 41–55.

———. *The Hélène Cixous Reader.* Ed. Susan Sellers. New York: Routledge, 1994.

———. "Sorties." *La jeune née.* Paris: Union Générale des Écrivains, 1975. 114–244.

"La conquête des femmes." *Le Soleil* (26 March 1993): 10.

Cornell, Drucilla. *The Imaginary Domain: Abortion, Pornography and Sexual Harassment.* London: Routledge, 1995.

Crowder, Michael. *Senegal: A Study in French Assimilation Policy.* London: Oxford UP, 1962.

Cruise O'Brien, Donal B. "Langue et nationalité au Sénégal: L'enjeu politique de la wolofisation." *L'Année Africaine.* Paris: Pédone, 1979. 319–35.

———. "Le 'contrat social' sénégalais à l'épreuve." *Politique Africaine* 45 (1992): 9–20.

———. *Saints and Politicians: Essays in the Organization of a Senegalese Peasant Society.* Cambridge: Cambridge UP, 1975.

Csórdas, Thomas J. "Introduction: The Body as Representation and Being-in-the-World." *Embodiment and Existence: The Existential Ground of Culture and Self.* Ed. Thomas J. Csórdas. Cambridge: Cambridge UP, 1994. 1–24.

D'Alméïda, Irène Assiba. "Femme? Féministe? Misovire? Les romancières africaines face au féminisme." *Notre Librairie* 117 (1994): 48–51.

———. *Francophone African Women Writers: Destroying the Emptiness of Silence.* Gainesville: U Presses of Florida, 1994.

Davies, Carole Boyce. "Private Selves and Public Spaces: Autobiography and the African Woman Writer." *Neohelicon* 17.2 (1990): 183–210.

Davies, Carole Boyce and Ogundipe-Leslie, Molara. "Women as Oral Artists: Introduction." *Research in African Literatures* 25.3 (1994): 1–6.

Demane, M. and P. B. Sanders. *Lithoko: Sotho Praise Poems.* Oxford: Clarendon Press, 1974.

Derrida, Jacques. *De la grammatologie.* Paris: Ed. de Minuit, 1967.

———. Trans. Gayatri Chakravorty Spivak. *Of Grammatology.* Baltimore: Johns Hopkins UP, 1976.

———. *Given Time: Counterfeit Money.* Trans. Peggy Kamuf. Chicago: U of Chicago P, 1992.

———. "La structure, le signe et le jeu dans le discours des sciences humaines." *L'Ecriture et la différence.* Paris: Seuil, 1967. 409–28.

Dia, Mamadou. *Réflexions sur l'économie de l'Afrique noire.* Paris: Présence Africaine, 1960.

Diallo, Nafissatou. *De Tilène au Plateau: Une Enfance dakaroise.* Dakar: Nouvelles Editions Africaines, 1975.

———. *A Dakar Childhood.* Trans. Dorothy S. Blair. Harlow: Longman, 1982.

———. *Le fort maudit.* Paris: Hatier, 1980.

———. *La princesse de Tiali.* Dakar: Les Nouvelles Editions Africaines, 1987.

Diaw, Abdoulaziz. *Un Vocabulaire wolof de la faune au Sénégal. Les Langues nationales au Sénégal* 67. Dakar: Centre de Linguistique Appliquée de Dakar, 1976.

———. *Un Vocabulaire wolof de la flore au Sénégal. Les Langues nationales au Sénégal* W16. Dakar: Centre de Linguistique Appliquée de Dakar, 1981.

Diaw, Aminata. "La démocratie des lettrés." *Sénégal: Trajectoires d'un état.* Ed. Momar Coumba Diop. Paris: Karthala, 1992. 299–329.

Dictionnaire volof-français: Précédé d'un abrégé de la grammaire volofe. Holy Ghost Fathers. Congrégation de St. Esprit et du St. Coeur de Marie. St. Joseph de Ngasobil: Mission de la Sénégambie, 1902.

Dieng, Bassirou. *L'Epopée de Kajoor*. Dakar: Editions Khoudia, 1993.

Dieng, Bassirou and Lilyan Kesteloot, eds. *Contes et mythes du Sénégal*. Paris: C.I.L.F.-IFAN, 1986.

——, eds. *Contes et mythes Wolof II: Du Tieddo au Talibé*. Paris: Présence Africaine, 1989.

Dièye, Alioune B. "Rap, *tassou*, 'kébetou.'" *Sud Quotidien Online*. Online. 24 December 1996. Available: http: www.rapide-pana.com.

Diop, Abdoulaye Bara. *La famille wolof: Tradition et changement*. Paris: Karthala, 1985.

——. "Jeunes filles et femmes de Dakar: Conditions de vie et attitudes rélatives à la famille, au mariage, et à l'éducation sexuelle." Bulletin de l'IFAN, Série B 44.1–2 (1982): 162–212.

——. *La société wolof: Systèmes d'inégalité et de domination*. Paris: Karthala, 1981.

Diop, Momar Coumba and Mamadou Diouf. *Le Sénégal sous Abdou Diouf: État et société*. Paris: Karthala, 1990.

Diop, Samba. *The Oral Hi ory and Literature of the Wolof People of Waalo, Northern Senegal. T' .Aaster of the Word (Griot) in the Wolof Tradition*. African Studies, vol. 6. Lewiston: Edwin Mellen Press, 1995.

Diouf, Madior. *Nini, mulâtresse du Sénégal: Étude critique*. Dakar: Editions Khoudia, 1990.

Dorsinville, Roger. "Vies d'Afrique: Une collection vérité." *Notre Librairie* 81 (1985): 147–50.

Drewal, Margaret Thompson. "The State of Research on Performance in Africa." Paper prepared for the Joint Committee on African Studies of the American Council of Learned Societies and the Social Science Research Council, 1990.

——. *Yoruba Ritual: Performers, Play, Agency*. Bloomington: Indiana UP, 1992.

DuCille, Ann. "The Occult of True Black Womanhood: Critical Demeanor and Black Feminist Studies." *Signs* 19.3 (1994): 591–629.

Duranti, Alessandro. "The Audience as Co-Author: An Introduction." *Text* 6.3 (1986): 239–47.

Eakin, Paul John. *Fictions in Autobiography: Studies in the Art of Self-Invention*. Princeton: Princeton UP, 1985.

——. "The Referential Aesthetic of Autobiography." *Studies in the Literary Imagination* 23 (1990): 129–44.

——. *Touching the World: Reference in Autobiography*. Princeton: Princeton UP, 1992.

Ekeh, Peter P. "Colonialism and the Two Publics in Africa: A Theoretical Statement." *Comparative Studies in Society and History* 17.1 (1975): 91–112.

Erlmann, Veit. *Die Macht des Wortes: ⁻reisgesang und Berufsmusiker bei den FulBe des Diamaré (Nordkamerun)*. Hohenschäftlarn: Klaus Renner, 1980.

Fabian, Johannes. "Ethnographic Misunderstanding and the Perils of Context." *American Anthropologist* 97.1 (1995): 41–50.

Fal, Arame, Rosine Santos, and Jean Léonce Doneux. *Dictionnaire Wolof-Français*. Paris: Karthala, 1990.

Fall, Pape. "Lekku Ndey: Les dessous d'un commerce lucratif." *Le Soleil* (19 August 1993): 8–9.

Fatton, Robert. "Clientelism and Patronage in Senegal." *African Studies Review* 29 (1986): 61–78.

Finnegan, Ruth. *Literacy and Orality: Studies in the Technology of Communication.* Oxford: Basil Blackwell, 1988.

———. *Oral Literature in Africa.* Oxford: Clarendon Press, 1970.

———. *Oral Poetry: Its Nature, Significance, and Social Context.* Cambridge: Cambridge UP, 1977.

Foley, John Miles. *The Singer of Tales in Performance.* Bloomington: Indiana UP, 1995.

Foucault, Michel. "Faire vivre et laisser mourir: La naissance du racisme." *Les temps modernes* 46.535 (1991): 37–61.

———. *The History of Sexuality.* Vol. 1: An Introduction. Trans. Robert Hurley. New York: Vintage, 1990.

———. "What Is an Author?" *The Foucault Reader.* Ed. Paul Rabinow. New York: Pantheon, 1986. 101–20.

Fox-Genovese, Elizabeth. *Feminism without Illusions: A Critique of Individualism.* Chapel Hill: U of North Carolina P, 1991.

Freccero, John. "Autobiography and Narrative." *Reconstructing Individualism: Autonomy, Individuality and the Self in Western Thought.* Eds. Thomas C. Hiller and Christine Brooke-Rose. Stanford: Stanford UP, 1986. 16–29.

Fresco, Alain. "'Les vies africaines': A Series of Popular Literature." *African Literature Today* 12 (1982): 174–80.

Gadjigo, Samba. *Ecole blanche, Afrique noire.* Paris: L'Harmattan, 1990.

Gallop, Jane. *Thinking through the Body.* New York: Columbia UP, 1988.

Gates, Henry Louis. *Loose Canons: Notes on the Culture Wars.* New York: Oxford UP, 1992.

———. *The Signifying Monkey: A Theory of African-American Literary Criticism.* Oxford: Oxford UP, 1988.

Gerhart, Mary. *Genre Choices, Gender Questions.* Norman: U of Oklahoma P, 1992.

Gilmore, Leigh. *Autobiographics: A Feminist Theory of Women's Self-Representation.* Ithaca: Cornell UP, 1994.

Gilroy, Paul. *Small Acts: Thoughts on the Politics of Black Cultures.* London: Serpent's Tail, 1993.

Goffman, Erving. *The Presentation of Self in Everyday Life.* Garden City, N.Y.: Doubleday, 1959.

Gunner, Elizabeth. "Songs of Innocence and Experience: Women as Composers and Performers of *Izibongo,* Zulu Praise Poetry." *Women and Writing in South Africa: A Critical Anthology.* Ed. Cherry Clayton. London: Heinemann, 1989. 12–39.

Gusdorf, Georges. "Conditions and Limits of Autobiography" [1956]. *Autobiography: Essays Theoretical and Critical.* Ed. James Olney. Princeton: Princeton UP, 1980. 28–48.

Guy-Grand, V. J. *Dictionnaire français-volof.* 3rd ed. St. Joseph de Ngasobil, 1890.

Heath, Debora. "Fashion, Anti-fashion, and Heteroglossia in Urban Senegal." *American Ethnologist* 19 (1992): 19–33.

———. "The Politics of Signifying Practice in Kaolack, Senegal: Hegemony and the Dialectic of Autonomy and Domination." Diss. Johns Hopkins U, 1988.

———. "The Politics of Appropriateness and Appropriation: Recontextualizing Women's Dance in Urban Senegal." *American Ethnologist* 21.1 (1994): 88–103.

———. "Spatial Politics and Verbal Performance in Urban Senegal." *Ethnology* 29 (1990): 209–23.

Hill, Jane H. and Judith T. Irvine, eds. Introduction. *Evidence and Responsibility in Oral Discourse.* Cambridge: Cambridge UP, 1993. 1–23.

Hountondji, Paulin. "Scientific Dependence in Africa Today." *Research in African Literatures* 21.3 (1990): 5–15.

Howard, Rhoda E. "Group Versus Individual Identity in the African Debate on Human Rights." *Human Rights in Africa: Cross-Cultural Perspectives.* Eds. Abdullahi Ahmed An-Na'im and Francis Deng. Washington, D.C.: Brookings Institution, 1990. 159–83.

Howarth, William. "Some Principles of Autobiography." *Autobiography: Essays Theoretical and Critical.* Ed. James Olney. Princeton: Princeton UP, 1980. 84–115.

Interview with Oulimata Diom: "La promotion de la femme indéniable." *Le Soleil* (5 May 1993): 10.

Interview with Awa Diop: "Les femmes sont fatiguées." *Le Soleil* (5 May 1993): 10.

Irvine, Judith T. "Caste and Communication in a Wolof Village." Diss. U of Pennsylvania, 1973.

———. "How Not to Ask a Favor in Wolof." *Papers in Linguistics* 13.1 (1980): 3–49.

———. "Insult and Responsibility: Verbal Abuse in a Wolof Village." *Responsibility and Evidence in Oral Discourse.* Eds. Jane H. Hill and Judith T. Irvine. Cambridge: Cambridge UP, 1993. 105–34.

———. "Language and Affect: Some Cross-Cultural Issues." *Contemporary Perceptions of Language: Interdisciplinary Dimensions.* Georgetown University Roundtable on Languages and Linguistics. Ed. H. Byrnes. Washington, D.C.: Georgetown UP, 1982. 31–47.

———. "Registering Affect: Heteroglossia in the Linguistic Expression of Emotion." *Language and the Politics of Emotion.* Eds. Catherine A. Lutz and Lila Abu-Lughod. Cambridge: Cambridge UP, 1990. 126–61.

———. "When Talk Isn't Cheap: Language and Political Economy." *American Ethnologist* 16.2 (1989): 248–68.

Jaccomard, Hélène and Jean-Marie Volet. "Pacte autobiographique et écrivaines francophones d'Afrique noire." *Présence Francophone* 41 (1992): 9–26.

Jackson, Michael. *Paths toward a Clearing: Radical Empiricism and Ethnographical Inquiry.* Bloomington: Indiana UP, 1989.

Jakobson, Roman. "Le folklore, forme spécifique de création." *Questions de poétique.* Trans. Jean-Claude Duport. Paris: Seuil, 1986. 59–72.

James, Stanlie M. "Mothering: A Possible Black Feminist Link to Social Transformation?" *Theorizing Black Feminisms: The Visionary Pragmatism of Black Women.* Eds. Stanlie M. James and Abena P. A. Busia. London: Routledge, 1993. 44–54.

Jameson, Fredric. "Third-World Literature in the Era of Multinational Capitalism." *Social Text* 15 (1986): 65–88.

Jeyifo, Biodun. *The Truthful Lie: Essays in a Sociology of African Drama.* London: New Beacon Books, 1985.

Joseph, George. "The Wolof Oral Praise Song For Semu Coro Wende." *Research in African Literatures* 10.2 (1979): 145–78.

Julien, Eileen. *African Novels and the Question of Orality.* Bloomington: Indiana UP, 1992.

———. "The Horror! The Horror! Going Native in Ken Bugul's Brussels." Unpublished paper presented at the MLA conference, New York, 1992.

Kâ, Aminata Maïga. "Ramatoulaye, Aïssatou, Mireille et . . . Mariama Bâ." *Notre Librairie* 81 (1985): 129–34.

Kane, Francine. "Femmes prolétaires du Sénégal, à la ville et aux champs." *Cahiers d'Études Africaines* 65.17–1 (1977): 77–93.

Kéïta, Abdoulaye. "Approche ethnolinguistique de la tradition orale wolof (contes et taasu)." M.A. thesis, Université de Cheikh Anta Diop de Dakar, 1986.

Kéïta, Anta Diouf. "L'écriture autobiographique dans le roman féminin sénégalais." *Autobiographies et récits de vie en Afrique.* Itinéraires et Contacts de Cultures 13. Ed. Paris: L'Harmattan, 1991. 135–44.

Ken Bugul. *Le baobab fou.* Dakar: Nouvelles Editions Africaines, 1983.

———. *The Abandoned Baobab.* Trans. Marjolijn de Jager. Chicago: Lawrence Hill Books, 1991.

———. *Cendres et braises.* Paris: L'Harmattan, 1994.

Knipp, Thomas. "Poetry as Autobiography: Society and Self in Three Modern West African Poets." *African Literature in its Social and Political Dimensions.* Annual Selected Papers of the Ninth African Literature Association. Meeting at the University of Illinois, Champaign/Urbana, 1983. Eds. Eileen Julien, Mildred Mortimer, and Curtis Schade. Washington, D.C.: Three Continents Press, 1983. 41–50.

Kobès, Mgr. and R.P.O. Abiven. *Dictionnaire volof-français.* Dakar: Mission Catholique, 1923.

Koné, Amadou. "Tradition orale et écriture du roman autobiographique: L'exemple de Camara Laye." *Autobiographical Genres in Africa/Genres autobiographiques en Afrique: Actes du 6e symposium International Jahnheinz Jahn.* Eds. János Riesz and Ulla Schild. Berlin: Reimer, 1996. 53–64.

Kurke, Leslie. *The Traffic in Praise.* Ithaca: Cornell UP, 1991.

Lâm, Maivân Clech. "Feeling Foreign in Feminism." *Signs* 19.4 (1994): 865–93.

Lambrech, Régina. "Three Black Women, Three Autobiographers." *Présence Africaine* 123 (1982): 136–43.

Larrier, Renée. "Reconstructing Motherhood: Francophone African Women Autobiographers." *The Politics of (M)Othering: Womanhood, Identity, and Resistance in African Literature.* Ed. Obioma Nnaemeka. New York: Routledge, 1997. 192–204.

Lawrence, Cecile Anne. "Racelessness." *American Mixed Race: The Culture of Microdiversity*. Ed. Naomi Zack. Lanham, Md.: Rowman and Littlefield, 1995. 25–38.

Laye, Camara. *L'enfant noir*. Paris: Plon, 1953.

Le Cour Grandmaison, Colette. "Activités économiques des femmes dakaroises." *Africa* 39 (1969): 138–52.

———. *Femmes dakaroises*. Annales de l'Université d'Abidjan, Série F, vol. 4, 1972.

———. "La natte et le manguier." *La natte et le manguier: Les carnets d'Afrique de trois ethnologues*. Eds. Ariane Deluz, Colette Le Cour-Grandmaison, and Anne Retel-Laurentin. Paris: Mercure de France, 1978. 3–83.

Lederman, Rena. *What Gifts Engender: Social Relations and Politics in Mendi, Highland Papua New Guinea*. Cambridge: Cambridge UP, 1986.

Lejeune, Philippe. *On Autobiography*. Ed. Paul John Eakin. Trans. Katherine Leary. Minneapolis: U of Minnesota P, 1989.

Leonardo, Micaela di. "Gender, Culture, and Political Economy: Feminist Anthropology in Historical Perspective." *Gender at the Crossroads of Knowledge: Feminist Anthropology in the Postmodern Era*. Ed. Micaela di Leonardo. Berkeley: U of California P, 1991. 1–48.

Lestrade, G. P. "Traditional Literature." *The Bantu-Speaking Tribes of South Africa*. Ed. I. Schapera. London: Routledge, 1973. 291–308.

Lévinas, Emmanuel. *Entre nous: Essais sur le penser-à-l'autre*. Paris: Grasset, 1991.

Lévi-Strauss, Claude. *The Elementary Structures of Kinship*. Boston: Beacon, 1969.

———. *The Savage Mind*. Trans. George Weidenfeld and Nicolson, Ltd. Chicago: U of Chicago P, 1966.

Leymarie, Isabelle. "Role and Function among the Griots of Senegal." Diss. Columbia U, 1978.

Lionnet, Françoise. *Autobiographical Voices: Race, Gender, Self-Portraiture*. Ithaca: Cornell UP, 1989.

———. *Postcolonial Representations: Women, Literature, Identity*. Ithaca: Cornell UP, 1995.

Littératures autobiographiques de la francophonie. Ed. Martine Mathieu. Paris: L'Harmattan, 1996.

Lüsebrink, Hans-Jürgen. *Schrift, Buch und Lektüre in der französischsprachigen Literatur Afrikas: Zur Wahrnehmung und Funktion von Schriftlichkeit und Buchlektüre in einem kulturellen Epochenumbruch der Neuzeit*. Tübingen: Niemeyer Vlg., 1990.

Magel, Emil. *Folktales from the Gambia: Wolof Fictional Narratives*. Washington, D.C.: Three Continents Press, 1984.

Magnier, Bernard. "Ken Bugul ou l'écriture thérapeutique." *Notre Librairie* 81 (1985): 151–55.

Manchuelle, François. "Assimilés ou patriotes africains? Naissance du nationalisme culturel en Afrique française (1853–1931)." *Cahiers d'études africaines* 138.139 (1995): 333–68.

Mason, Mary G. "The Other Voice: Autobiographies of Women Writers." *Autobiography: Essays Theoretical and Critical*. Ed. James Olney. Princeton: Princeton UP, 1980. 207–35.

Mauss, Marcel. *The Gift: Forms and Functions of Exchange in Archaic Societies*. Trans. Ian Cunnison. New York: W. W. Norton, 1967.

Mbaye, Kéba. "L'Afrique et les droits de l'homme." *Revue juridique et politique* 48 (1994): 2–11.

Miller, Christopher. *Blank Darkness: Africanist Discourse in French*. Chicago: U of Chicago P, 1985.

———. "Literary Studies and African Literature: The Challenge of Intercultural Literacy." *Africa and the Disciplines: The Contributions of Research on Africa to the Social Sciences and Humanities*. Eds. Robert H. Bates, V. Y. Mudimbe, and Jean O'Barr. Chicago: U of Chicago P, 1993. 213–31.

———. "Nationalism as Resistance and Resistance to Nationalism in the Literature of Francophone Africa." *Yale French Studies* 82 (1993): 62–100.

———. *Theories of Africans: Francophone Literature and Anthropology in Africa*. Chicago: U of Chicago P, 1990.

Modic, Kate. "Negotiating Power: A Study of the *Ben Ka Di* Women's Association in Bamako, Mali." *Africa Today* 41.2 (1994): 25–37.

Mortimer, Mildred. *Journeys Through the French African Novel*. Portsmouth, N.H.: Heinemann, 1990.

Mudimbe, V. Y. *The Idea of Africa*. Bloomington: Indiana UP, 1994.

———. *The Invention of Africa: Gnosis, Philosophy, and the Order of Knowledge*. Bloomington: Bloomington UP, 1988.

———. *L'Odeur du père: Essai sur des limites de la science et de la vie en Afrique noire*. Paris: Présence Africaine, 1982.

Mudimbe-Boyi, Elisabeth. "The Poetics of Exile and Errancy in *Le baobab fou* by Ken Bugul and *Ti Jean L'Horizon* by Simone Schwarz-Bart." *Yale French Studies* 83 (1993): 196–212.

Ndiaye, Adja Ndeye Boury. *Collier de cheville*. Dakar: Les Nouvelles Editions Africaines, 1984.

Ndiaye, Catherine. *Gens de sable*. Paris: P.O.L., 1984.

Ndione, E.D. *Le don et le recours: Ressorts de l'économie urbaine*. Dakar: Enda Editions, 1992.

Ndione, Tidiane Cheikh Ah. "Woyi Ceet: Traditional Marriage Songs of the Lebu." Trans. R. H. Mitsch. *Research in African Literatures* 24 (1993): 89–100.

Ndoye Mbengue, Mariama. *Introduction à la littérature orale léboue: Analyse ethno-sociologique et expression littéraire*. Diss. Université Cheikh Anta Diop, Dakar, 1982.

Neuberger, Benyamin. *National Self-Determination in Postcolonial Africa*. Boulder, Colo.: Lynne Rienner, 1986.

Nfah-Abbenyi, Juliana Makuchi. *Gender in African Women's Writing: Identity, Sexuality, and Difference*. Bloomington: Indiana UP, 1997.

Ngandu Nkashama, Pius. "L'autobiographie chez les femmes africaines." *Notre Librairie* 117 (1994): 129–37.

Niang, Mamadou. "Gender Differences in Speech Behavior—Who Has the Best Speech?" *Theoretical Approaches to African Linguistics*. Ed. Akinbiyi Akinlabi. Trenton, N.J.: Africa World Press, 1994. 393–401.

Niang, Fatou Siga. *Reflets de modes et traditions Saint-Louisiennes*. Dakar: C.A.E.C./Ed. Khoudia, 1990. 134.

Okely, Judith and Helen Callaway, eds. *Anthropology and Autobiography*. London: Routledge, 1992.

Olney, James. *Metaphors of Self: The Meaning of Autobiography*. Princeton: Princeton UP, 1972.

———. "Some Versions of Memory/Some Versions of *Bios*: The Ontology of Autobiography." *Autobiography: Essays Theoretical and Critical*. Ed. James Olney. Princeton: Princeton UP, 1980. 236–67.

———. *Tell Me Africa: An Approach to African Literature*. Princeton: Princeton UP, 1973.

Ormerod, Beverley and Jean-Marie Volet. *Romancières africaines d'expression française: Le Sud du Sahara*. Paris: L'Harmattan, 1994.

———. "Ecrits autobiographiques et engagement: Le cas des Africaines d'expression française." *French Review* 69.3 (1996): 426–44.

Paredes, Américo. "On Ethnographic Work among Minority Groups: A Folklorist's Perspective." *New Directions in Chicano Scholarship*. Eds. Ricardo Romo and Raymund Paredes. La Jolla, Calif.: Chicano Studies Monograph Series, 1978. 1–32.

Pascal, Roy. *Design and Truth in Autobiography*. Cambridge, Mass.: Harvard UP, 1960.

Pateman, Carole. *The Sexual Contract*. Oxford: Polity Press, 1988.

Paul, Peter. "Le système réferentiel personnel en wolof." *Bulletin IFAN* Série B 34 (1972): 607–16.

Phillips, Anne. *Democracy and Difference*. University Park, Pa.: Pennsylvania State UP, 1993.

Polanyi, Karl. *The Great Transformation*. New York: Farrar and Rinehart, 1944.

Rabain, Jacqueline. *L'enfant du lignage: Du Sévrage à la classe d'âge*. Paris: Payot, 1979.

Rajan, Rajeswari Sunder. *Real and Imagined Women: Gender, Culture, and Postcolonialism*. London: Routledge, 1993.

Renan, Ernest. "What Is a Nation?" Trans. Martin Thom. *Nation and Narration*. Ed. Homi Bhabha. London: Routledge, 1990. 8–22.

Representations of Motherhood. "Introduction." Eds. Donna Bassin, Margaret Honey and Meryle Mahrer Kaplan. New Haven: Yale UP, 1994. 1–25.

Riesz, János. "Autobiographische Gattungen in Afrika und Europa—Historische Einbindung und Vision eines anderes Lebens." *Koloniale Mythen— Afrikanische Antworten*. Europäisch-afrikanische Literaturbeziehungen, Vol. 1. Frankfurt: Vlg. für interkulterelle Kommunikation, 1993. 265–88.

Riss, Marie-Denise. *Femmes africaines en milieu rural: Les Sénégalaises du Sine-Saloum*. Paris: L'Harmattan, 1989.

Robert, Stéphane. *Approche énonciative du système verbal: Le Cas du wolof*. Paris: Ed. du CNRS, 1991.

Rosaldo, Michelle Zimbalist. "Woman, Culture, and Society: A Theoretical Overview." *Woman, Culture and Society*. Stanford: Stanford UP, 1974. 17–42.

Rosaldo, Renato. *Culture and Truth: The Remaking of Social Analysis*. Boston: Beacon Press, 1989.

Rubin, Gayle. "The Traffic in Women: Notes on the 'Political Economy' of Sex." *Toward an Anthropology of Women.* Ed. R. Rayner. New York: Monthly Review Press, 1975. 157–210.

Ruddick, Sara. *Maternal Thinking: Toward a Politics of Peace.* Boston: Beacon Press, 1989.

———. "Thinking Mothers, Conceiving Birth." *Representations of Motherhood.* Eds. Donna Bassin, Margaret Honey and Meryle Mahrer Kaplan. New Haven: Yale UP, 1994. 29–45.

Rush, Norman. "The Woman in the Broken Mirror." *New York Times Book Review* (Dec. 15, 1991): 1–28.

Sadji, Abdoulaye. *Nini, mulâtresse du Sénégal.* Paris: Présence Africaine, 1965.

Samb, Amar. "L'Evolution de la 'dot' au Sénégal de la tradition à la modernité." *Notes africaines* 140 (1973): 85–99.

———. "Folklore wolof du Sénégal." *Bulletin de l'I.F.A.N.* 37, Série B, 4 (1975).

Sarr, Moustapha. *Louga et sa région: Essai d'intégration des rapports ville-campagne dans la problématique du développement.* Dakar: IFAN, 1973.

Scarry, Elaine. *The Body in Pain: The Making and Unmaking of the World.* Oxford: Oxford UP, 1985.

Schapera, I. *Praise-Poems of the Tswana Chiefs.* Oxford: Clarendon Press, 1965.

Scheub, Harold. "Review of African Oral Traditions and Literature." *African Studies Review* 28 (1985): 1–73.

Schenck, Celeste. "All of a Piece: Women's Poetry and Autobiography." *Life/Lines: Theorizing Women's Autobiography.* Ed. Bella Brodzki and Schenck, Celeste. Ithaca: Cornell UP, 1988. 281–305.

Schipper, Mineke. "Emerging from the Shadows: Changing Patterns in Gender Matters." *Research in African Literatures* 27 (1996): 155–71.

———. "Knowledge Is Like an Ocean: Insiders, Outsiders, and the Academy." *Research in African Literatures* 28.4 (1997).

———. "Mother Africa on a Pedestal: The Male Heritage in African Literature and Criticism." *African Literature Today* 15 (1987): 35–53.

Seck, Papa Ibrahima. *La Stratégie culturelle de la France en Afrique: L'Enseignement colonial (1817–1960).* Paris: L'Harmattan, 1993.

Senghor, Léopold Sédar. *Liberté I: Négritude et humanisme.* Paris: Seuil, 1964.

———. *Liberté II: Nation et voie africaine du socialisme.* Paris: Seuil, 1971.

———. *Liberté V: Le Dialogue des cultures.* Paris: Seuil, 1993.

———. *Poèmes.* Paris: Seuil, 1964.

Seye, Mamadou. "Canons de beauté: Ah, ces diongomas." *Le Soleil* (21–22 August 1993): 6.

Shivji, Issa G. *The Concept of Human Rights in Africa.* London: CODESRIA, 1989.

Siegel, Reva B. "Abortion as a Sex Equality Right: Its Basis in Feminist Theory." *Mothers in Law: Feminist Theory and the Legal Regulation of Motherhood.* Eds. Martha Albertson Fineman and Isabel Karpin. New York: Columbia UP, 1995. 43–72.

Smith, Sidonie. "Construing Truth in Lying Mouths: Truthtelling in Women's Autobiography." *Studies in the Literary Imagination* 23 (1990): 145–63.

―――. "The (Female) Subject in Critical Venues: Poetics, Politics, Autobiographical Practices." *Auto/Biography Studies* 6.1 (1991): 109–30.

―――. *A Poetics of Women's Autobiography: Marginality and the Fictions of Self-Representation.* Bloomington: Indiana UP, 1987.

―――. *Subjectivity, Identity and the Body: Women's Autobiographical Practices in the Twentieth Century.* Bloomington: Indiana UP, 1993.

Smith, Sidonie and Julia Watson. Introduction. *De/Colonizing the Subject: The Politics of Gender in Women's Autobiography.* Eds. Sidonie Smith and Julia Watson. Minneapolis: U of Minnesota P, 1992.

Sow, Fatou. "Femmes, socialité et valeurs africaines." *Notes africaines* 168 (1980): 105–12.

Sow Mbaye, Amina. *Mademoiselle.* Paris: EDICEF, 1984.

Spacks, Patricia Meyer. "Selves in Hiding." *Women's Autobiography: Essays in Criticism.* Ed. Estelle C. Jelinek. Bloomington: Indiana UP, 1980. 112–32.

Spaulding, Carol Roh. "The Go-Between People: Representations of Mixed Race in Twentieth-Century American Literature." *American Mixed Race: The Culture of Microdiversity.* Ed. Naomi Zack. Lanham, Md.: Rowman and Littlefield, 1995. 97–114.

Spengemann, William C. *The Forms of Autobiography: Episodes in the History of a Literary Genre.* New Haven: Yale UP, 1980.

Spickard, Paul R. *Mixed Blood: Intermarriage and Ethnic Identity in Twentieth-Century America.* Madison: U of Wisconsin P, 1989.

Spillers, Hortense J. "Notes on an Alternative Model—Neither/Nor." *The Difference Within: Feminism and Critical Theory.* Eds. Elizabeth Meese and Alice Parker. Amsterdam: John Benjamins, 1989. 165–87.

Spivak, Gayatri Chakravorty. "Imperialism and Sexual Difference." *The Oxford Literary Review* 8 (1986): 225–40.

Sprinker, Michael. "The End of Autobiography." *Autobiography: Essays Theoretical and Critical.* Ed. James Olney. Princeton: Princeton UP, 1980. 321–42.

Stanley, Liz. *The Auto/biographical I: The Theory and Practice of Feminist Auto/biography.* Manchester: Manchester UP, 1992.

Stanton, Domna C. "Autogynography: Is the Subject Different?" *The Female Autograph: Theory and Practice of Autobiography from the Tenth to the Twentieth Century.* Ed. Domna C. Stanton. Chicago: U of Chicago P, 1987. 3–20.

Steady, Filomina Chioma. "African Feminism: A Worldwide Perspective." *Women in Africa and the African Diaspora.* Eds. Rosalyn Terborg-Penn, Sharon Harley, and Andrea Benton Rushing. Washington, D.C.: Howard UP, 1987. 3–24.

Stoler, Ann Laura. *Race and the Education of Desire: Foucault's History of Sexuality and the Colonial Order of Things.* Durham: Duke UP, 1995.

Stone, Ruth. *Let the Inside Be Sweet: The Interpretation of Music Event among the Kpelle of Liberia.* Bloomington: Indiana UP, 1982.

Strathern, Marilyn. *The Gender of the Gift: Problems with Women and Problems with Society in Melanesia.* Berkeley: U of California P, 1988.

Stringer, Susan. "Innovation in Ken Bugul's *Le baobab fou.*" *Cincinnati Romance Review* 10 (1991): 200–207.

————. "Nafissatou Diallo—A Pioneer in Black African Writing." *Continental, Latin-American, and Francophone Women Writers.* Selected Papers from the Wichita State University Conference on Foreign Literature II, 1986–1987. Eds. Ginette Adamson and Eunice Myers. Lanham, Md.: UP of America, 1987. 165–71.

————. *The Senegalese Novel by Women: Through Their Own Eyes.* Francophone Cultures and Literatures, Vol. 7. New York: Peter Lang, 1996.

Suleri, Sara. "Woman Skin Deep: Feminism and the Postcolonial Condition." *Critical Inquiry* 18 (1992): 756–69.

Swigart, Leigh. "Cultural Creolization and Language Use in Postcolonial Africa: The Case of Senegal." *Africa* 64.2 (1994): 175–89.

————. "Women and Language Choice in Dakar: A Case of Unconscious Innovation." *Women and Language* 15 (1992): 11–20.

Sylla, Assane. *La philosophie morale des Wolof.* Dakar: Sankore, 1978.

Syr, Diagne Oumar. "Les frais du mariage Saint-Louisien. Origines. Principaux aspects et conséquences." *Notes africaines* 34 (1947): 8–13.

Taylor, Charles. *Multiculturalism and "The Politics of Recognition."* Princeton: Princeton UP, 1992.

Thiam, Awa. *La parole aux négresses.* Paris: Denoël-Gonthier, 1978.

Thiam, Chérif. *Introduction à l'étude d'un genre satirico-laudatif: Le taasu wolof.* M.A. thesis, Université Cheikh Anta Diop, 1979.

Thioune, Babacar. "L'exploration de l'écriture féminine au Sénégal: La tentation autobiographique." Diss. Paris: Université de Paris-Sorbonne IV, 1987.

Todorov, Tzvetan. "L'origine des genres." *Les genres du discours.* Paris: Seuil, 1978. 44–60.

Traoré, Karim. "Kourouma's *Monnè* and the Aesthetics of Lying." Unpublished paper, presented at the African Studies Association Conference, Boston, 1992.

Trinh, Minh-ha T. "Aminata Sow Fall et l'espace du don." *French Review* 55.6 (1982): 780–89.

————. *Woman Native Other: Writing Postcoloniality and Feminism.* Bloomington: Indiana UP, 1989.

Turcotte, Denis and Hélèn Aubé. *Lois, règlements et texts administratifs sur l'usage des langues en Afrique occidentale française (1826–1959). Répertoire chronologique annoté.* Québec: Presses de l'Université de Laval, 1983.

Vail, Leroy and Landeg White. *Power and the Praise Poem: Southern African Voices in History.* Charlottesville: U of Virginia P, 1992.

"Vers une évolution du mariage sénégalais." *Bulletin de l'Institut Français de l'Afrique noire* 13 (1951): 542–46.

Villalón, Leonardo A. "Democratizing a (Quasi) Democracy: The Senegalese Elections of 1993." *African Affairs* 93 (1994): 163–93.

————. *Islamic Society and State Power in Senegal: Disciples and Citizens in Fatick.* Cambridge: Cambridge UP, 1995.

Volet, Jean-Marie. *La Parole aux Africaines: L'idée du pouvoir chez les romancières d'expression française de l'Afrique sub-Saharienne.* Amsterdam: Rodopi, 1993.

Wallerstein, Immanuel. "The Insurmountable Contradictions of Liberalism: Human Rights and the Rights of Peoples in the Geoculture of the Modern World-System." *Nations, Identities, Cultures.* Ed. V. Y. Mudimbé. Durham: Duke UP, 1997. 181–98.

Wane, I. "Sur une forme de solidarité. Le Baptême toucouleur." *Notes africaines* 97 (1963): 42–46.

Watson, Julia. "Unruly Bodies: Autoethnography and Authorization in Nafissatou Diallo's *De Tilène au Plateau* (A Dakar Childhood)." *Research in African Literatures* 28.2 (1997): 34–56.

Wills, Dorothy Davis. "Economic Violence in Postcolonial Senegal: Noisy Silence in Novels by Mariama Bâ and Aminata Sow Fall." *Violence, Silence and Anger: Women's Writing as Transgression.* Ed. Deirdre Lashgari. Charlottesville: U of Virginia P, 1995. 158–71.

Wimsatt, William and Monroe C. Beardsley. "The Intentional Fallacy." *The Verbal Icon: Studies in the Meaning of Poetry.* Lexington: U of Kentucky P, 1954. 3–18.

Wright, Bonnie L. "The Power of Articulation." *Creativity of Power: Cosmology and Action in African Societies.* Eds. W. Arens and Ivan Karp. Washington, D.C.: Smithsonian Institution Press, 1989. 39–58.

Young, Iris Marion. *Throwing Like a Girl and Other Essays in Feminist Philosophy and Social Theory.* Bloomington: Indiana UP, 1990.

Zima, Peter. *Die Dekonstruktion.* Tübingen: Francke, 1994.

INDEX